NATO AND THE FUTURE
OF EUROPEAN SECURITY

NATO AND THE FUTURE OF EUROPEAN SECURITY

Sean Kay

ROWMAN & LITTLEFIELD PUBLISHERS, INC.
Lanham • Boulder • New York • Oxford

ROWMAN & LITTLEFIELD PUBLISHERS, INC.

Published in the United States of America
by Rowman & Littlefield Publishers, Inc.
4720 Boston Way, Lanham, Maryland 20706

12 Hid's Copse Road
Cumnor Hill, Oxford OX2 9JJ, England

British Library Cataloguing in Publication Information Available

Library of Congress Cataloging-in-Publication Data

Kay, Sean, 1967–
    NATO and the future of European security / Sean Kay.
        p.   cm.
    Includes bibliographical references and index.
    ISBN 0-8476-9000-8 (cloth : alk. paper). — ISBN 0-8476-9001-6
(pbk. : alk. paper)
        1. North Atlantic Treaty Organization—History.   2. North Atlantic
Treaty Organization—Membership.   3. National security—Europe.
4. Europe—Defenses.   I. Title.
UA646.3.K377   1998
355′.031091821—dc21   98-18649
                                                                              CIP

Printed in the United States of America

♾ ™ The paper used in this publication meets the minimum requirements of
American National Standard for Information Sciences—Permanence of Paper for
Printed Library Materials, ANSI Z39.48–1984.

Contents

Acknowledgments

A number of people have given considerable time and effort in support of my research for this book. As always, the content and conclusions are the sole responsibility of the author. I am very grateful to Eric S. Einhorn, Peter M. Haas, Stephen Pelz, James Der Derian, M. J. Peterson, Karl Ryavec, and Ronald Tiersky in Amherst, Massachusetts. Each played a critical role in commenting on various stages of my writing. I am also grateful to my colleagues of the Institute for National and Strategic Studies at the National Defense University in Washington, D.C., for the opportunity to take what I learned from this research and apply it in a US government setting at a time of momentous change for NATO and European security. I am grateful to the late Joseph Kruzel who took time from his busy schedule to facilitate the research that went into this book. His efforts on behalf of security in Europe remain an inspiration for all who continue to pursue efforts towards lasting peace. I am particularly appreciative to Jamie P. Shea at NATO headquarters in Brussels for his professional support and personal friendship. Also, thanks go to Chris Donnelly and Nicholas Sherwin at NATO for taking an interest in this project and helping see it to publication. My thanks go to S. Victor Papacosma and Mark Rubin of the Lemnitzer Center for NATO Studies at Kent State University for providing an opportunity to present early stages of this research and for their encouragement, friendship, and patient counsel. I am forever in debt to three outstanding scholars who first introduced me to European security issues—Boleslaw Boczek, Robert W. Clawson, and Lawrence S. Kaplan. Many senior US, European, and NATO officials provided key off-the-record interviews. I am very grateful for their insights and enthusiasm about this book. At Rowman and Littlefield, I would like to thank Susan McEachern and her associates Karen Johnson, Matt Hammon, and Dorothy Bradley for their professionalism and editorial expertise.

I am especially in debt to my family, in particular my parents, Jennifer and David Kay, and my mother-in-law Anna Madigan, for their continued support and encouragement. My wife Anna-Marie and our wonderful children have been my bedrock of support and inspiration. Finally, I am grateful to my father-in-law Matt Madigan. Our many conversations about all things European were a great inspiration, and my ongoing research is a tribute to his living memory.

Acronyms

AFSOUTH	Allied Forces Southern Europe
ARRC	Allied Rapid Reaction Corps
AWACS	Airborne Warning and Control System
CFE	Conventional Forces in Europe Treaty
CFSP	Common Foreign and Security Policy
CIA	Central Intelligence Agency
CIS	Commonwealth of Independent States
CJCIMIC	Combined Joint Civil-Military Cooperation
CJTF	Combined Joint Task Forces
CMO	NATO Crisis Management Organization
CSCE	Conference on Security and Cooperation in Europe
DPC	Defense Planning Committee
EAPC	Euro-Atlantic Partnership Council
EC	European Community
EDC	European Defense Community
EMU	European Monetary Union
ESDI	European Security and Defense Identity
EU	European Union
FSC	Forum for Security Cooperation
G-7	Group of Seven
GDP	Gross Domestic Product
GNP	Gross National Product
IEPG	Independent European Programme Group
IFOR	Bosnia Peace Implementation Force
IGC	Inter-Governmental Conference
IMF	International Monetary Fund
INF	Intermediate-Range Nuclear Forces Treaty
IPP	Individual Partnership Program
JRDF	Joint Rapid Deployment Force
LTDP	Long Term Defense Plan

MAD	Mutual Assured Destruction
MBFR	Mutual and Balanced Force Reductions
MLF	Multilateral Force
NAA	North Atlantic Assembly
NAC	North Atlantic Council
NACC	North Atlantic Cooperation Council
NADGE	NATO Air Defense Ground Environment
NAEWF	NATO Airborne Early Warning Force
NATO	North Atlantic Treaty Organization
NBMR	NATO Basic Military Requirement
NPG	Nuclear Planning Group
NSC	United States National Security Council
OECD	Organization for Economic Cooperation and Development
OMB	Office of Management and Budget
OSCE	Organization for Security and Cooperation in Europe
PARP	[Partnership for Peace] Planning and Review Process
PCG	Policy Coordination Group
PFP	Partnership for Peace
PJC	NATO-Russia Permanent Joint Council
PMSC	Political Military Steering Committee
PPS	Policy Planning Staff (US Department of State)
SACEUR	Supreme Allied Commander Europe
SACLANT	Supreme Allied Commander Atlantic
SFOR	Bosnia Stabilization Force
SHAPE	Supreme Headquarters Allied Powers Europe
SRG	Strategy Review Group
START	Strategic Arms Reduction Treaty
UN	United Nations
UNHCR	United Nations High Commissioner for Refugees
US	United States of America
USSR	Union of Soviet Socialist Republics
WEAG	Western European Armaments Group
WEU	Western European Union
ZOS	Zone of Separation

1

NATO and European Security

European Security after the Cold War

Shortly following the collapse of communism in Eastern Europe and the end of the Cold War, Czech leader Vaclav Havel met with Manfred Wörner, the secretary general of the North Atlantic Treaty Organization (NATO). Havel remarked that "we have a country that is run by dissidents, but none of whom have studied tax law."[1] What was most telling about Havel's comment was the person, and the institution, to which it was directed. NATO's founding mission of collective defense organized against the Soviet threat has been fundamentally transformed. Its members have adapted NATO with the hope of meeting new challenges that affect their security. Yet as NATO approached its fiftieth anniversary in 1999, the relationship between its institutional characteristics and security was uncertain. This book examines the institutional development of NATO to make conclusions about what, if anything, NATO can do to enhance the future of European security. My central conclusion is that NATO is likely to survive well into the next century. Whether that survival will increase or decrease security in Europe will be dependent upon the institutional form that NATO takes.

As Vaclav Havel implied, post–Cold War European security has multiple aspects including political, economic, societal, and environmental dimensions. Nevertheless, national security remains the primary factor motivating states in an uncertain international environment. During the current general peace, security in Europe is enhanced when states and their leaders are content with their relative position in the international system. European security is also enhanced when states are assured that events occurring in one state or region will not adversely affect their interests. The United States and its European allies have sought to shield themselves from the consequences of international anarchy in Europe through a myriad of international institutions designed to secure the existing peace. NATO, in particular, has sought to stabilize post-communist democracies, expanded its membership and sphere of influence,

promoted a special relationship with Russia, and helped manage Balkan security—to list just a few of its activities.

If in the future NATO is to enhance European security, it must do more than
expand its agenda. NATO will have to address three interrelated challenges to
the security of its member states.

The first, and most critical, challenge to European security is sustaining the
US political and military engagement in Europe. US involvement in Europe
gives NATO credibility as a multilateral defense planning organization. This
institutional activity discourages European members of NATO from pursuing
costly and provocative nationalistic defense strategies. However, domestic
pressures in the US and the political unwillingness of Europeans to assume
greater responsibility for their own security may precipitate an American disengagement from Europe. Without the US military presence in Europe, NATO
would be a hollow shell and traditional security dilemmas it has helped to
ameliorate among members and aspirant members could be undermined.

The second challenge is the promotion of stability in the region between
Germany and Russia. Security competition between Germany and Russia has
historically led to war in Europe. With Germany's relative power on the rise
and Russia in an ongoing state of weakness, it is not unthinkable that such
competition might resume in the twenty-first century. NATO enlargement into
Central and Eastern Europe would, in theory, prevent this by establishing a
hedge between Germany and Russia via the extension of American influence.
This was a central justification for the NATO decision made in Madrid, Spain,
in July 1997, to invite Poland, Hungary, and the Czech Republic to negotiate
membership in NATO. However, NATO enlargement is a power strategy implemented with institutional means. New members will enter NATO without
a direct guarantee of their borders. Additionally, to ease strong Russian opposition to NATO enlargement, Moscow may have been granted an opportunity
to exercise an informal veto over NATO decision-making via the creation of
a NATO–Russia Permanent Joint Council. NATO enlargement may have thus
set the alliance on a trend in the direction of a diluted collective security
institution. The transformation of NATO into an ineffective talk-shop might
also precipitate an American disengagement from Europe.

The third challenge to European security is the management of regional
crises. Left unattended, regional crises can draw in larger European powers
and lead to escalating security competition at a more general level. The former
Yugoslav republics and other potential flash points, such as between NATO
members Greece and Turkey, will require continued international attention for
years to come. To date, NATO's role in these conflicts has been highly responsive, ad hoc, and incomplete. If NATO does not have the capacity to prevent
or end wars in Europe then its relevance will be in serious doubt. Its members
may thus question NATO's utility and pursue unilateral security goals instead.
Ultimately, Europe's most critical security challenge, maintaining the trans-

atlantic relationship, may hinge on the European members of NATO engaging credibly in such conflicts without always involving the US.

Institutional Adaptation and Security

This chapter establishes a framework for thinking about NATO as an international institution. The analysis draws from international relations theories of realism and institutionalism and their relationship to security. Subsequent chapters address NATO's founding, Cold War development, post–Cold War adaptation and role in the Balkans, enlargement, and efforts to restructure the transatlantic relationship.

International institutions are persistent and connected sets of rules that prescribe behavior roles, constrain activity, and shape expectations through international regimes and organizations like NATO. Institutions are characterized by the principles, norms, rules, and decision-making procedures around which state expectations converge in a given issue area.[2] A security institution is a formal international arrangement, specifically identified by its members as responsible for enhancing their security.

This book shows that NATO's institutional tasks; organizational capacity; norms, principles, rules, and procedures; and capacity for change have yet to have an independent impact on security in Europe. It is with this in mind that some international relations scholars suggest that institutions like NATO do not independently enhance national security and cannot cause peace. States, national interests, and the international distribution of power are seen as the primary determinants of national security, and this explains how and under what circumstances states cooperate. Power is anything that aids in the control of man over man. It can be measured in terms of capacity to use force, which is the ability to use authority or influence to attain voluntary or involuntary cooperation from another. Power includes the "hard" military and resource capabilities that a state possesses. It also includes "soft" attributes such as socioeconomic strengths and the ability to use international institutions to promote national interests.[3]

Realist scholars generally assume that, at best, international institutions are intervening variables affecting security outcomes.[4] Institutions are thought to promote a false sense of security, while states seek to maximize power within or outside the institutional context. Even the perception that one state is making gains at the expense of another can prompt a state to maximize its own national security and lead to instability and conflict—which institutions can do little to prevent. For example, as John J. Mearsheimer maintains: "Another state may be reliably benign, but it is impossible to be certain of that judgment because intentions are impossible to divine with 100 percent certainty."[5] As Joseph M. Grieco has shown, "even states that are currently allies may become competitors or enemies in the future."[6] In this sense, institutions are not likely to have an independent impact on security outcomes and states cannot afford to rely on them when their survival is at stake.

This realist view of institutions is important for testing the proposition that the institutional characteristics of an organization like NATO increase security. The US and Europe are behaving in ways that suggest their decision-makers believe that international institutions increase national security. Therefore, it is essential to maintain a realist understanding of what NATO can, and cannot, do to meet these state demands. Realism helps scholars and policymakers consider both what to avoid when using institutions to promote security and what can go wrong if institutions fail to do what is expected of them. That is not to say that institutional approaches to understanding European security have no value. It is impossible to discuss European security without considering the role of institutions. Institutionalist scholars are on the forefront of a critical area of international relations research. Submitting institutions to a hard test of their relevance to national security will, one hopes, help scholars and policymakers construct policies that will make institutions more effective.

There is historical justification for a skeptical view of security institutions. Three major efforts to institutionalize security architectures based on the ideals of collective security have been attempted in Europe, and each failed to prevent war or end conflict. Collective security is an effort by states to manage security challenges by organizing power on the basis of all-against-one crisis management. The goal is to create an international environment in which stability emerges through cooperation rather than competition. Violators of norms and principles will be punished through collective action.[7]

The Concert of Europe, which formed the basis of nineteenth-century collective security, had some nascent institutional functions. However, it was a system of Great Power management, which worked well only while there was a general agreement among the five major actors and the individuals representing them. Once interests diverged, the institution could not adapt to shifts in the distribution of power. Over time, Europe's security architecture disintegrated, ultimately leading to World War I.

Following World War I, states sought to secure the general European peace through a hierarchical collective security institution in the League of Nations. Its members sought to redefine national security as a collective good through legal enforcement mechanisms. The League of Nations members committed to apply multilateral sanctions or to intervene on the principle of all against one when institutional norms, rules, and principles were violated. However, the League of Nations was neither collective or secure. The League of Nations was an institutional shell under which anarchy ruled and from which World War II emerged.

From 1991 through mid-1995 Europe embarked on a concerted effort to build an amalgamated form of collective security based on interlocking institutions. This was a period of considerable institutional activity. However, the United Nations (UN), European Union (EU), Conference on Security and Cooperation in Europe (CSCE—renamed OSCE [Organization for Security and Cooperation in Europe] in 1995), and NATO were unable to prevent or end war in the Balkans. Some 250,000 people were killed or went missing in the Balkan wars. Europe's institutions proved unable to manage the continent's worst conflict since World War II. While they eventually contributed to peace in Bosnia-Herzegovina, the capacity of international institutions to enhance long-term security was seriously limited.

Realism is a limited analytical tool if its proponents assume that an institutional analysis intrinsically means a belief that collective security is attainable. In fact, there are three institutionalist approaches to understanding national security. The first school, neoliberal institutionalism, stresses national interest and the mutual gains that states make by cooperating in institutions. Neoliberal institutional scholars maintain that some institutionalized security arrangements can help states better understand each other's aims. Institutions thus reduce uncertainty, which lowers the risk of misperceptions that could lead to conflict. International institutions are also thought to facilitate the flow of information among states so that the transaction costs of organizing international coalitions are lowered. The second school includes advocates of collective security who believe a hierarchical security architecture for contemporary Europe can make up for the failings of the League of Nations. The third school focuses on security communities. This approach suggests that institutions can help eliminate the possibility of war between two or more states. For example, by adapting membership rules from restricted to conditionally open, an institution might impact the behavior of states seeking to join a particular organization and thus be an important tool of community-building and environment-shaping.[8]

NATO's role in the future of European security is a critical test for the value of institutionalist claims about security. If NATO's institutional attributes alone can be shown to enhance security, then the empirical evidence of its transition will be of central importance to students of international relations. However, if NATO fails to increase security, then the strength of realism as an analytical and predictive tool may be enhanced. In either case, the outcome of the debate between realists and institutionalists is a critical test for understanding the future of international security relationships. NATO's transformation, in particular, will be one of the most important issues confronting the study of international relations, international organization, and foreign policy in the twenty-first century.

Realism and NATO

Contemporary realism is essential to testing the relationship between NATO's institutional characteristics and security. For example, without the

Soviet threat uniting NATO, some contemporary realists conclude that the US will inevitably leave Europe, and the continent will enter a state of anarchy—with a strong and united Germany exerting more influence over European security.[9] Mearsheimer writes:

> NATO provides a good example of realist thinking about institutions. NATO is an institution, and it certainly played a role in preventing World War III and in helping the West win the Cold War. Nevertheless, NATO was basically a manifestation of the bipolar distribution of power in Europe during the Cold War, and it was that balance of power, not NATO per se, that provided the key to maintaining security on the continent. NATO was essentially a tool for managing power in the face of a Soviet threat. Now with the collapse of the Soviet Union, realists argue that NATO must either disappear or reconstitute itself on the basis of the new distribution of power in Europe.[10]

Mearsheimer concedes that "with the United States serving as a night watchman, fears about relative gains among the Western European states were mitigated, and furthermore, those states were willing to allow their economies to become tightly interdependent."[11] Yet as Kenneth N. Waltz concludes, after the Cold War, "NATO's days are not numbered, but its years are."[12] To Waltz, the most pertinent question is: "How can an alliance endure in the absence of a worthy opponent?"[13]

Alliances are usually short-lived responses by states organizing to defend against a specific threat. When the threat goes away, interests normally begin to diverge and alliances dissolve. Some realists conclude that because of its institutional qualities, NATO may survive—for a time—on bureaucratic inertia and familiarity, but in this context NATO will eventually become a hollow shell due to an inevitable decline of the American political and military role in Europe. However, realists do not necessarily discount institutional shells for, once created, it is easier to maintain an existing institutional arrangement than to create a new one. As Richard K. Betts puts it: "Shells are far from useless—they can maintain the base from which remobilization and coordination can be accomplished in a shorter time than if they had to be accomplished from scratch—but they do not provide the animation or originality that revolutionary political changes seem to mandate."[14]

Institutionalized patterns of allied behavior can be adapted to changed realities in the international system. While the original foundations of an alliance may no longer have relevance, its members may give it life beyond its original purpose. As Stephen M. Walt has shown, an alliance can have appeal not just because of the current capabilities a threat possesses, but also because of a perceived danger or the aggressiveness of a particular state's intentions.[15] While a threat may not be immediate, or even likely, perceived dangers and uncertainties can give value to an alliance even in the absence of a major threat.

Fear of instability and the unknown can be as much a unifying factor as a clear and present danger. In this sense, sustained cooperation in NATO may be an important element of self-help. As Charles L. Glaser notes, a policy is thought to provide a state with gains when it increases what the state values, not when it increases the instruments the state has available or employs.[16] A state will primarily value security. If it perceives an institution as aiding that goal, then membership can be an important part of self-help even if the members have different immediate reasons for participating.

The most forceful realist argument for maintaining NATO would be to enhance security by expanding the alliance into Central and Eastern Europe. NATO enlargement would consolidate the new status quo after the Cold War by reassuring Germany's neighbors about its growing power and increasing the West's deterrence capacity against Russia. In this view, NATO will not be sustainable unless it is expanded to constrain Great Power security competition in Central and Eastern Europe. Even if Russia does not pose an immediate threat, NATO enlargement would contain instability in the former Soviet Union. NATO enlargement would also ensure American primacy over Europe by preventing rising competitors from challenging America's dominant role in Europe or around the world.[17]

Alliance enlargement as the solution to NATO's uncertain role after the Cold War is not embraced by all realists. Some realists warn that enlargement is a gain by the West at Russia's expense, unnecessarily provokes political confrontation between NATO and Russia, and undermines pro-Western politicians in Moscow. Given Russia's conventional weaknesses, Moscow may eventually deter further NATO enlargement (for example to include former Soviet republics) with an increased reliance on decaying nuclear weapons. Moreover, NATO enlargement may overextend American security commitments at a time when Europe's future may include a decreasing US operational role on the continent. Alternatively, a threat-based analysis might conclude that Europe's immediate security challenges are actually in Southern Europe and not in its central region. If so, NATO should not have prioritized inviting the Czech Republic and Hungary, which would then have little geostrategic importance. Instead, NATO should have been initially expanded to include Poland, Slovenia, and Romania.

Realism has limited explanatory power if its conclusions are not based on detailed analyses of security institutions and how particular variations in institutional form can affect security outcomes. However, while institutional approaches to the study of NATO often provide good descriptions of its institutional activity, institutionalism has yet to offer rigorous proof that such activity will independently increase security. It is not enough to claim that because institutions exist, they matter. Scholars exploring the relationship between international institutions and security must be able to show that institutions actually increase security for states. This is especially true regarding post–Cold War Europe because, as Jack Snyder warns, "institution building will do great damage if it is attempted, but doesn't work. . . . It will damage the West by embroiling it deeply in the possibly insoluble problems of the East."[18]

Institutionalism and NATO

Institutionalists are optimistic that international institutions can enhance security. Institutions are seen by some international relations scholars as relevant to security because they can make international cooperation easier to attain than it would be in their absence. Such cooperation, conducted over time, is likely to become the international norm as states are socialized into new patterns of security behavior. Security will be enhanced because states will have a greater opportunity to learn about each other and their intentions.

Institutions are seen as having an important contribution to relations among states because, as Robert Axelrod and Robert O. Keohane suggest, the shadow of the future and the uncertainty of anarchy in the international system allow for an environment in which international institutions both embody and affect state expectations.[19] Neoliberal institutionalists, in particular, claim to have considerable explanatory power because their approach sees institutions as fundamentally rooted in the realities of power and interests. As Keohane and Lisa Martin assert, "liberal institutionalists . . . do not argue that NATO could have maintained stability under any imaginable conditions. . . . What we argue is that institutions make a significant difference in conjunction with power realities."[20]

Since the end of the Cold War, scholars have increasingly turned their attention to the potential for institutions to enhance security. For example, Keohane and Joseph S. Nye demonstrate how some types of security institutions aid the exercise of influence, constrain bargaining strategies, balance or replace other institutions, signal governments' intentions by providing others with information and making policies more predictable, specify obligations, and impact both the interests and preferences of states.[21] Charles A. Kupchan shows that institutions are relevant to security because they increase the level of information available to all parties by enhancing transparency, raise the costs of defection and define what constitutes defection, increase the likelihood of issue linkage, and advance interstate socialization by promoting the concept of an international community.[22] Regarding Europe, Keohane asserts, "If the theories of institutions have any validity, the rich tapestry of institutions should both constrain states, through the operation of rules, and provide them with opportunities without positing the threats to other states that are so characteristic of realistic anarchy."[23]

Addressing NATO, John G. Ruggie notes that among the options the US had when establishing its post–World War II security ties, the US pursued an explicitly institutional approach via NATO.[24] Thus institutions, adapted to reflect fluctuations in the international power structure, have been an important element of transatlantic relations since NATO's founding. Stephen Weber observes that as the alliance developed over time, NATO facilitated communication through a network of permanent and intermittently meeting bodies, as well as ad hoc groups set up at the request of member states.[25] Explaining NATO's post–Cold War adaptation, John Duffield asserts that "NATO's institutional character has probably contributed to the alliance's persistence. . . . [NATO's] supranational bodies and the individuals who head them have almost certainly helped the alliance to adapt to changing external circumstances by defining new tasks, identifying ways to achieve them, forging compromises, and otherwise providing leadership."[26] Robert McCalla describes NATO's persistence after the Cold War in institutional terms, but without assessing whether or not institutional activity is relevant to security.[27]

Despite this increased attention to NATO, little detailed consideration has been given to the basic realist challenge: Do institutions affect the degree of national security and, if so, how? Neoliberal institutionalism suggests that NATO can lower the transaction costs of forming coalitions for acting in crises when its members' interests are challenged. In this "cooperative security" perspective, the security of one state is viewed as intrinsically linked to, and dependent on, the security of others. This interdependence of security thus motivates states to utilize multilateral forums, including formal institutions, to make cooperation easier.[28] NATO has demonstrated a capacity to function along these lines in Bosnia-Herzegovina. However, NATO has been unable to redistribute military responsibility in the organization. Absent an immediate threat to American interests, a redistribution of primary responsibility for European security will be critical to ensuring that American engagement can be sustained within the institution.

Alternatively, some high-level US policymakers view NATO as a "club" of democracies expanding a zone of peace and stability, drawing on the idealism that drives collective security. Wanting to accelerate NATO toward enlargement in late 1994, a senior Clinton administration official opined that the Partnership for Peace "is like getting guest privileges at the club—you can play golf once in a while. . . . Now we want to send the bylaws and ask, 'Do you want to pay the dues?' "[29] Such comments reflect hollow utopian wishes to overcome a practical understanding of just what NATO is and whether it has adapted sufficiently to the post–Cold War security environment. NATO is not a club. NATO is an international organization that performs critical security functions in the heart of a continent that witnessed the horror of millions of dead through two world wars. If NATO did have an internal collective security function, it worked because of the primacy of threat-driven collective defense and American power.

The assumption that NATO embodies a security community is also problematic. A security community, as defined by Karl Deutsch, is a region in which there is virtually no prospect for war among a group of states.[30] Deutsch argued that NATO might contribute to the evolution of a security community by developing its economic and social potential to make it "more than a military alliance."[31] Stephen Weber asserts that NATO has always been a peculiar mix of alliance and security community. He suggests that a security community can be institutionalized as equivalence is favored over hierarchy, with decisions requiring unanimity and the formal organization existing primarily to enhance transparency and to facilitate the transfer of information among states.[32]

Rhetorically, NATO enlargement seems designed for community building. US Secretary of State Madeleine K. Albright has claimed that "by adding Poland, Hungary, and the Czech Republic to the alliance, we will expand the area within Europe where wars simply do not happen," and that:

> NATO defines a community of interest among the free nations of North America and Europe that both preceded and outlasted the Cold War. America has long stood for the proposition that the Atlantic community should not be artificially divided and that its nations should be free to shape their destiny. We have long argued that the nations of Central and Eastern Europe belong to the same democratic family as our allies in Western Europe.[33]

Yet, as Emanuel Adler has shown, a more appropriate geographic basis for a well-defined security community is more likely to be found in the European Union.[34]

NATO is a security institution that is at the heart of international organization in Europe. It has some institutional attributes that are, in part, reflective of each institutionalist approach to security—neoliberal, collective security, and security community. Indeed, part of NATO's strength and persistence comes from its attractiveness for many disparate interests at the analytical and policy level. Nevertheless, NATO's institutional functions must be shown to have a specific relationship to particular security outcomes if institutionalist arguments about security are to be relied on. If states are defining their national security in an institutional context, then it is imperative that decision-makers have a sound understanding about what works in international institutions and why.

An Alliance Transformed

In the absence of a major threat, NATO must ensure the sustainability of the transatlantic relationship if it is to increase European security in the twenty-first century. If NATO is unable to stabilize Eastern Europe without diluting its internal cohesion, the transatlantic relationship may be at risk. Indeed, if

NATO's commitment to an open-door process of enlargement is not managed carefully, the alliance may drift out of control—evolving into an ineffectual general collective security framework for Europe. Moreover, if NATO's old and new European members are unwilling or unable to demonstrate a capacity to assume the lead role for regional crisis management, then the transatlantic relationship may also be at risk. NATO's post–Cold War adaptation has been determined by ad hoc responses to changes in the international environment. As a result, its capacity for positively affecting the future of European security exists, but may be increasingly in decline.

2

The Formative Period

The Origins of NATO

After World War II European security was challenged by a number of factors. To the east stood a massive Soviet presence consolidating its gains through the creation of puppet regimes throughout Eastern Europe. The Soviet Union maintained approximately thirty divisions in Eastern Europe, including nine tank and eleven motorized infantry divisions. Western intelligence estimates concluded that in the immediate postwar years, the Soviet Union had some five million men in the armed forces, with 175 divisions in the western Soviet Union and another 125 divisions in strategic reserve.[1]

Western Europe was so economically devastated and militarily weak that it could not balance Soviet power alone. Economic disaster, fragile democracies, and dispirited populations also made the West European states susceptible to internal Soviet-backed communist influence and destabilizing nationalism. At the same time, the US was dramatically reducing its troop presence in Europe, and those troops that remained had low combat potential. The US position in Western Europe was especially tenuous because the Americans were unable to send more than a division anywhere without resorting to partial mobilization. As a result, the entire defense of Western Europe relied on American air power and its nuclear component.[2]

Toward the end of the war, Britain had considered alternative postwar international developments and sought to institutionalize the integrated wartime cooperation between the combined US and British military staffs. In September 1943 British Prime Minister Winston Churchill noted in a speech at Harvard University: "It would be a most foolish and improvident act on the part of our two Governments, or either of them, to break up this smooth-running and immensely powerful machinery the moment the war is over. . . . We are bound to keep it working and in running order after the war—probably for a good many years."[3] On 9 November 1944 the British chiefs of staff issued a classified report which concluded that Britain's security interests lay in the formation of a West European security group that would cooperate with the British Commonwealth and the US. Such a security group would begin with an Anglo-French alliance and expand to include closer cooperation with Belgium, Holland, Denmark, and perhaps Germany. At Potsdam in 1945 the British chiefs of staff suggested that the US and Britain have continued machinery for the mutual exchange of information.[4]

By early 1946 sustained allied security cooperation took on a sense of urgency. On 22 February, George Kennan, the top US government expert on Soviet affairs, warned that the West faced a political force committed "fanatically to the belief that with the US there can be no permanent *modus vivendi*, that it is desirable and necessary that the internal harmony of our society be disrupted, our traditional way of life destroyed, the international authority of our state broken, if Soviet power is to be secured."[5]

On 5 March Churchill gave a speech in Fulton, Missouri, warning of an "iron curtain" descending on Eastern Europe in the form of Soviet domination. Churchill proposed a "fraternal association" between Britain and the US. This required "not only the growing friendship and mutual understanding between our two vast but kindred systems of society, but the continuance of the intimate relationship between our military advisers, leading to common study of potential dangers, the similarity of weapons and manuals of instruction, and to the interchange of officers and cadets at technical colleges."[6] Churchill concluded: "If there is to be a fraternal association of the kind I described, with all the extra strength and security which both our countries can derive from it, let me make sure that great fact is known to the world, and that it plays its part in steadying and stabilizing the foundations of peace. . . . Prevention is better than cure."[7]

American involvement in postwar European security had become increasingly important for the Europeans because of the immediate concern over Soviet intentions in the east, the potential for a renewal of German nationalism, and the inability of Britain to maintain its traditional stabilizing influence on the continental balance of power. To address the German question, Britain and France signed the Dunkirk Treaty on 4 March 1947. The treaty committed them to mutual assistance in the event of German aggression and to cooperation in their postwar reconstruction efforts.[8] At the same time, the decline of British influence on continental affairs became apparent in Greece, where the Western-oriented Greek monarchy was engaged in an intense civil war against Soviet-backed communist rebels. London could no longer afford to furnish military and economic assistance as they had been doing; Britain hoped the Americans would fill the void.

The US responded with the Truman Doctrine, announced on 12 March 1947 in a presidential address to Congress. President Harry S. Truman specifically promised American aid to Greece and Turkey, based on extending the universal principles of freedom, democracy, and peace.[9] In June, US Secretary of

State George Marshall announced a plan of economic assistance for Western Europe designed to prevent the rise of nationalism, promote democracy, and establish economic containment of the Soviet Union. The Marshall Plan implicitly recognized the growing convergence between interdependence, stability, and security. However, the plan's purpose was to promote independence from, and not dependence on, the US.[10] With the Truman Doctrine and the Marshall Plan, the US entered a gradual process of institutionalizing regional commitments intended to promote security in areas understood to be vital to its national interest.

The Rio Treaty

In December 1947 Congress approved the Rio Treaty, which bound the US to a regional security guarantee in the Americas. The accord stressed mutual aid and raised hope among the Europeans that it might have broader implications for preserving peace in Europe. While primarily an institutionalization of the Monroe Doctrine, the Rio Treaty was an important signal to the world that the US favored regional security institutions as the basis for its postwar global involvement. This pact was justified by Article 51 of the UN charter, which guarantees states the "inherent right of individual or collective self-defence."[11]

The Rio Treaty provided for mutual assistance in the event of an aggressive action against any American state. Internal procedures were created to promote the peaceful settlement of regional disputes prior to referring them to the UN. Such a regional pact promoted the principles reflected in the UN charter, but at the same time, circumvented a Soviet veto over security issues in areas of vital US national interest. The treaty condemned war, and its signatories agreed to resort to the threat or the use of force only in a manner consistent with that provided for by the UN. Following passage of the treaty on 8 December 1947, by a vote of 72 to 1, the chairman of the US Senate Foreign Relations Committee, Arthur Vandenberg, stated: "We are building upon mutual trust. . . . This is a true partnership which represents the greatest advance ever made in the business of collective peace."[12]

On 15 December *New York Times* columnist James Reston noted that some American officials hoped "to negotiate a regional alliance within the United Nations for the defense of those areas of Western and Southern Europe that are considered by our strategic experts to be essential to our own security." He concluded, "It is gradually becoming recognized in the Capital that economic security and political security, like peace, are indivisible, and that classic diplomatic statements of concern are no answer to the problem of communist internal power."[13] Reston, who had close ties to senior US officials, reflected a growing understanding that the threat to European security was more complicated than a direct Soviet invasion. West European democracies struggling with economic disaster after the war needed a sense of reassurance about their relative safety and stability in order to deter the political challenge that communism, or nationalism, might pose.

The Brussels Pact

On 15 December 1947 British Foreign Secretary Ernest Bevin met with Secretary of State Marshall in London, following the collapse of the four-power (US, Britain, France, and the USSR) dialogue over the future of Germany. Bevin told Marshall that Europe and America must increase their commitment to each other. He suggested that this need not necessarily come through a formal alliance, but rather an "understanding backed by power, money and resolute action . . . sort of a spiritual federation of the West."[14] Summarizing his view of the Soviet challenge, Bevin said:

> I am convinced that the Soviet Union will not deal with the West on any reasonable terms in the foreseeable future and that the salvation of the West depends upon the formation of some form of union, formal or informal in character, in Western Europe, backed by the United States and the Dominions—such a mobilization of moral and material force will inspire confidence and energy within, and respect elsewhere.[15]

Marshall generally supported Bevin's sentiments. However, he was adamant that Bevin proceed under the same formula as the Marshall Plan and that the Europeans should first institutionalize a defense community in Western Europe. Marshall advised Bevin that the Europeans should "come together for their own protection, see what they could do, and then turn to the United States, and see what we could do to make up the difference between what the situation required and what they were able to do by their own efforts."[16] Thus the US established that any peacetime alliance with Europe should enhance European's responsibility for their own security.

On 13 January 1948 Bevin informed Washington that, in his view, Marshall Plan aid alone would not prevent further Soviet encroachment on the West. "Political and indeed spiritual forces must be mobilized in our defense," Bevin suggested. This would be attained by seeking "to form with the backing of the Americans and the Dominions a Western democratic system comprising Scandinavia, the Low Countries, France, Italy, Greece and possibly Portugal. . . . As soon as circumstances permit we should, of course, wish also to include Spain and Germany without whom no Western system can be complete."[17]

The American response was positive, but not as specific as Bevin might have liked. In a 20 January letter to Lord Inverchapel, the British ambassador in Washington, Marshall wrote: "As in the case of the recovery program, we heartily welcome European initiative in this respect and Mr. Bevin may be assured of our wholehearted sympathy in this undertaking."[18] The next day

John Hickerson, director of the State Department's Office of European Affairs, told Inverchapel that the US hoped to help create "a third force which was not merely the extension of US influence but a real European organization strong enough to say 'no' both to the Soviet Union and to the United States, if our actions should seem so to require."[19]

On 22 January Bevin informed Parliament that he had instructed British representatives in France and the Benelux countries to begin negotiations on the creation of a Western Union. The rationale for this departure from Britain's traditional avoidance of continental security commitments was placed in the context of West European integration. Bevin asserted: "The nations of Western Europe have much to unite them—common sacrifice in two wars, their parliamentary democracy, and their striving for economic rights and conceptions of and love for democracy."[20] However, a Western Union alone would have been inadequate for the security of Western Europe. As Belgian Prime Minister Paul-Henri Spaak asserted: "Any defense arrangement which did not include the United States would be without practical value."[21] The Western Union was a bold initiative that risked prompting an aggressive Soviet response, which would have taken advantage of the Union's institutional weakness. The Western Union thus was primarily designed to establish a framework for a broader, transatlantic institution involving an American security guarantee.

American reassurance was a primary concern for France. Because any real defense of Western Europe would require meeting the Soviet challenge as far east as possible, Germany would have to be a part of Western defense plans and such a forward defense strategy would require German rearmament to be credible. Additionally, the success of the Marshall Plan and European integration would likely hinge on economic development in Western Germany. France promoted the idea of forward defense and hoped to make substantial gains from Marshall Plan aid and European integration. However, France could not easily forget its adversarial history with Germany and its recent Nazi occupation. Nevertheless, as Kennan concluded, only a Western Union "holds out any hope of restoring the balance of power in Europe without permitting Germany to become again the dominant power."[22] While Kennan was correct in this assessment, he appeared not to understand that a successful Western Union, which would ultimately rest on Franco-German reconciliation, could not emerge in the absence of direct American reassurance of its commitment to West European security.

On 28 February 1948 Marshall related French fears about the German question to the continued presence of American troops:

> The French are secure against Germany as long as (the) occupation continues. In view of Communist integration of a third of Germany and the likelihood of continuing stringent economic conditions, a united Germany bereft of Western occu-

pation force would be an easy prey to Communist domination. As long as European Communism threatens US vital interests and national security we could ill afford to abandon our military position in Germany. The logical conclusion is that three power occupation may be of unforeseeable and indefinite duration, thus offering protracted security guarantees and establishing a firm community of interests.[23]

This desire to reassure France was shared in London where Bevin wrote to Prime Minister Clement Atlee on 1 March:

Instead of being bottled up in Central Europe, we feel the Germans have a great contribution to make to the world's industrial and social development. Our aim is to protect ourselves against any further aggression by Germany and at the same time to bring her back into the community of nations as a united entity on a democratic basis, with democracy as Western civilization understands it. In this connection of course, you must not forget the French. We all talk too much about Germany. Our approach, therefore, to a reorganization of economic, social and defence weapons is a good neighbourly policy, first with the French and now with Benelux. In view of the fact that France has been invaded so many times and paid such a price, we must therefore arrange our defences and our responsibilities to give the French the assurance of her security as far as we humanly can.[24]

Marshall and Bevin had signaled a clear understanding of the need to alleviate French fears by institutionalizing a policy of reassurance in the form of a general US commitment to European security.

After Soviet-backed communists took over Czechoslovakia in late February and the pro-Western Czech Foreign Minister Thomas Masaryk was murdered on 10 March, western states became fearful of so-called fifth-column Soviet invasions. Such Soviet actions might use covert activity to rally communist forces in a fragile democracy and turn that state's policy toward the Soviet sphere of influence. Western concerns were heightened by the ongoing civil war in Greece, scheduled elections in April showing the possibility of a communist victory in Italy, and Soviet pressure on Finland and Norway to enter into nonaggression pacts with Moscow. French national security concerns in particular were intensified by these developments as France had recently undergone major work stoppages and had a large communist presence in its National Assembly.

France had few options for increasing its national security. France could not isolate Germany, as it had in the early 1920s, for fear that such a policy could push Western Germany into the Soviet orbit. Going it alone was no longer an option, as the threat was much greater than the resources France could marshal. Establishing bilateral alliances in Eastern Europe was not possible as long as the Soviet Union occupied the region, nor was political accommodation with Moscow an option. France was left with little choice but to seek hard security guarantees from Britain and the US. Even the French nationalist Charles de Gaulle said on 7 March:

> It is necessary that there be formed among the free states of Europe an economic, diplomatic, and strategic grouping, joining their productions, their moneys, their exterior action, and their means of defense . . . It is necessary that the effort of old Europe and that of America be joined to put our poor world back on its feet again. Their support must extend at the same time to the domain of defense and in a manner as precise and explicit on the one hand as in the Marshall project in the matter of credits and imports.[25]

France especially wanted direct military assistance to rebuild its national security capabilities.

France maintained a deep concern, based on the failure of the League of Nations before World War II, about reliance on institutional promises of its national security. During the Versailles negotiations, which established the League of Nations, France proposed creating a permanent military staff prepared to intervene immediately in the case of aggression. France proposed that the League Council should have standing troops at its disposal, recruited specifically for the League of Nations or composed of national forces put under League of Nations command. These forces would include a standing military staff, to be organized by the League of Nations, which would train contingents and take responsibility for military planning in advance of war. The French plan received no serious consideration by the US or British governments, however, which led to a growing skepticism among the French about the reliability of its allies in the absence of credible military guarantees.[26]

A Western European security institution was created in Brussels by the United Kingdom, France, and the Benelux countries on 17 March 1948.[27] The Western Union, as it was informally called, sought to promote integration and mutual assistance in a range of political, economic, and military activities. The Western Union established a Consultative Council to "promote the attainment of a higher standard of living by their peoples and to develop on corresponding lines the social and other related services of their countries" (Article 2). The members agreed to make "every effort in common to lead their peoples towards a better understanding of the principles which form the basis of their common civilization and to promote cultural exchanges by conventions between themselves or by other means" (Article 3).

Article 4 of the Brussels Treaty stated that if any member should be the object of attack in Europe, the others will, "in accordance with the provisions of Article 51 of the Charter of the United Nations, afford the party so attacked all the military and other aid and assistance in their power." Article 7 specifi-

cally mentioned Germany but had greater implications for the emerging Soviet challenge. It mandated consultation in the event of aggression at the
request of any member, "in whatever area this threat should arise; with regard
to the attitude to be adopted and the steps to be taken in case of a renewal by
Germany of an aggressive policy; or with regard to any situation constituting
a danger to economic stability." Additionally, the treaty established a principle of internal conflict resolution by requiring member states to resolve internal conflicts according to the rules of the International Court of Justice
(Article 8).

Worried about a potential isolationist backlash at home, the Truman administration was careful not to associate publicly with the formation of the
Western Union. However, the Western Union was encouraged privately by
Washington as a prerequisite for negotiating a transatlantic security institution.
By building a security institution from the ground up, the West European
countries had made substantial progress toward coordinating shared national
security objectives. While collective security had failed in the League of Nations thirty years before, an emerging community of shared interests between
the US and Western Europe held promise that an alliance built upon power
and community would succeed.

Framing the Transatlantic Community

On the day the Brussels Treaty was signed, President Truman delivered a foreign policy speech to a joint session of Congress. Truman suggested that national security must be understood in a broad context. Western Europe needed
to integrate its economic resources in order to escape its history of war and
defend itself against the Soviet Union. However, if Western Europe were
going to unite economically, it must be reassured of its security. Truman said:

> The free nations of Europe realize that economic recovery, if it is to succeed,
> must be afforded some measure of protection against internal and external ag-
> gression. The movement toward economic cooperation has been followed by a
> movement toward common self-protection in the face of the growing menace to
> their freedom. . . . This development deserves our full support and I am confident
> that the United States will, by appropriate means, extend to the free nations the
> support which the situation requires.[28]

On 22 March American, Canadian, and British officials began secret discussions deep within the Pentagon about the prospect of creating a formal transatlantic institution based on either the Brussels Pact or the Rio Treaty.

These three-way talks were preliminary but resulted in a draft working
paper presented by the US, written primarily by John Hickerson. The central
recommendations included having the president of the United States invite

thirteen other countries—the United Kingdom, France, Canada, Belgium, Luxembourg, the Netherlands, Norway, Sweden, Denmark, Iceland, Ireland, Portugal, and Italy—to negotiate a collective defense agreement for the North Atlantic area. Pending conclusion of an agreement, the president would issue a unilateral declaration that the US would consider an armed attack against any signatory of the Brussels Treaty as an armed attack against itself.[29]

The two main Soviet specialists in the US State Department, George Kennan and Charles Bohlen, opposed a formal treaty and had serious reservations about the conclusions drawn by the working group. They argued that West European defense was an inappropriate security commitment for the US to make and that it might foreclose on a political settlement with Moscow.[30] Kennan's and Bohlen's views were dismissed by their colleagues in favor of a formal security commitment to Western Europe, based on a combination of shared values and a common threat.[31]

Its founders wanted the transatlantic alliance to reflect the political, moral, even "spiritual" elements that united the North Atlantic community of nations. As Escott Reid, a key figure in the Canadian Ministry of Foreign Affairs, had written in an internal draft memorandum to the prime minister on 13 March:

> The purpose of the pact is to rally the spiritual as well as the military and economic resources of western Christendom against Soviet totalitarianism; [and] it must therefore not be merely a negative anti-Soviet military alliance but must be the basis for a dynamic liberal counter-offensive. The pact may succeed in giving us a long period of peace if it results in creating an overwhelming preponderance of force against the Soviet Union, but the force to be overwhelming must not only be military and economic force; it must be the force that comes from ability to rally to our side all non-Communists in all countries, including our own, who are now apathetic, fearful or doubtful. A bold move is necessary to raise the hearts and minds and spirits of all those in the world who love freedom that confidence and faith which will restore their vigor. The pact must set forth the gospel—the good news of our faith—for which we are willing to live and die. It must make as clear as possible the methods which the peoples and governments of the Free World intend to follow to make good their faith in human rights and fundamental freedoms, in the worth and dignity of man and in the principles of parliamentary democracy, personal freedom and political liberty.[32]

Reid's suggestion became formal Canadian policy. On 29 April Canadian Foreign Minister Louis St. Laurent stated that it may be necessary for free countries of the West to establish a security league whose purpose would be to "create a dynamic counter-attraction of a free, prosperous, and progressive society."[33] On 27 May British Prime Minister Attlee denied that what was sought was a "power pact," but rather "an association of free peoples, based

on a community of ideas, cooperating economically and defensively to provide a firm material basis toward spiritual unity."[34]

The Vandenberg Resolution

Gaining the necessary two-thirds majority for US Senate approval of a
treaty establishing an entangling peacetime alliance in Europe required a
strong bipartisan effort to ensure final success. Key State Department officials,
especially Undersecretary of State Robert Lovett, worried about the disparate
attitudes in the Republican-controlled Senate, ranging from isolationists to
UN supporters to anti-Russian hawks. They therefore consulted early with
Senate Foreign Relations Committee Chairman Vandenberg, who indicated
his conditional support for a treaty.[35] Passed by the Foreign Relations Committee on 19 May and approved by the full Senate on 11 June, the "Vandenberg Resolution" endorsed the "progressive development of regional and
other collective arrangements for individual and collective self-defense in accordance with the purposes, principles and provisions of the [UN] Charter."[36]
The Vandenberg Resolution showed that the US security commitment
would proceed according to clearly defined constitutional means and that it
would rest on the principle of popular legitimacy. Popular support for the
alliance was essential in promoting a positive view of the world based on
shared democratic principles. The resolution reaffirmed American support for
the UN, but at the same time endorsed the idea of going outside the UN when
necessary to avoid a Soviet veto. It also sought to assure internationalists that
the new pact would remain consistent with the general principles of international relations that the US had initially hoped would prevail in the UN.
The Vandenberg Resolution stressed that American association with regional and other collective arrangements must be "based on continuous and
effective self-help and mutual aid." By this clause Vandenberg sought to ensure that the Europeans would be producers, and not solely consumers, of
security. This principle was included to strengthen European integration as a
front line of containment and to help gain Senate support for a treaty based
on burdensharing principles.
The Europeans were not pleased with this provision. They continued to feel
vulnerable without assurances of direct military aid from the US. However,
they would have to agree to the burdensharing principle if they wished to
make the American commitment to European security lasting by maintaining
US domestic support.

Uniting Power and Community

Formal negotiations began in Washington, D.C., on 6 July 1948 to shape
the institutional form of a peacetime security pact among the US, Canada, and
the Brussels Pact states. During the talks, two differing perspectives on the

alliance emerged among the participants. The first view was represented by Kennan, who intervened at the beginning and the end of the discussions. At the outset, Kennan proposed that the institutional form should be based on a "dumbbell concept" of alliance, in which the Europeans would assume primary military responsibility.[37] In this view, the US would provide aid while reducing its presence on the ground. Kennan also warned of potential consequences from over-promising what the alliance would do to enhance agreed principles and build a transatlantic community. He asked what would happen in a future situation "in which the countries of Eastern Europe might come out from under the Iron Curtain and be able to come into the European family?"[38]

The second, and prevailing, view came from the Americans most involved in the Washington negotiations—Hickerson and Theodore C. Achilles of the State Department's European Desk—who each held the view that any transatlantic treaty should be more than a traditional alliance. Both were influenced by a book published in 1939 by American journalist Clarence K. Streit, titled *Union Now*. Streit called for the unification of the North Atlantic democracies based on citizenship, defense, customs union, currency, and postal/communications systems.[39] In his memoirs, Achilles noted that both he and Hickerson had read and been impressed by *Union Now* and that they "shared enthusiasm for negotiating a military alliance and getting it ratified, as a basis for further progress toward unity."[40] Hickerson and Achilles entertained "a lot of generalization about common interests, democratic values, Atlantic civilization and the threat of Communism."[41] For example, the British representative Sir Oliver Franks noted that whatever their differences over the form of the alliance, all of the countries at the meetings shared a common conception of democracy—"the conviction that the state existed for the individual"—and that the Soviet challenge was a "collective concern for all members of the North Atlantic community."[42]

Though principles and ideals were important in Paris, France's representatives came to Washington seeking urgent military assistance.[43] The French also wanted the US to ensure that if a third world war broke out, it would be fought east of the Rhine and that American forces and military supplies would be available from the start to defend French territory.[44] The French were adamant to the point of intransigence about direct military assistance programs coming in conjunction with a formal institution. As Lester Pearson, head of the Canadian delegation, reported to Ottawa, "The attitude of the French is causing increasing impatience and irritation here and is incomprehensible to everybody."[45] The Americans were more blunt in their assessment. In a personal letter to American Ambassador Jefferson Caffery in Paris, Lovett complained: "Dear Jeff: The French are in our hair."[46]

The French concerns were eased when their representative Henri Bonnet was given a lengthy opportunity to air his position in an informal discussion at the home of Robert Lovett.[47] This style of formal and informal multilateral airing of grievances, compromise, and consensus-building played a key role in the development of the institutional form of a mutual defense pact. The founders saw a clear benefit in formalizing a process to facilitate the exchange of information among the member states and their representatives. As Achilles observed:

> The "NATO spirit" was born in the Working Group. Derick Hoyer-Miller [of the British delegation] started it. One day he made a proposal which was obviously nonsense. Several of us told him so in no uncertain terms, and a much better formulation emerged from the discussion. Derick said: "Those were my instructions. All right. I'll tell the Foreign Office I made my pitch and was shot down, and try to get them changed." He did. From then on we all followed the same system. If our instructions were sound and agreement could be reached, fine. If not, we'd work out something that we all, or most of us, considered sound, and whoever had the instructions undertook to get them changed. It always worked, though sometimes it took time.[48]

While the end result might not necessarily be exactly what one country had wanted, short-term interests were set aside for long-term mutual gains.

The negotiators believed that such forms of multilateral security cooperation might spill over into issue areas beyond collective defense. The Canadians, in particular, wanted to establish formal consultative forums addressing nonmilitary issues. Canada felt that a peacetime alliance required a political foundation, so that it would have longevity, provide a positive alternative to communism, deepen transatlantic political and economic integration, and promote cultural cooperation.[49] Pearson was quite prescient in his desire that security cooperation not be tied too closely to Soviet intentions. He argued that this "might mean that if the danger were removed, or appeared to be removed, this justification for a collective system would disappear. . . . Such a system was justifiable on broader grounds and should have a positive and not merely a negative purpose."[50]

Pearson's comment demonstrates that the actors who designed NATO's early institutional form had a forward-looking concept of power, threat, and alliances. They sought to preempt problems related to alliance cohesion by creating an institutional form with a broader purpose than collective defense. Such an approach represented a sophisticated assessment that détente could be as much a challenge to alliance cohesion as war and that the Soviet Union might use peace initiatives to divide the alliance. The new transatlantic security institution was given a broad foundation upon which it could survive Cold War tension, détente, and even peace—if the member states so desired.

Interestingly, Kennan endorsed this analysis, emphasizing that "the community of interests of the participating governments was wider than military, it was traditional, historical, and would continue. . . . Association was necessary entirely aside from the troubles of the moment and might well go far beyond the military sphere."[51] Nevertheless, the Washington working group was careful not to endorse too broad a concept of an Atlantic Community. The British in particular did not want to intrude on efforts to promote European integration via the Brussels Pact. France saw deeper multilateral cooperation as irrelevant to their immediate quest for military assistance. The US was also concerned that language promoting too much cultural cooperation, for example, would hurt the treaty's chances for approval in the Senate, which might have worries about intrusions on sovereignty.[52]

All of the parties except Britain supported the creation of a high-level council for political consultation, cooperation, and information exchange. The British worried that excessive consultative structures could delay a response to a crisis rather than facilitate military action, but London did not force this position and the decision was made to give the alliance a mandate to create an organizational structure. However, the working group did not envisage NATO as a supra-sovereign or heavily bureaucratized political authority.[53] States would remain the final arbiters of how the institution would be utilized. At its founding, NATO was not intended to be an independent actor in international relations. Instead, it would be a standing structure designed to aid the needs of its member states.

The Rationale for a Treaty and a Realist Backlash

On 9 September 1948 the Washington working group completed a highly classified document for home government review explaining the rationale for a North Atlantic security pact.[54] The report—referred to as the "Washington Paper"—concluded that the nature of the problem facing transatlantic relations was "to consider how the countries of Western Europe and those of the North American continent can most effectively join together for mutual aid against this common danger and achieve security." The common danger was identified as any Soviet attempt to use indirect or direct aggression. The Soviet Union was termed an "implacable enemy of western civilization." However, the Soviet threat was not to be the sole purpose of the institution. The purpose would be to deter a Soviet attack and to restore confidence among the people of Western Europe. "United States and Canadian association in some North Atlantic security arrangement would be a major contribution to this," the report concluded.

The presence of American forces in Germany guaranteed US involvement in any hostility in Central Europe. However, the report stressed that "If the arrangement is . . . to contribute to the restoration of confidence among the peoples of Western Europe, it would not be possible to base it on the presence of U.S. troops in Germany." A broader American commitment to Europe was necessary to guarantee successful reassurance for America's allies.

The Washington Paper concluded that a formal treaty was essential to meeting the dual objective of collective defense and reassurance. To make a treaty more palatable at home and to score propaganda points vis-à-vis the Soviet Union, the report recommended: "Soviet criticism could be offset by fitting the arrangement squarely into the framework of the United Nations and by providing not merely for defense but also for the advancement of the common interests of the parties and the strengthening of the economic, social and cultural ties which bind them." However, the report underscored that the political concept of the treaty went beyond propaganda and that a North Atlantic pact "should be more than an arrangement for defense alone; it should serve both to preserve the common civilization and to promote its development by increasing the collaboration between the signatories and advancing the conditions of stability and well-being upon which peace depends."

The working group concluded that a pact would require "adequate machinery for implementing its terms, in particular for organized coordination and strengthening of the defense capacities of the parties, beginning immediately as it comes into force." The working group summarized Canada's position, noting that cooperation in fields other than security would contribute to general security. "The Canadians," the Washington Paper stated, "felt that the purpose of a treaty should not be merely negative and that it should create the dynamic counter-attraction of a free, prosperous and progressive society as opposed to the society of the Communist world."

As the negotiators moved toward formal treaty language, their efforts were reinforced by the actions of Soviet leader Joseph Stalin. Stalin had begun implementing what would become a lengthy blockade of Berlin designed to break Western resolve over Germany. The Dutch representative suggested that the preamble to the treaty read simply: "Dear Joe."[55] However, in late September, George Kennan reentered the discussions and expressed serious reservations about the alliance's institutional characteristics and their potential impact on security. On 26 September Kennan prepared a draft memorandum for Marshall and Lovett in which he concluded:

> Instead of the development of a real federal structure in Europe which would aim to embrace all free European countries, which would be a political force in its own right, and which would have behind it the logic of geography and historical development, we will get an irrevocable congealment of the division of Europe into two military zones: a Soviet zone and a U.S. zone. Instead of the ability to divest ourselves gradually of the basic responsibility for the security of Western Europe we will get a legal perpetuation of that responsibility. In the long run, such a legalistic structure must crack up on the rocks of reality; for a divided Europe is not permanently viable, and the political will of the U.S. people is not sufficient to enable us to support Western Europe indefinitely as a military appendage.[56]

In late November a formal memorandum from the Policy Planning Staff (PPS 43) drafted by Kennan emerged. The memo warned: "There is a danger that we will deceive ourselves, and permit misconceptions to exist among our own public and in Europe, concerning the significance of the conclusion of such a pact at this time."[57]

Kennan was especially concerned that a military alliance could prevent a permanent settlement with the Soviet Union. He continued to stress that the primary Soviet challenge was political and that, for Moscow, "military force plays a major role only as a means of intimidation."[58] Thus:

> A North Atlantic Security Pact will affect the political war only insofar as it operates to stiffen the self-confidence of the western Europeans in the face of Soviet pressures. Such a stiffening is needed and desirable. But it goes hand in hand with the danger of a general preoccupation with military affairs, to the detriment of economic recovery and of the necessity for seeking a peaceful solution to Europe's difficulties. . . . We should have clearly in mind that the need for military alliances and rearmament on the part of the western Europeans is primarily a subjective one, arising in their own minds as a result of their failure to understand correctly their own position. Their best and most hopeful course of action, if they are to save themselves from communist pressures, remains the struggle for economic recovery and for internal political stability.[59]

Kennan concluded that a North Atlantic pact should not be the main answer to the Soviet challenge in Europe. A transatlantic institution could not substitute for "the other steps which are being taken and should be taken to meet the Russian challenge, nor should they be given priority over the latter."[60]

Kennan wanted an integrated Western Europe to be the main political and military component of containment in Europe. However, the European unity that Kennan sought could only be attained after these countries had been sufficiently reassured of their security. Thus Kennan's arguments were rejected on the basis that, with its nuclear umbrella and troops in Germany, the US could institutionalize a security guarantee to its weaker allies and thereby provide the reassurance Western Europe needed to build its resources for self-help. As Ernest Bevin had suggested in an April 1948 memo, the most important result of a treaty would be to provide confidence, which would make a Western Union more effective. "If the new defense system is so framed that it relates to any aggressor, it would give all the European states such confidence that it might well be that the age-long trouble between Germany and France might tend to disappear," Bevin concluded.[61] Thus emerged what became the unspoken but often-repeated rationale for NATO—keeping the Americans in, the Russians out, and the Germans down.

Membership Criteria: Geostrategic or Principles?

Early in the Washington talks, the geographical scope of membership was discussed. Options ranged from concluding an agreement only among the core nations involved, to inviting other countries to join with "graded" or "associate" status.[62] The group ultimately decided that all members must be full members and share in the benefits, risks, and costs that would come from collective defense.

The working group also worried that membership not be viewed as an effort to encircle Russia—perhaps provoking a preventive war. The French representative asked: "Would it be wise, for example, to enlarge the system in such a way that could, however wrongly, be considered by Russia as encirclement?"[63] At the outset the decision was made that, where possible, membership would reflect shared values and principles—but the primary factor would be geostrategic.

Norway, Denmark, and Sweden had hoped to create a regional collective security institution of their own based on shared cultural identity, commonality of interests, and (at Sweden's insistence) neutrality. This neutrality policy suited Sweden, which had not been occupied during World War II, but it was of less interest to Norway and Denmark who had suffered from direct Nazi occupation. Additionally, Norway shared a border with the Soviet Union and Moscow placed considerable pressure on Oslo either to take measures to enhance its security or to negotiate a compromise with Moscow. Thus recent Norwegian and Danish historical experiences made Sweden's insistence on neutrality unappealing. At the same time, the US wanted Iceland, Norway, and Denmark (which was located at an important position at the entrance to the Baltic Sea and possessed the territory of Greenland) in the alliance because of their strategic importance as stepping-stones to Europe. Early in 1949 Norway came under strong pressure from Moscow to sign a nonaggression pact (as had been previously signed between the Soviet Union and Finland). This accelerated the collapse of the Scandinavian defense pact discussions and caused Norway and Denmark to move toward the Atlantic alliance.[64]

The Republic of Ireland too was invited to join the discussions on membership. Dublin responded that it would join the negotiations only as representatives of a united Ireland. While the Americans wanted the island state in the treaty within the context of "stepping-stones" (as a base for antisubmarine warfare), Dublin's linkage of the partition issue was unacceptable. The US neither wanted to incorporate a problem of the nature of Ireland's partition into the treaty nor offend its key ally, the United Kingdom. According to Achilles, Washington's response to Dublin was, in effect, "It's been nice knowing you."[65]

The US and Britain also wanted Portugal as one of the original treaty members. The Azores and the position of the Iberian peninsula as a gateway to the Mediterranean placed a strong geostrategic priority on Portuguese membership. However, the authoritarian dictatorship of Antonio Salazar stood in direct contrast to the nonmilitary foundations of the institution. In this early test of institutional norms and principles defining membership criteria, strategic priorities won.

Salazar labeled the proposed preamble of the North Atlantic Treaty as "manifestly unfortunate." Nevertheless, he added, "Be that as it may, we feel bound by the obligations of the treaty and by its general aims—not [in any way] by a doctrinal affirmation pointing to the uniformity of political regimes, of whose virtues in our country we have learnt enough."[66]

Canada raised fundamental concerns about Portuguese membership. Pearson told a British representative early in the negotiations: "If a pact were to be worked out which included declarations of belief in democracy, free institutions, etc., such as were included in the Brussels pact, it would be a little anomalous to have Portugal as an original signatory."[67] In the US, Sen. Forrest Donnell questioned whether Portugal was a democracy.[68] Sen. Henry Cabot Lodge asked Achilles in a confidential meeting how the US could square the "common heritage of freedom with the Portuguese tradition." To this Achilles responded that "although its government is not the same form of democracy as we have it, it is authoritarian, but it is not totalitarian. . . . If it is a dictatorship, it is because the people freely voted for it."[69] Portugal's entry into NATO required some careful diplomatic maneuvering in selling a treaty based on shared principles. It also set a Cold War precedent that when considering rules for membership, geostrategic needs would outweigh the stated institutional norms and principles.

Italy, Greece, and Turkey presented additional problems for the negotiators. In April 1948 Italian voters had overwhelmingly rejected communism, despite direct Soviet support for the Italian communists.[70] Nevertheless, there was a general concern among the negotiators that if Mediterranean states were admitted, they would diminish the "North Atlantic" character of the pact. Having secured Scandinavian participation, there was a legitimate concern that extending the scope of the treaty could harm the principle of mutual aid. Broadening the geographic membership raised a fundamental question of collective defense: Would Norway go to war to defend Mediterranean states or vice versa? Moreover, would an institution covering too large an area make effective decisions, or would it lose cohesion and collapse in a crisis?

The negotiators in Washington agreed that Italy had an important role to play in Central Europe and should be invited to join the final treaty negotiations.[71] Greece and Turkey were not invited because of concerns that they would dilute the North Atlantic element of the pact and possibly force the consideration of inviting Iran to join the treaty as well. There was, however, a general understanding that the Truman Doctrine made Greece and Turkey part of the area covered by the treaty. Greece and Turkey would have been defended by the US whether or not they were part of NATO because it was in America's interests to do so.

The North Atlantic Treaty

In his first public comments following his appointment as secretary of state, Dean Acheson said on 27 January 1949:

> We North Atlantic peoples share a common faith in fundamental human rights, in the dignity and worth of the human person, in the principles of democracy, personal freedom and political liberty. . . . We believe that these principles and this common heritage can best be fortified and preserved and the general welfare of the people of the North Atlantic advanced by an arrangement for cooperation in matters affecting their peace and security and common interest.[72]

Shortly thereafter, key elements of the security pact between the US, Canada, and Western Europe were carefully leaked to the press. On 18 March 1949 the treaty was made public in advance of signing ceremonies planned for early April. The public presentation of the accord prompted the Belgian prime minister to call it "diplomacy on the open market."[73] However, despite claims of transparency, the accord was the result of over a year of highly secret negotiations. The NATO treaty was neither open-market diplomacy or, as Acheson would later call it, "an open covenant openly arrived at."[74]

The pact institutionalized a balance-of-power security arrangement and reflected a growing sense of a transatlantic community among those who crafted the institutional form. As Acheson said in a radio address to the nation on 18 March:

> It is important to keep in mind that the really successful national and international institutions are those that recognize and express underlying realities. The North Atlantic community of nations is such a reality. It is based on the affinity and natural identity of interests of the North Atlantic powers. The North Atlantic treaty which will formally unite them is the product of at least 350 years of history and perhaps more.[75]

Similar sentiments had been repeatedly stressed in both public statements and classified documents throughout the negotiations over the treaty; they were the primary focus of the speeches given by the signatories at the treaty signing ceremonies; and they were formalized in the language of the North Atlantic Treaty, which was signed by representatives of the participating states on 4 April 1949.[76]

The preamble to the North Atlantic Treaty commits the members to "faith in the purposes and principles of the Charter of the United Nations and their desire to live in peace with all peoples and all governments." The institution was to be built by the members "to safeguard the freedom, common heritage and civilization of their peoples, founded on the principles of democracy, individual liberty and the rule of law." Members agree to "promote stability and well-being in the North Atlantic area" through collective defense.[77]

Article 1 of the treaty requires that the members not use force in "any manner inconsistent with the purposes of the United Nations." Article 2 incorporates the Canadian design for general security: "The Parties will contribute toward the further development of peaceful and friendly international relations by strengthening their free institutions, by bringing about a better understanding of the principles upon which these institutions are founded, and by promoting conditions of stability and well-being. They will seek to eliminate conflict in their international economic policies and will encourage economic collaboration between any or all of them." Burdensharing was identified as a priority institutional goal through Article 3: "The Parties, separately and jointly, by means of continuous and effective self-help and mutual aid, will maintain and develop their individual and collective capacity to resist armed attack." Should any member feel threatened by any state (including another member), Article 4 facilitates consultation within the institutional structure of the alliance, and Article 5 provides the security guarantee (under the right to individual or collective self-defense under Article 51 of the UN Charter) that an "armed attack against one or more of them in Europe or North America shall be considered an attack against them all."

The treaty provides for formal organization to aid multinational cooperation and consensus through a North Atlantic Council (Article 9), which would "set up such subsidiary bodies as may be necessary." Also, the treaty allows for enlargement in a manner that furthers its principles and contributes to the security of the North Atlantic area (Article 10). The treaty affirms that member states are the key actors by ensuring that the treaty "shall be ratified and its provisions carried out by the Parties in accordance with their respective constitutional processes" (Article 11). The spirit of this article would come to include ratification of changes in treaty membership through subsequent enlargements.

More Than an Alliance

The primary reason for NATO's founding was the Soviet challenge in Eastern Europe. NATO was an alliance created in response to a threat. As Charles Bohlen wrote in his memoirs: "Our participation in the North Atlantic Treaty arrangement was entirely due to Soviet policy and power. . . . Had the Soviet Union not chosen to prevent the unification of Germany in 1947 and 1948, there would have been no North Atlantic Treaty."[78] However, to explain primary causality is insufficient to understanding why the states chose the particular institutional form that emerged in April 1949. A variety of factors beyond the Soviet threat coalesced to determine the form that the NATO alliance would take in its early years.

First, the national representatives who negotiated the NATO treaty placed a high value on using the alliance to enhance the principles that they believed united their countries—peaceful international relations and democracy. The negotiators recognized that if a peacetime alliance were to withstand the ebbs and flows of the Cold War, it would have to reflect a broader purpose than collective defense. Second, the negotiators had a concept of national security challenges that went beyond the Soviet threat. They saw states challenged by fragile economies, weak political systems, and the potential for internal Soviet influence or traditional nationalism spreading from within and threatening regional stability. Third, the US insisted on a specific institutional form that would prioritize burdensharing and strengthen the capacity of the European allies to help themselves. Washington sought to make certain that the European members would be more than security consumers—that they would have to contribute as well. Fourth, during the negotiations, a pattern of consultation and information exchange developed in which short-term compromises were made in the interest of shared long-term interests. This "NATO spirit" of consultation and consensus was viewed as so beneficial to the negotiations that it was institutionalized in the North Atlantic Council and its subsidiary organs.

Critics of NATO, such as George Kennan, were present during the negotiations. Later, some realist observers would discount the nonmilitary tasks given to NATO as mere window dressing designed to sell an entangling alliance with Europe to the US Senate. Indeed, the 9 September 1948 Washington Paper recommended that if the treaty were placed within a UN context, it could have positive propaganda results. US Secretary of State Acheson endorsed the Canadian proposals primarily to appeal to internationalist senators. In 1949, Acheson spoke of NATO in colorful language stressing its foundations in Western civilization but in 1966 he admitted:

> The plain fact, of course, is that NATO is a military alliance. Its purpose was and is to deter and, if necessary, to meet the use of Russian military power or the fear of its use in Europe. This purpose is pretty old-fashioned. Perhaps to avoid this stigma, Canadian draftsmen had Article 2 inserted into the treaty.[79]

Reflecting on NATO's founding, Henry Kissinger writes: "America would do anything for the Atlantic Alliance except call it an alliance. It would practice a historic policy of coalition so long as its actions could be justified by the doctrine of collective security."[80]

These assessments stand in contrast to those of the widely recognized founder of contemporary realism, Hans J. Morgenthau. In his *Politics among Nations*, Morgenthau declares: "In its comprehensive objectives and the techniques used to accomplish them, NATO indeed moves beyond the traditional alliance toward a novel type of functional organization."[81] A purely realist view of NATO's non-alliance functions implies that statesmen such as Bevin, St. Laurent, Pearson, Lovett, Marshall, Acheson, and Truman intentionally misinformed public opinion. Similar sentiments were pervasive in the confidential treaty negotiations, and the records show that the participants placed a high value on the principles on which the institution would be founded. Realism was not rejected by those who created NATO. Realism was transformed by pragmatic diplomats into an understanding that a particular institutional form would shield this peacetime alliance because it was founded upon a broader concept of security challenges than the Soviet threat alone.

NATO was intended to perform four tasks at its founding. The first, and primary, function was to promote collective defense by signaling to the Soviet Union the will of the member states to come to each other's aid in the event of an attack. The second was to reassure the West European members of their safety so they could assume responsibility for their security and thus enhance allied burdensharing. The third was to strengthen and expand an international community based on democratic principles, individual liberty, and the rule of law in the context of a peaceful international society. The fourth was to build institutional structures to aid the completion of these goals.

The organizational capabilities present at NATO's founding were minimal. The institutional form was premised on state dominance and avoidance of hierarchy. NATO was never intended to have institutional autonomy. Even in the event of an attack on a member, Article 5 only committed states to respond "individually and in concert with the other Parties, such actions as it deems necessary." It would be incumbent upon the member states to implement the security guarantee, and the response would not necessarily be automatic.

In its earliest days, NATO had no standing organization and relied on the underdeveloped Western Union for military planning. The North Atlantic Council was created to facilitate international cooperation and it was tasked to establish a Defense Committee responsible for making recommendations on meeting the needs of collective defense. Early NATO meetings initially consisted only of the foreign ministers of the member states meeting on an ad hoc basis with no standing procedures or structures to facilitate or implement institutional objectives.

Principles and norms were defined in the treaty negotiations and were enshrined in the preamble and the treaty language. Specific rules and procedures were narrow and were left for further development. Yet it was also clear that collective defense needs outweighed principle in the decision to include Portugal as a founding member. Procedurally, Article 4 promoted formal consultation in the event that a member felt threatened from any source. The treaty also established procedures for national adherence to the constitutional procedures of each member. The institution was restricted in its membership rules. Becoming a new member would require a contribution to the principles of the treaty and to the security of the North Atlantic area. However, it was primarily restricted by the distribution of power in the international system and the division of Europe into competing spheres of influence.

The founders of NATO hoped to instill the institution with a capacity for change. The decision to endow this alliance with institutional characteristics was designed to aid the process of adaptation. For example, the NAC was empowered to set up subsidiary bodies as might be necessary; NATO could enlarge; the treaty was open to review by the members after a ten-year period; and after twenty years in force, any party could leave one year after a notice of denunciation had been given. Nevertheless, the decision on how to advance variations in institutional form was reserved for the member states.

During the intensive information exchange in the treaty negotiations, a sophisticated understanding of the complex security challenge was attained, which affected the institutional form of NATO. By institutionalizing a US security commitment, Europe attained a period of reassurance in which military assistance could flow to them and in which Marshall Plan aid could stabilize their economies. The information exchange created a better understanding of national security concerns among allies. The participants learned to work together, and make concessions when necessary, toward common objectives. However, at its founding, NATO held considerable potential as a false promise of security. In fact, little actually changed immediately following the signing of the North Atlantic Treaty. The choice of songs to be played at the treaty signing ceremonies was suitably ironic: "It Ain't Necessarily So" and "A Whole Lot of Nothin' " from the musical *Porgy and Bess*.[82]

3

Who Put the "O" in NATO?

Collective Defense

At its founding, NATO was an institutional shell promoting reassurance for Western Europe. The US security guarantee was mostly political in nature and had no organizational structure to facilitate the tasks of the alliance.

In September 1949 the North Atlantic Council was identified as the principal authority of the alliance. The NAC would meet at the request of any of its members and periodically as the situation required. Soon a pattern emerged of the NAC meeting in formal ministerial session biannually at the ambassadorial level in weekly meetings at NATO headquarters established outside Paris (relocated to Brussels, Belgium, in 1967).[1] The NAC established a Defense Committee consisting of defense ministers responsible for defense planning. A Military Committee was created to meet at the chiefs-of-staff level to advise the NAC on military issues. A Defense Financial and Economic Committee and a Military Production and Supply Board soon followed.

Significantly missing from this military institution was an organized military capability. As US Secretary of State Dean Acheson asserted, NATO was conceived as a "pre-integration organization, aimed to produce general plans for uncoordinated and separate action in the hope that in the event of trouble a plan and forces to meet it would exist and would be adopted by a sort of spontaneous combustion."[2] NATO had no integrated forces, no defense plan, and no real means of mobilizing against a Soviet attack. However, dramatic global events prompted a major adaptation of NATO's institutional form. The Soviet attainment of nuclear weapons, the victory of the communists in mainland China, and the war in Korea globalized the Cold War and had a major impact on NATO as it was transformed into a highly formal military alliance.[3]

In Europe, the divide between East and West had become startlingly unbalanced by the early 1950s. Twelve divisions and under 1,000 combat aircraft were available to defend NATO against an estimated 210 Soviet divisions accompanied by over 6,000 aircraft. President Truman asked Congress for a substantial military assistance program for Western Europe which included a planned increase of US troops stationed in Europe from 145,000 to 346,000 by 1952. NATO members agreed to establish a formal military command structure to be headed by the Supreme Allied Commander Europe (SACEUR). The first SACEUR was the World War II hero and popular American general Dwight D. Eisenhower.

Initially, Eisenhower led a military command with no military structure. NATO planning had previously been based on limited chiefs-of-staff cooperation that had begun in the Western Union and on regional national commands. US defense plans assumed an evacuation strategy, in the event of a Soviet attack, that would seek to hold a line at the Pyrenees.[4] Gradually this planning was extended to promise a defense of the Rhine and eventually the Elbe rivers after Eisenhower became SACEUR.

In 1952 the NATO ministers met in Lisbon and agreed to establish a US-dominated military structure and to build a force structure including twenty-five to thirty divisions stationed in Central Europe—primarily in western Germany. Development of such an ambitious force goal would require multilateral consultation to avoid duplication in defense planning. However, as Eisenhower observed of early NATO planning "devising an organization that satisfies the nationalist aspirations of twelve different countries or the personal ambitions of affected individuals is a very laborious and irksome business."[5] The NATO members thus created an international political and military bureaucracy to aid the process of multilateral defense planning. A political organization was created by the member states, to be headed by a secretary general in charge of an International Secretariat staffed by representatives from the member states. The secretary general was to speak for and prepare matters for the NAC, and implement NAC decisions with the help of the International Secretariat.[6] A tradition was born that the position of secretary general would be held by a European.

Political Consultation

Consultation and consensus became the primary decision-making procedures in NATO. Each was essential to alliance cohesion and became institutionalized over time.

The "habit of consultation," as Eisenhower described it in 1958, did not come easily.[7] The demand for increased consultation among NATO members arose primarily from the need to prevent conflicts that occurred outside the NATO area, and involved its members, from negatively affecting alliance cohesion. Several international events accelerated this demand. In 1954 the fall of Dien Bien Phu and the departure of France from Indochina strained relations between Paris and Washington as the US was quick to fill the strategic void left by the French. Both French and British relations with the US were strained during the Suez crisis of 1956. Additionally, the inability to coordinate a unified political response to the Soviet repression of Hungarian reform movements in 1956 made NATO appear ineffective and irrelevant in a time of crisis. De-Stalinization in the Soviet Union and the potential for an East–West détente also placed political pressure on NATO to respond or risk appearing irrelevant as external events outpaced its ability to adapt.

In 1956 a Committee on Non-Military Cooperation was established by the NAC, to be headed by the foreign ministers from Italy, Norway, and Canada— commonly referred to as the "Three Wise Men."[8] They concluded that

> consultation within an alliance means more than letting the NATO Council know about national decisions that have already been taken; or trying to enlist support for those decisions. . . . It means the discussion of problems collectively, in the early stages of policy formation, and before national positions become fixed. At best, this will result in collective decisions on matters of common interest affecting the Alliance. At the least it will ensure that no action is taken by one member without a knowledge of the views of the others.[9]

In accepting the report, the NAC empowered the secretary general to take a lead role in settling disputes among the allies. If the parties consented, the secretary general could initiate or facilitate procedures of inquiry, mediation, conciliation, or arbitration. In addition to the increased scope of activity for the secretary general, NATO further enhanced its organizational structures, and consultation was increased at all levels of the organization.[10]

Despite this expanded institutional activity, many problems emerged from NATO's consultative procedures and have persisted during and beyond the Cold War.[11] First, the sharing of information on sensitive issues of national security policy, even among the closest of allies, is something that states are hesitant to undertake. Second, members tend to utilize consultative mechanisms solely to enhance national interests—not necessarily those of the collective good of the institution. Third, excessive consultation can be time-consuming and members are likely to circumvent the institution if a situation requires quick decisions. Fourth, national bureaucracies can frustrate, delay, or even block collective action due to their own decision-making procedures. Fifth, the flow of information can highlight differences among allies and contribute to a political crisis of cohesion and lower the deterrent value of the alliance.

Most importantly, NATO's formal political structures were not designed to have an independent impact on outcomes. The decision-making heads of state met rarely and then only to endorse previously debated and approved documents. Foreign, defense, and military staff leaders would generally meet just twice a year. It was in the lower-level NATO committees, chaired by representatives of the International Secretariat (to ensure continuity of committee mandates and provide a neutral voice), that the everyday institutional activity occurred.[12]

Committees were often instructed by the NAC or other organs to conduct particular tasks such as short- and long-term studies (for example, assessments of the Soviet threat or Warsaw Pact capabilities). If, in committee work, an impasse arose that could not be resolved via consensus, the dispute would be referred to the NAC or to home governments for instructions. After completion of their work, committees might forward their recommendations to the NAC for action. This advice would be reviewed by member state governments and a final decision made by national ambassadors in the NAC acting on instructions from their home governments. NATO's committee activity did aid the flow of information and expertise—but committees did not make independent decisions. Moreover, the decisions that were eventually made generally reflected the desires of the stronger and more influential members of the alliance.

Despite these obstacles, NATO members saw benefit from political consultation. Larger states gained by obtaining in advance better knowledge of other members' national security perspectives to avoid confrontation when seeking support for a policy. Alternatively, bargaining or coercive strategies could be more readily developed by the larger states when attempting to bring others toward a particular position. Smaller members also gained, as diplomatic proximity at NATO headquarters facilitated the organization of coalitions to influence the larger states. Also, since each member of the NAC had an informal veto over NATO activity in the consensus process, maintaining alliance cohesion often required bargaining with a state for its support in the NAC. Thus a small state could exact concessions from a larger member via the consultative and consensus process.

In this environment, the most effective form of consultation that developed in NATO was informal. "Hallway negotiations" among national representatives were often the best way to get an understanding of the reasoning behind another member's formal positions or to work toward building consensus on a particular initiative. However, the very nature of such negotiations— personal and confidential—makes it difficult to demonstrate specific linkage to an increase in national security. The same is true of semiofficial discussions between member states held in the private office of the secretary general. Such meetings are held primarily absent staff and held in strict confidentiality.

One indication that states saw benefit from informal consultation was the emergence in the early 1960s of a scheduled lunch among the NAC ambassadors at which no subject was barred. The lunch occurred prior to the weekly NAC ambassadors meeting so that the participants had a better sense of what to expect in the NAC. The meetings were institutionalized but remained informal and off the record. Each member state hosted the lunch on an alphabetical rotation. This allowed Iceland or Luxembourg as much opportunity to shape the agenda as France or the US. The secretary general was invited to participate as an equal voice among the member states at the table. Participants gave personal views of international events occurring in or out of NATO. The ambassadors were free to challenge or debate their own national instructions—possibly leading to a request for a change of instruction if it would facilitate consensus.[13] Nevertheless, consensus among NATO ambassadors did not guarantee that anything substantive would result in the NAC. In their formal activity, representatives still had to act according to their national instructions.

By the 1990s, the weekly lunch meeting had become deeply ingrained in the institutional culture of NATO. It is held at the private residence of each NATO ambassador as well as those of the secretary general and deputy secretary general on a rotating basis. The agenda is usually set by the secretary general or his deputy as well as by the host country and the remaining ambassadors as required. Generally, the substance of the next day's formal ambassadors' meeting in the NAC will be discussed and national positions made informally known to the others at the meeting. This gives the ambassadors an opportunity to correspond with their home governments and either confirm or seek changes in government policy in advance of stating their formal position in the NAC. It also gives the secretary general an opportunity to raise issues to the national delegates on behalf of the organization and explain how particular decisions might affect NATO as an institution. Informally, the lunch also serves as an opportunity for ambassadors to blow off steam around their colleagues in a less formal manner than that provided by the NAC if there are serious disagreements within NATO. The lunch thus continues to be one of the most important informal patterns of consultative behavior within the state-dominated process of NATO decision-making. Indeed, to a certain degree the informal lunch process diminishes the importance of the official NAC meetings themselves as actual business occurs the day before.

Defense Planning

NATO's Cold War military organization was based on integrated regional command headquarters under the command of SACEUR at the Supreme Headquarters Allied Powers Europe (SHAPE). SACEUR, by tradition, has always been a senior American general.[14] The standing NATO military command headquarters were assigned personnel by member states and organized as an integrated military staff. Three kinds of forces were made available for military planning in NATO: forces assigned to NATO that were either under the operational control or command of SACEUR, or that would come under SACEUR's operational control or command during periods of emergency; forces from certain nations that agreed to assign them to the operational command or control of a NATO commander at some future date; and land, sea, and air forces under national command not specifically assigned to or earmarked for a NATO command but which might be placed under the operational command, control, or cooperation with a NATO command under certain circumstances.

Effective collective defense required that national military planning take into consideration the interests of the Alliance. NATO was thus tasked to lower the transaction costs of collective defense planning by overcoming disparities between collective defense needs and national military planning. This process was completed through a defense planning cycle conducted by NATO.[15]

The process was initiated with ministerial guidance as approved by the NATO defense ministers. Once guidance was given to the NATO staff, military planners developed force goals to be met by the member states. Then a follow-up was carried out to review national actions during the current year and adapt lessons learned into the next cycle of defense planning. NATO enhanced transparency via an annual exchange of information on national military planning. Additionally, NATO conducted command-post and live-action exercises to refine the planning process and expose national militaries to the technical requirements of collective defense. This annual defense review was incorporated into a common NATO Force Plan, which provided the basis for NATO defense planning over a five-year period.

If collective defense planning were to be effective, NATO would have to promote the national adoption of common standards, which would assure interoperability of forces and equipment and promote efficiency in multinational military planning and effectiveness in multilateral military operations. NATO standardization goals included equipment, components and parts for systems, and maintenance and training systems that assured the most effective use of the research, development, production, and logistical resources of member states.[16]

NATO made numerous attempts to promote standardization, including aiding the development of common military equipment via the NATO Basic Military Requirement (NBMR) procedure in the late 1950s. However, the NBMR could not overcome national perspectives on defense requirements and was abandoned in 1966.[17]

Subsequent efforts, including statements endorsing standardization in formal NATO communiqués, proved equally ineffective. By the 1980s NATO efforts were limited to promoting "interoperability" of equipment, designed to enhance the degree of compatibility between national military equipment. Though not based on one standard, the new goal was that national planning would promote systems that could be integrated into a NATO command on an effective basis.

Member states endorsed the principle of standardization, but in practice each state supported standardization only to the extent that its own model was to be the standard for common NATO purchases. For example, in the cases where NATO did attain some standardization of equipment (the M-44 torpedo, the F-104F fighter, and several missile systems), it was on the American model—attained only after hard leverage was exerted by the US and its related defense industries.[18] The inability of NATO to effect the collective defense requirement of standardization demonstrated the weakness of NATO's institutional functions and the primacy of its member states. As one observer concluded of NATO's standardization efforts, "The biggest impediment stemmed from the need for unanimity at each individual decision level; centralized control proved to be impossible because the [members] jealously guarded their independence."[19]

The identification of areas for infrastructure development—fixed military installations for the deployment and operation of integrated armed forces in the event of war—was another major task for NATO defense planning. NATO infrastructure needs included airfields, signals and telecommunications installations, military headquarters, fuel pipelines and storage, radar warning and navigational aid stations, port installations, and missile installations.

Infrastructure facilities could also provide early warning and enhance information available to decision-makers. For example, the NATO Air Defense Ground Environment (NADGE) was established as a linked system of standing sites ranging from Norway to Turkey and was equipped with radar and communications systems designed to alert NATO military authorities of an incoming air attack. This early-warning capacity was adapted further in the 1980s with the acquisition of a NATO-commanded fleet of E-3A Airborne Warning and Control System (AWACS) aircraft which served as mobile information-gathering systems and control centers as part of NATO's Airborne Early Warning Force (NAEWF). At NATO Headquarters, crisis management was aided by the NATO Situation Center, which was linked to the major NATO commands and infrastructure warning systems as well as to the member state capitals.

NATO was granted authority to identify infrastructure needs and to aid the flow of budgetary resources for infrastructure activities. The NATO member states would then jointly contribute to a common NATO infrastructure fund. The impetus remained with host countries (those who would host the infrastructure) and user nations (those who would contribute forces to the program). NATO civilian and military committees played an important advisory role in the multinational planning process, but initiative and implementation remained with the member state representatives acting on instructions from home governments. Pressure for infrastructure expansion grew from smaller states, who saw it as a means of enhancing their security and as having spillover economic benefits. However, once implemented and running, NATO could not justify or originate program expansion, as it had no independent control over funding.

The primary criteria for national contributions to the common infrastructure program were state-based and did not result in substantial financial resources. These criteria included the contributing capacity of the member countries, the advantage accruing to the user countries, and the economic benefit for the host countries. Though it was central to NATO's military effectiveness, the infrastructure program on average totaled less than .3 percent of combined NATO national defense spending.[20]

NATO did not administer the distribution of infrastructure funds. The members entered into mutual financial commitments and paid each other the requested amounts as needed. NATO's primary administrative role was to keep account of such transactions. The responsibility for actual administration lay in the Infrastructure Payments and Progress Committee, composed of member state delegations operating under national instructions.

Integration or Disintegration?

By the 1960s, NATO had the appearance of accelerating transatlantic integration, based on its increased consultative and defense planning characteristics. However, within NATO the trend was actually toward disintegration as the Cold War ebbed and flowed.[21] The successful Soviet launch of the Sputnik rocket in 1957 fueled a perception in the US that Moscow now had the capacity to reach American territory with intercontinental ballistic missiles carrying nuclear weapons. The Cuban Missile Crisis of 1962, in which the Soviet Union deployed intermediate range missiles ninety miles off the US coast, gave the world a glimpse of a superpower standoff bordering on nuclear war. Ongoing crises in Berlin, leading to the construction of the Berlin Wall, heightened tensions between the US and the Soviet Union in Europe. This new strategic environment tested the credibility of NATO's collective defense function and contributed to France's withdrawal from the integrated military command in 1966.

Initially, the ultimate deterrent behind NATO was the principle of Mutual Assured Destruction (MAD), which threatened massive retaliation by US nuclear forces in the event of a Soviet attack. But by the late 1950s, MAD was undermined by a fundamental challenge to the principle of collective defense: Would the US risk its own territory for that of its NATO allies now that the Soviet Union could threaten American soil? Since the US controlled nuclear decisions in NATO, reassurance had decreasing credibility for some European members. With nuclear parity emerging between the US and the Soviet Union, the concept of MAD actually increased the potential for a lower-level conventional attack in Europe, should the Soviet Union wish to test US resolve to defend Western Europe. As Roger Hilsman, a senior State Department official, wrote in 1959: "In the face of this new strategic situation, Europeans have begun to translate $E = mc^2$ into local terms."[22]

To reassure its European allies, and prevent any conventional war in Europe from escalating into a global nuclear exchange, the US initially appeared to support a plan (conceived by SACEUR Gen. Lauris Norstad) for a Multilateral

Force (MLF), which would make NATO a fourth nuclear power. The US would not put all of its nuclear forces under NATO command, but would grant NATO a collective role in the decision to use nuclear weapons. The primary hope behind creating the MLF was to reassure France in particular about the quality of the security guarantee it received in NATO and thereby convince Paris not to develop an independent nuclear force. However, to President Charles de Gaulle, the MLF was an insincere effort to enhance European reassurance that strengthened NATO integration, increased the US role in Europe, and thus constrained independent French action.

De Gaulle's concerns were heightened when, after first appearing to promote the MLF, the Kennedy administration decided that crisis decision-making required maximum US control over nuclear forces and that multiple decision-making centers would cloud the capacity to respond quickly. As an alternative, the US advanced a policy of "flexible response" in which NATO would respond step by step to a crisis by continually assessing the degree to which escalation might be necessary. The US would eventually offer reassurance to the Europeans by supporting the creation of a minister-of-defense–level Defense Planning Committee (DPC) with primary responsibility for military affairs (replacing the Defense Committee) and a Nuclear Planning Group (NPG) to increase smaller NATO members' involvement in the development of nuclear policy.

None of these institutional efforts satisfied General de Gaulle, who worried about the US commitment to French security. For several years, the US had used NATO planning structures to soothe French worries, but strategic concerns and national pride were still driving France away from NATO. To the extent that France was participating in NATO, it was as an obstacle to NATO planning.

In 1966, France informed its allies that it would withdraw from the NATO integrated military command and that all NATO installations should be removed from French territory. De Gaulle was careful to distinguish between NATO and the "Western alliance," in which France still considered itself a member. Moreover, France did not completely withdraw from NATO's political structure, thereby confirming the proposition that states found value in nonmilitary participation in NATO. By continuing its political role, France could continue to raise concerns about, and even block, NATO policy, should it wish.[23]

Little changed with the French withdrawal from NATO integrated military planning. The structure of the international system remained intact and NATO cohesion was actually enhanced as the remaining allies were able to proceed with decisions that had been held up by France. France also maintained its role in areas where it felt that NATO increased its security—such as in the NADGE early warning system, of which France continued to pay about 12 percent of the costs. Realizing that little had actually changed with the withdrawal of France, the US was not especially critical. The US remained committed to West European security, and the premise of collective defense remained forward defense in Germany. That policy was revised to account for nuclear planning via flexible response, but it was unaffected by the absence of France from NATO planning. Paris and Bonn negotiated a new status-of-forces accord allowing France to maintain its forces in West Germany outside of the NATO command structure, and thus the balance of power remained unchanged.

The dramatic external and internal changes that created crisis in NATO in the 1960s produced a reassessment of NATO's institutional tasks. The Harmel Report of 1967, as accepted by the NAC, broadened NATO's scope to include coordinating a multilateral détente strategy to relax tensions with the Soviet Union.[24] The report concluded:

> Military security and a policy of détente are not contradictory but complementary. Collective defense is a stabilizing factor in world politics. It is the necessary condition for effective policies directed towards a greater relaxation of tensions. The way to peace and stability rests in particular on the use of the Alliance constructively in the interests of détente.[25]

The report recommended that NATO coordinate a multilateral approach to bridging gaps between East and West, commit the major powers to full consultation with NATO allies on German reunification, overcome the division of Germany and foster European security, and coordinate and consult on arms control and mutual and balanced force reductions between East and West.[26] Despite this continued adaptation, the balance of power attained between east and west made NATO increasingly appear as an alliance that had outlived its usefulness and that was struggling to find new missions.

In a comprehensive overview of NATO's consultative functions written in 1969, Robert Hunter noted that NATO's institutions have "been unable, perhaps inevitably, to affect seriously the complicated process of diplomatic bargaining that have been the life-blood of the Alliance and the relations conducted among fifteen nations within that context."[27] A short list of major challenges to international security during the Cold War shows that NATO had little if any direct role. During the Suez, Cuban, and Vietnam crises, the views of European allies were largely ignored by the US. Major decisions related to Berlin and Germany were taken by the US, Britain, and France outside of the consultative framework of NATO.

The US and its allies were in disarray by the mid-1970s over disputes related to the Middle East. In the 1980s, Britain ignored its allies' concerns over its war in the Falkland Islands, and the US launched air attacks on Libya over the objections of all of its allies except Britain. On the other hand, by the 1980s, the Soviet deployment of SS-20 intermediate-range nuclear missiles targeted at Western Europe, the Soviet invasion of Afghanistan, and the violent repression of the Solidarity reform movement in Poland renewed the American commitment to a global Cold War strategy, with NATO its centerpiece. However, the same kinds of problems that the institution failed to ameliorate in the 1950s and 1960s returned to divide NATO in this new phase of Cold War tension. In particular, differences between the US and Western Europe over the perceived danger of the Soviet threat prompted resentment in Washington, D.C., over the failure of Europe to share in the burdens of collective defense.

For example, the Soviet invasion of Afghanistan signaled what the Americans viewed as a threat to US and European access to Persian Gulf oil. The US hoped to get European commitments to offset any reallocation of American resources from the continent to the Gulf theater of operations while establishing a US–led Rapid Deployment Force for the region. However, the Europeans did not share this assessment and rejected American opposition to a planned sale of gas pipeline materials to the Soviet Union. US Sen. Ted Stevens, representing a growing frustration in the US, commented: "If [the Europeans] feel so secure in their relationship with the Russians, then I think it is time for us to re-examine the number of troops we have in Europe."[28]

Burdensharing

NATO failed to ensure burdensharing. The primacy of NATO's alliance functions contributed to a political economy of West European military dependence on the US, as George Kennan had warned during NATO's formative period. This shortcoming constrained Europe's capacity to act on its own and became a constant irritant for many American members of Congress. Many Americans felt that the European allies were "free-riding" on the US, which spent disproportionate amounts of its gross national product (GNP) securing Western Europe.[29] The lack of burdensharing in NATO became ingrained in the political economy of West European integration.

Disproportionate cost-sharing in NATO is demonstrated by comparing relative defense expenditures as a percentage of GNP among major alliance members.[30] For example, in 1953 the US spent 14.7 percent of its GNP on defense while France and Britain spent around 11 percent, and in the Federal Republic of Germany, the spending was less than 5 percent. As the US level fell, so too did those of the allies. By 1970 the American percentage had leveled off, while European contributions continued to fall. By 1980 the US figure fell to 5.5 percent, but only Britain raised its percentage. At the height of the early 1980s Cold War tensions, US defense spending rose to 6.5 percent while European spending remained unchanged. At the end of the Cold War in 1991, defense spending by the major NATO allies fell again. Over time, European contributions hovered just above or below 3.0.

As a global power, the US naturally maintained greater total defense expenditures, which appear as a larger percentage of the defense burden in NATO as measured by GNP. Adjusting for the non–NATO portion of national defense expenditures is difficult, especially for the US which saw its defense spending rise considerably during the Korean and Vietnam wars. Yet, as one study has shown, the US, with 48 percent of the aggregated NATO gross domestic product, provided 66 percent of NATO defense costs when Vietnam is excluded from the assessment. For equity to have been attained, the US would have to have spent $1.1 trillion less on defense between 1961 and 1988.[31]

Other major NATO powers did maintain a relatively high level of peacetime defense spending. For example, the Federal Republic of Germany maintained a large standing army as a frontline state in Europe. However, the internal and external constraints on West Germany assuming any role outside its own territory kept its defense expenditures relatively low. France maintained a relatively high share of the defense burden because of its perception that the American commitment to its security could not always be counted on. Nevertheless, France's defense expenditures actually fell following its withdrawal from NATO's integrated military command. This suggests that, in part, France was seeking to have the benefits of NATO without sharing in the costs of collective defense.

American gains in political and military influence in NATO were offset by opportunity costs in soft security while Europe made economic gains by avoiding heavy defense expenditures. European investment in human and industrial resources through welfare states was part of a strategic effort to provide an alternative economic model to Soviet communism. Yet as the European welfare states grew, so did domestic bureaucracies resistant to reallocating resources that might have reassured the US that European promises to share the costs of security were sincere. Even if there had been a desire to contribute more to the costs of collective defense, the political economy of NATO and European integration made this an unlikely policy option in Europe. Forced to choose among continued free-riding on the US, raising taxes, reducing popular welfare-state spending, or increasing budget deficits, European leaders were left with an easy political decision. Though often publicly berating NATO and the US, Europe continued to support the alliance. West European security dependence on Washington thus became deeply ingrained in the political economy of European integration.

The European Pillar

The day after signing the NATO treaty, the Brussels Pact countries submitted a formal request to the US for military and financial aid.[32] This request fueled State Department and congressional concern that the US would be expected to underwrite the economic and military recovery of Western Europe. Kennan lobbied against military aid to Europe. He argued that the militarization of NATO would hinder efforts toward a political settlement with the Soviet Union. Senator Vandenburg felt that it was inappropriate to overemphasize the military and cost aspects of NATO, as the Senate was about to debate treaty ratification. A compromise was reached to postpone congressional debate on military assistance until after the treaty was approved.[33]

Adequate collective defense required a forward defense strategy centered on Germany and its rearmament. Thus, early on, defense planning and burdensharing were linked. As President Truman wrote in his memoirs:

> Without Germany, the defense of Europe was a rearguard action on the shores of the Atlantic Ocean. With Germany there could be a defense in depth, powerful enough to offer effective resistance to aggression from the East. Any map will show it, and a little arithmetic will prove what the addition of German manpower means to the strength of the joint defense of Europe.[34]

As Lawrence S. Kaplan asserts: "Not only was it illogical to omit the German component to NATO, it was also unfair. . . . Why should Americans—and Europeans—labor to defend a West that includes Germany without the Germans participating in the common defense?"[35]

France insisted that German rearmament be carried out through an all-European army which would grant Paris authority over German military activity. To that end, French Premier René Pleven proposed creating a European Defense Community (EDC), which would also accelerate European economic integration via the creation of a supranational integrated planning structure. The EDC would be based on a Special European Force with its own European minister of defense and with an independent command staff under the authority of existing NATO command structures. Germany would contribute manpower but would not have its own General Staff, defense ministry, or armaments industry. Unlike NATO, the EDC would decide the direction and control of arms industries on behalf of its member states.[36] The US endorsed the EDC as a means of strengthening the European contribution to collective defense while maintaining the primacy of NATO and attaining both objectives through the inclusion of West Germany in NATO.

The EDC treaty was signed on 27 May 1952, and a number of parliaments ratified it.[37] However, France—which had originated the concept—caused it to fail. Historical sensitivity toward military integration with Germany, concern that French colonial distractions in Indochina would allow Germany to increase its power in Europe, and intense differences of domestic opinion between pro–NATO forces and nationalist Gaullists, all prompted the French National Assembly to defeat the EDC treaty on procedural grounds on 30 August 1954. For its part, Washington had not eased French worries about

American reliability. For example, US Secretary of State John Foster Dulles had warned that failure of the EDC might prompt an "agonizing reappraisal" of the American commitment to Europe.[38]

As an alternative to the EDC, Britain suggested a NATO solution to manage Germany and promote reassurance for its neighbors. In September 1954 Foreign Secretary Anthony Eden proposed revitalizing the Brussels Pact to create a Western European Union (WEU), to include Germany and Italy. Because the security guarantees of the WEU would apply to the same states as the NATO guarantee, the WEU could become the means of bringing West Germany into NATO. This option would avoid militarizing the WEU and would thus be more a political event than an effort to create a functional European pillar of NATO.

The proposed modification to the Brussels Treaty specified that "recognizing the undesirability of duplicating the military staffs of NATO, the Council and its agency will rely on the appropriate military authorities of NATO for information and advice on military matters."[39] Nevertheless, the WEU proved to be a workable means of settling the question of forward defense. It included Britain, reassured France, and promoted the principle of a European pillar of NATO, thereby for a time satisfying the US. This institutional adaptation facilitated an acceptable compromise among disparate national security concerns in which the major participants believed that their security had increased.[40] Nevertheless, the European allies failed to achieve any capacity to contribute to operational burdensharing and their security dependence on the US deepened.

Sharing the Costs of Security

By the 1960s, the failure of Europe to establish an operational European pillar in NATO began to draw strong criticism in the US Congress. Such discontent was heightened by a growing dispute over balance-of-payments deficits between the US and Europe caused by the cost of maintaining troops and variations in currency exchange rate losses.[41] The issue took the political form of American pressure on Germany to provide offset payments to the US for maintaining forces there. Germany agreed to a program of arms purchases from the US and some direct payments for American troop activities. However, in Europe there was already a sense of shouldering the greatest burden. Any potential war with the Soviet Union would most likely take place on European territory. Additionally, the German public was increasingly frustrated with the permanent presence of foreign troops and their regular large-scale exercising.

In 1966, Sen. Mike Mansfield began introducing a series of Senate resolutions that asserted that NATO would not be harmed by substantial reductions in US troop levels in Europe. Sen. Mansfield hoped to use legislation to return

NATO to its origins of promoting a strong European pillar organized within the transatlantic context. The original Mansfield Resolution declared:

> The condition of our European allies, both economically and militarily, has appreciably improved since large contingents of forces were deployed. The commitment by all Members of the North Atlantic Treaty is based upon the full cooperation of all Treaty partners in contributing materials and men on a fair and equitable basis, but such contributions have not been forthcoming from all of the Members; relations between the two parts of Europe are now characterized by an increasing two-way flow of trade, people and their peaceful exchange; and the present policy of maintaining large contingents of US forces and their dependents on the US continent also contributes further to the fiscal and monetary problems of the US.[42]

Seeking to reassure the NATO allies, President-elect Richard Nixon wrote to NATO Secretary General Manlio Brosio in early 1969, "There will be no diminution of America's commitment to the defense of Western Europe or to the Organization you so ably serve."[43] The Nixon Administration persuaded the European allies to agree that any reductions in NATO troop levels be done in the context of mutual and balanced force reductions (MBFR) to be negotiated between NATO and the Warsaw Pact and not through unilateral declarations. The idea that support for Mansfield-style legislation might damage arms reduction efforts (and thus hinder military cost-reductions) therefore took some steam out of Mansfield's efforts.[44] Nevertheless, Mansfield had struck a chord in Congress, which was frustrated with maintaining 315,000 uniformed troops, 235,000 dependents, and 14,000 civilian employees stationed in Europe—all of which contributed to a dollar gap in foreign exchange amounting to a $1.5 billion annual deficit.[45]

In 1977 NATO members agreed to balance burdensharing as measured by percentage of GNP. As part of US President Jimmy Carter's Long Term Defense Plan (LTDP) to modernize conventional and nuclear capabilities and promote standardization of equipment among the allies, the NATO members agreed on 18 May 1977 to fund the project from 1979 to 1984, with a 3-percent annual increase in NATO-related defense expenditure in real terms required from each member state.[46] A senior Carter administration official told US senators in a closed meeting that the 3-percent solution was based on "our perception that we needed some kind of an agreed program whereby we could get the Allies to come along with us in the rearmament we saw as necessary in NATO."[47] Actually, the European defense expenditures had been rising at an average of about 3 percent during the 1970s as part of national force modernization programs—while US spending had been in decline.[48] Nevertheless, the political perception of the Europeans as free-riders remained strong in the US Congress.

By endorsing a 3-percent solution to promote burdensharing, the NATO members created a supranational guideline to which member states were expected to adhere. However, there was no mechanism for guaranteeing compliance. The DPC communiqué qualified the plan by adding "this annual increase should be in the region of three percent, recognizing that for some individual countries economic circumstances will affect what can be achieved." In Washington, the program sparked bureaucratic debate, with the Office of Management and Budget (OMB) insisting that only defense outlays for NATO should be counted and thus there was no need for an increase in US defense spending. Meanwhile, the National Security Council and the Department of Defense asserted (successfully) that the NATO plan should apply to the entire defense budget.[49]

The internal American debate over how to measure national commitments to this burdensharing plan suggested to the Europeans that creative legerdemain might allow members to circumvent the institutional objective. The result was a divisive program based on redundant military planning. Even if successful, the results would have maintained the perceived "unfairness" complaint over burdensharing—only measured at a higher proportionate level of GNP. Thus, as NATO moved toward the end of the Cold War, it had failed to achieve the institutional task of burdensharing. The objective of a reassured and economically strong Western Europe was attained in the form of West European economic integration, but it was built upon a security dependence on the US.

NATO Enlargement

Article 10 of the NATO treaty states: "The Parties may, by unanimous agreement, invite any other European state in a position to further the principles of this Treaty and to contribute to the security of the North Atlantic area to accede to this Treaty."[50] The relevant principles are "to safeguard the freedom, common heritage and civilization of their peoples, founded on the principles of democracy, individual liberty, and the rule of law."[51] NATO expanded three times during the Cold War—to include Greece and Turkey (1952), West Germany (1955), and Spain (1982). Each enlargement was done for strategic gain. Norms and principles were secondary and, in some cases, ignored entirely.

Greece and Turkey

Greece and Turkey were the focus of the Truman Doctrine and thus central to the US policy of containing the Soviet Union. However, they were not original NATO members. A number of strategic and political objections to Greek and Turkish membership were raised at NATO's founding by the negotiators. Central to these arguments were concerns over extending NATO's defense into the Middle East and up to the Caucasian border of the Soviet Union.

Neither country could really be considered "Atlantic." Moreover, as Greeks were Orthodox Christians and Turks Islamic, some founding members argued that neither country was representative of the early allied understanding of the Atlantic community. Finally, Britain was more interested in creating a separate alliance in the Mediterranean that would look toward the Middle East.[52]

The changed strategic environment of the early 1950s facilitated Greece and Turkey's entrance into NATO. Greece could serve as a containment point on the Balkan peninsula, and Turkey would cut off Soviet naval access to the Mediterranean Sea. Turkey would provide NATO planning with one of the largest standing armies in Europe—up to 25 divisions—which could tie down and distract the Soviet Union should it attack Central Europe. The two new members would also shore up NATO's southern command and open the way for US bases in Turkey.[53] In September 1950, Greece and Turkey were invited to coordinate with NATO defense planning. On 22 October 1951 Greece and Turkey signed protocols on their accession to the North Atlantic Treaty, which was formalized on 18 February 1952.

After joining NATO, Greece made initial steps to promote adherence to some NATO principles by encouraging civilian control over its military. For example, Athens sent officers to the NATO Defense College in Rome where democratic civil-military relations were studied. However, in 1967 Greek colonels staged a coup, using a NATO counterinsurgency plan (called *Prometheus*) intended for use in response to internal subversion.[54] NATO faced what one observer termed a "crisis of conscience" regarding one of its members.[55] However, NATO did nothing to discourage the Greek military. The Scandinavian NATO members did raise the issue of the Greek regime for discussion in the NAC. However, their efforts were deflected by more powerful members. NATO Secretary General Brosio also opposed discussion of the Greek regime—an act which the Scandinavian members argued went beyond the authority of his office.

American, British, and NATO officials met regularly with the Greek coup leaders.[56] Reflecting the realist policies of US Secretary of State Henry Kissinger, US and NATO officials believed that it was necessary to live with the Greek coup out of strategic necessity—even if it meant working with a military that was using NATO plans to subvert democracy.[57] The coup leader, George Papadopoulos, responded with decidedly pro-NATO policies.[58] However, NATO paid a price for this sacrifice of its founding principles. After the military government fell in 1974, the new civilian government quickly withdrew from the NATO integrated military command.[59] NATO's short-sighted policy had so alienated Greece that it actually decreased overall security in NATO by damaging collective defense capabilities in the Mediterranean.[60] Greece eventually decided that it could better constrain its historical enemy Turkey with a voice in NATO affairs. However, Athens was not able to negotiate readmission to the NATO integrated military command until 1980.

Greece's reentry was delayed due to obstacles raised by Turkey over command-and-control issues and territorial disputes in the Aegean sea.[61]

For its part, Turkey experienced a series of military coups, restrictions on the press, violent public protests, and martial law. In 1987, however, Turkey had parliamentary elections, showing momentum toward democracy. This movement continued in 1995 when parliamentary elections brought a peaceful change of government. Democracy appeared to be functioning marginally in Turkey—but not due to NATO. In these elections, the victorious islamic Welfare party campaigned on a platform that included withdrawing from NATO and establishing an "Islamic NATO." As a former US ambassador to Turkey asked, "How do you deal with a NATO ally led by a man who is fundamentally anti-NATO, fundamentally anti-Semitic and fundamentally pro-Islamist, even when he's largely behaving himself?"[62] In summer 1997, the secular Turkish military forced the Welfare party to stand down from government. This act was strategically appealing to some of Turkey's allies, but was extraconstitutional and undemocratic all the same.

NATO's record of managing relations between Greece and Turkey is also weak. In 1956 the NATO Secretary General Lord Ismay suggested that NATO could mediate Greek–Turkish disputes over what was then the British mandate of Cyprus. Though little came of this initiative, it was advanced again in 1957 by Secretary General Paul-Henri Spaak who proposed that the NAC sponsor a conference on Cyprus. Spaak advocated a federal arrangement for Cyprus, composed of Greek and Turkish assemblies, which would work with a British governor over a period of seven years. In the first case, a lack of consensus in the NAC prohibited NATO from acting, and in the second, the parties were unwilling to place good faith in NATO as a mechanism for resolving their disputes.

In 1964 Greece and Turkey were nearly drawn into a civil war on Cyprus, which held sizable Greek and Turkish populations. Like his predecessors, NATO Secretary General Dirk Stikker attempted to mediate on behalf of NATO.[63] There was also inconsequential debate in the NAC about the possibility of deploying a NATO peacekeeping force.[64] However, war was only deterred by the US acting unilaterally with power politics. On 5 June 1964 US President Lyndon Johnson dispatched a personal letter to Turkish Prime Minister Ismet Inonu asserting: "I hope you will understand that your NATO allies have not had a chance to consider whether they have an obligation to protect Turkey against the Soviet Union if Turkey takes a step which results in Soviet intervention without the full consent and understanding of its NATO allies."[65]

While Johnson appealed to the principle of peaceful settlement of disputes in his letter, it was the implied threat that the US might not come to Turkey's defense in the event of a Soviet attack that prompted a change in Turkish policy. The Turkish prime minister replied that the tone and substance of the US letter raised "great sorrow and concern" for Turkey. He specified that:

"Our understanding is that the North Atlantic Treaty imposes upon all member states the obligation to come forthwith to the assistance of any member victim of an aggression . . . [and] the only point left to the discretion of the member states is the nature and the scale of this assistance."[66] NATO did reassure Turkey somewhat as the NAC instructed Secretary General Stikker to observe Greek–Turkish disputes and report to the council. Given disparate views of NATO's role between Athens (which preferred the UN) and Ankara (which preferred NATO), it was necessary for Stikker to distinguish between facilitating the information flow and mediation. The NATO secretary general concluded, "I am a watch-dog trying to diminish tensions between Greece and Turkey."[67]

In 1967, renewed strains over Cyprus nearly brought Greece and Turkey to war again. NATO Secretary General Brosio was given a mandate by the NAC to use his office to lower tensions. Although the US approved Brosio's mission, President Johnson also appointed his own special envoy, Cyrus R. Vance, to mediate between the countries. Though the two worked in a complementary manner, it remained the influence of the US, and not NATO itself, that brought the two countries away from the brink of war.

Civil war in Cyprus again drew the two NATO allies to the brink of conflict in 1974. While negotiating with Greece in Geneva, Turkey quietly built up forty thousand troops on Cyprus, and then in a quick action took over 40 percent of the island in August. The US Senate responded by imposing an arms embargo on Turkey which lasted from 1974 to 1978. This restriction on Turkish freedom to act angered Ankara, and Turkey temporarily closed over two dozen US military installations on its territory.[68]

Turkish foreign policy toward Cyprus had been constrained by the balance of power on the island and by the US. NATO had no independent role to play beyond reinforcing the American pressure on Greece and Turkey in at least ten special sessions of the NAC. However, Turkey built up considerable resentment toward the US and, by association, NATO for the constraints it felt had been unjustly placed on its foreign policy.

In 1996 Greece and Turkey were still close to war (in this case over small rock islands in the Aegean Sea). NATO provided a forum in the NAC, where they were "read the riot act" for setting a poor example while NATO was implementing peacekeeping plans in nearby Bosnia-Herzegovina.[69] However, when NATO Secretary General Javier Solana offered his good offices for mediation, Athens rejected his participation, as it would imply there was even something to negotiate. In Greece's view the rocks were nonnegotiable and protected by international law. Once more, the tensions between Greece and Turkey were resolved by US diplomatic pressure—this time by President Bill Clinton and his top foreign policy representatives.

In 1997 further efforts were made by the US and NATO to lessen tensions between Greece and Turkey. The US appointed a special envoy to address the

future of Cyprus. Additionally, NATO Secretary General Solana advanced a
five-point plan for confidence building between Athens and Ankara. Solana
proposed regular bilateral meetings of senior Greek and Turkish officials on
the margins of the NATO ministerial meetings; a secure hotline linking the
secretary general with Athens and Ankara; efforts to resolve disputes over
command structure reform (particularly airspace issues); confidence building
measures such as exchanges of observers on naval vessels, a moratorium on
military exercises in July and August, and publishing military exercise plans;
and a ban on Cyprus overflights.[70]

The effects of these efforts were nonetheless minimal, as tensions continued
to escalate between Greece and Turkey over the European Union's 1997 decision not to extend an invitation to Turkey to be considered for membership
in that organization. Addressing his personal frustration with Greek–Turkish
disputes, President Clinton said on 12 June 1996, "As to Greece and Turkey
I can tell you that I am very concerned about it. . . . Both those nations are
our allies and Europe's allies through NATO, and I believe that the future of
the region which they both occupy would be immeasurably brighter if they
can resolve their problems and are immeasurably darker if they cannot."[71]

Ongoing differences between Greece and Turkey are time-consuming for
NATO and often distract its members from more important security issues. At
the same time, their differences often prevent NATO from effectively dealing
with their disputes because each can block NATO involvement. NATO has
played a constraining role and at times has served as a channel for information
between the two. This has lowered the risk that each other's military maneuvers, for example, might be misinterpreted as plans for an attack. However,
constant tension over Cyprus and the Aegean Sea ruined any chance of institutional cooperation enhancing security. From the mid-1970s through 1990
there were no significant joint military exercises between the two allies that
might have contributed to a culture of cooperation between the two. Most of
the exercises that Greece and Turkey have undertaken in the Aegean Sea since
1974 have not been with, but rather against, each other.[72]

Germany

West Germany's membership in NATO resulted from strategic defense
plans requiring West German rearmament and forward defense. Without a
solid defense of Germany, NATO defense policy would continue to rely on a
fallback strategy that would have ceded an advantage to the Soviet Union,
which had consolidated its presence in East Germany. To attain these goals,
NATO leaders looked to the alliance to allay Germany's neighbors' concern
over German rearmament. As the US representative in western Germany, John
J. McCloy, asserted in a classified memo in 1950 the challenge was, "to foster
the right kind of Germany and have that Germany accepted by other Western

powers, and indeed the whole democratic world, as an equal partner."[73] Even in France the issue was not whether Western defense plans should include West Germany, but rather how. West German Chancellor Konrad Adenauer believed that West Germany's future lay in identifying with Western institutions. Although the West German public largely opposed rearmament, Adenauer felt that West Germany's strategic position could be used to bargain for formal West German statehood.[74] For West Germany, statehood meant voluntary restraint within NATO guaranteed by the presence of US troops.

Meeting in Paris with its soon-to-be allies in October 1954, West Germany agreed as a condition of statehood not to manufacture atomic, chemical, or biological weapons; guided missiles; magnetic and influence mines; warships; or long-range bombers, except at the request of NATO.[75] West Germany also promised not to use its new military forces (which became the 500,000-man *Bundeswehr*) to force German unification. Upon entering NATO, West Germany agreed "never to have recourse to force to achieve the reunification of Germany or the modification of the present boundaries of the German Federal Republic, and to resolve by peaceful means any disputes which may arise between the Federal Republic and other states."[76] The US, Britain, and France added that any event that would "threaten the integrity and unity of the Atlantic alliance" from within, would result in the offending government "having forfeited its rights to any guarantee and any military assistance provided for in the North Atlantic Treaty" and would cause the other members to act with a view to "taking other measures which may be appropriate."[77]

The entrance of the Federal Republic of Germany into NATO was a compromise among diverse national interests. As Richard Kugler writes, "Each participant was required to undertake important, enduring obligations of the sort that sovereign nations do not normally accept. . . . [The Paris Agreements] made these obligations acceptable by offering each participant offsetting strategic gains that exceeded the costs of these commitments."[78] Moreover, as Joseph Joffe concluded, the resolution of the German question created a situation in which "collective gain could overwhelm the zero-sum logic of rivalry and relative gain."[79] This transparency and reassurance in turn provided an opportunity for complementary institutional activity—especially economic integration—to bind Germany to the West as a stable and peaceful democracy.

West German public opinion occasionally ran counter to NATO interests and periodic popular movements supporting German neutrality as a means of gaining unification arose during the Cold War. In the 1980s considerable anti-NATO public opposition grew in West Germany over the US nuclear deployment strategy during the INF crisis. Nonetheless, West Germany remained firmly embedded in NATO.

The end of the Cold War has shown the continued validity of this "dual-containment" function of NATO. When proposing "2-plus-4" negotiations on German unification to Soviet President Mikhail Gorbachev in February 1990,

US Secretary of State James Baker asked, "Would you prefer to see a united Germany outside of NATO and with no U.S. forces, perhaps with its own nuclear weapons? . . . Or would you prefer a unified Germany to be tied to NATO, with assurances that NATO's jurisdiction would not shift one inch eastward from its present position?"[80] By 1991 Germany was unified as a member of NATO—with Soviet approval.

Spain

Although NATO was willing to accept dictatorships in Portugal and Greece, the Spanish dictator Gen. Francisco Franco's relationship with Adolf Hitler during World War II prevented Spain from entering NATO. Nevertheless, the US viewed Franco as a useful ally because of his virulent anticommunism and Spain's strategic location at the entrance to the Mediterranean Sea. In 1953 the US began providing Spain with economic assistance in return for basing rights on Spanish territory.[81] Spain gained economic assistance and aid in military modernization from the bilateral relationship but ceded considerable sovereignty through a secret accord granting US access to Spanish territory in the event of war without previous consultation with the Spanish government.[82]

After Franco's death in 1974, Spain began a period of gradual democratic reform. Spain suffered only one major setback, during a failed coup attempt by armed forces associated with the Franco regime in 1981. Under Franco the primary function of the Spanish military was to prevent domestic unrest, with no independent civilian oversight of this responsibility. In its planning and operations, the Spanish military was oriented toward domestic police functions. To maintain loyalty to this arrangement, Franco established an officer-heavy patronage system. When democratization and military reform arrived in the late 1970s, the military thus became a formidable source of resistance.[83] The 1981 coup attempt demonstrated that weak civil–military relations posed a serious challenge to democratization in Spain.

Spain's path to NATO was guided by a desire among post-Franco political elites to use European institutions to aid democracy and decrease the likelihood of another coup. Once Spain joined NATO, the Socialist government of Felipé Gonzalez resolved to hold a referendum on Spanish membership. While the political leadership backed membership, the public was hostile to the US (and, by association, NATO) for its past support of Franco.[84]

Two strategies combined to win public support for Spain's membership in NATO. First, foreign leaders and domestic politicians informally linked Spain's membership in NATO to a path to the European Community—a more popular proposition.[85] Second, the Gonzalez government made concessions to public opinion on the status of Spain's membership in NATO: Spain would remain in NATO without joining the integrated military command, there would be no deployment of nuclear weapons in Spain, and efforts would be made to reduce the role of the US military on Spanish territory. With these concessions to public opinion, the 12 March 1986 referendum affirmed Spain's conditional membership in NATO by a vote of 52 percent in favor to 40 percent opposed. NATO and democracy had been procedurally linked through the Spanish referendum. However, other key variables besides NATO included the US desire to include the entire Iberian peninsula in NATO defense planning and Spain's quest to join the European Community.

Though it did not join the integrated military command, NATO's military goals were incorporated into Spain's national security planning. The Spanish military began preparing and organizing for external activity rather than civil-control functions. The Spanish armed forces assumed five key tasks to complement NATO planning: assure security on the Iberian peninsula; contribute to the strengthening of the defense of the western Mediterranean flank; participate in keeping the Atlantic routes open and assure the aero-naval passage between the US and Spain in the event of conflict; monitor and control the approaches to the Strait of Gibraltar; and integrate the Spanish air-warning network into the NATO–wide early warning systems.[86]

The Spanish government also instituted a comprehensive reform of its civil–military relations. Reforms included a pardon for those who had been punished for support of democracy in the military, and full civilian control over the Ministry of Defense.[87] Since the end of the Cold War, the trend in Spain has been toward increased support for NATO—with Spain sending considerable peacekeeping forces, first under a UN mandate and then under NATO command, in the Balkans. In November 1996, the Spanish parliament voted to join the NATO integrated military command. While Spain's military integration was delayed by a dispute with Britain over the status of Gibraltar, its path to integration was largely completed by December 1997.

The Primacy of Alliance

As NATO developed during the Cold War, it played a critical role in facilitating the collective defense of its member states. At the same time, a number of institutional weaknesses were demonstrated by the primacy of a US–dominated alliance and the limits of bipolarity. NATO failed to facilitate burdensharing in the transatlantic relationship. Indeed, west European economic integration became largely dependent upon the American security guarantee. NATO did fulfill its treaty goal of enlargement. However, it was done for strategic reasons rather than to enhance specific principles. Once new members joined NATO, the capacity of the institution to influence domestic or international outcomes was very limited. Change in NATO was responsive, slow, and dependent on the international distribution of power. The capacity of the alliance to shape the international environment after the Cold War would thus require a radical adaptation of its institutional identity and functions if NATO were to survive.

4

NATO after the Cold War

Winning the Peace

By the late 1980s, military overextension and internal economic crises forced the Soviet Union to withdraw from the Cold War stalemate in Europe. This process began in December 1987 when the US and the Soviet Union eliminated an entire class of nuclear weapons in Europe through the Intermediate-Range Nuclear Forces (INF) Treaty. A year later Soviet President Mikhail Gorbachev announced a reduction of 500,000 personnel from the Soviet military, to include a withdrawal of the most threatening Soviet forces from Eastern Europe. In November 1990, the Conventional Forces in Europe Treaty (CFE) was concluded by all NATO and Warsaw Pact countries.

CFE limits the deployment of military equipment between NATO and the former Warsaw Pact by restricting weaponry levels to defensive postures including tanks, armored fighting vehicles, artillery, attack helicopters, and combat aircraft to be implemented by each participating country with intrusive verification procedures. CFE troop restrictions within the Atlantic to the Urals region would seek to lower (between 1989 and 1997) NATO's collective force level from 3,410,600 persons to 2,158,000; the combined East European (Polish, Czech, Hungarian, Bulgarian, and Hungarian) levels from 820,200 persons to 452,000; and former Soviet levels from 4,260,000 to 2,124,000 persons. This included a reduction in the size of the Russian armed forces of around 1,500,000 personnel by 1997. Conventional reductions were followed by agreements between the US and the Soviet Union to reduce strategic nuclear weapons through the Strategic Arms Reduction Treaties (START) I and II. Together, the two nuclear treaties would eliminate nearly two-thirds of existing strategic nuclear forces.

Eventually, a revitalized nationalistic Russia might challenge European security with its large inventory of nuclear and conventional weapons and the capacity to promote instability in its neighboring states. However, there would be considerable warning time of a direct Russian threat to Central Europe as it would require large-scale violations of the verifiable CFE treaty. The most serious danger from post–Cold War Russia was not expansion but implosion, disintegration, and the proliferation of conventional and nuclear materials.

The end of a divided Europe, however, also elevated historical concerns about German power and the potential for security competition between Germany and Russia. Democracy appeared to be spreading in Central and Eastern Europe after the dramatic post-communist revolutions of 1989. Yet democracy did not necessarily mean stability and the potential for larger states to seek relative gains in a security vacuum was a factor that states had to consider in their strategic planning.

As NATO Secretary General Manfred Wörner observed in 1993, NATO's members and many countries from Central and Eastern Europe expected NATO to maintain the transatlantic relationship; manage international conflict; serve as a forum for multilateral diplomacy toward the East, backed by substantial military resources; alleviate traditional conflicts within Western Europe and contain a united Germany; provide predictability and reassurance in European–American relations in a time of increasing economic competition; and lower the costs of national security by pooling defense resources in cooperation with like-minded states.[1] Additionally, because NATO command and control arrangements, logistics, communications, and some forces were used indirectly with considerable success in the 1991 Persian Gulf War, some of its members hoped that NATO could facilitate the multinational use of force outside the NATO area. Indeed, the Gulf War was the first and only time that a NATO country has invoked Article 5's collective defense premise in response to Iraqi threats to Turkish territory. With its standing structures and years of consultative patterns and mutual trust, its members preferred NATO as the forum for addressing national security concerns to the Group of Seven (G-7) nations, the Organization for Economic Cooperation and Development (OECD), or the Conference on Security and Cooperation in Europe (CSCE).

Contrary to many theoretical assumptions about alliances dissolving in the absence of a threat, NATO moved to the core of an emerging European security architecture. Yet, for a time, it also became the center of false hopes of security for some areas of Central and Eastern Europe. While its members used NATO to make overtures toward winning the post–Cold War peace, little security was provided on the Balkan peninsula between 1991 and 1995. Events in the former Yugoslavia outpaced the ability of NATO to adapt to new security challenges and the willingness of states to make it function. Other organizations such as the EU and UN suffered even more from their institutional weaknesses. At times they caused more problems than they provided solutions for in the Balkan crises. Nevertheless, there were some important successes. A secure environment was established, in part by NATO, in Bosnia-Herzegovina from 1995 to 1998. NATO played a pivotal role in facilitating peace. However, its capacity to enhance long-term security was limited.

Promoting Stability in the East

Meeting in London in July 1990, the NATO heads of state stressed the continued institutional task of collective defense, while acknowledging that challenges to that mission had been radically transformed:

> We recognize that, in the new Europe, the security of every state is inseparably linked to the security of its neighbors. NATO must become an institution where Europeans, Canadians and Americans work together not only for the common defense, but to build new partnerships with all the nations of Europe. The Atlantic Community must reach out to the countries of the East which were our adversaries in the Cold War, and extend to them the hand of friendship.[2]

NATO invited East European leaders, including Soviet President Gorbachev, to address the NAC and to establish regular diplomatic liaison with the alliance. "This will make it possible for us to share with them our thinking and deliberations in this historic period of change," the NATO leaders proclaimed.[3]

In November 1991 NATO adopted a new strategic concept, after sixteen months of work and twelve different drafts by its Strategy Review Group (SRG). The process was completed with the understanding that the new strategic concept would represent the collective diplomacy of the NATO members. Reflecting the political nature of the drafting process, France joined the SRG, but only participated when it became clear that major strategic decisions affecting the future of European security were being made in its absence.

NATO members agreed that the primary challenge to their security was uncertainty and instability in the East, specifically:

> the adverse consequences of instabilities that may arise from the serious economic, social, and political difficulties, including ethnic rivalries and territorial disputes, which are faced by many countries in Central and Eastern Europe. The tensions which may result, as long as they remain limited, should not directly threaten the security and territorial integrity of members of the Alliance. They could, however, lead to crises inimical to European stability and even to armed conflicts, which could involve outside powers or spill over into NATO countries, having a direct effect on the security of the Alliance.[4]

NATO outlined four "fundamental tasks" for the alliance after the Cold War:

1. To provide one of the indispensable foundations for a stable security environment in Europe, based on the growth of democratic institutions

and commitment to the peaceful resolutions of disputes, in which no country would be able to intimidate or coerce any European nation or to impose hegemony through the threat or use of force.

2. To serve, as provided for in Article 4 of the North Atlantic Treaty, as a transatlantic forum for Allied consultations on any issues that affect their vital interests, including possible developments posing risks for members' security, and for appropriate coordination of their efforts in fields of common concern.
3. To deter and defend against any threat of aggression against the territory of any NATO member state.
4. To preserve the strategic balance of power within Europe.[5]

During the drafting there were divisions within the SRG.[6] Some members opposed the stress on preserving the strategic balance of power in Europe. This gave NATO an appearance of wanting to maintain the previous status quo at a time when the Warsaw Pact was in rapid dissolution. Additionally, some alliance officials and member states were deeply divided on whether NATO's successful adaptation would require amending its mission to include action outside of its territorial area. Among senior NATO officials there was considerable enthusiasm for giving NATO an out-of-area role—some arguing that NATO's future depended on it. However, France, in particular, opposed any "out-of-area" language in the document insisting that NATO should be maintained in reserve as a hedge against any new Soviet threat and not take on new missions.[7] NATO was in consensus on the need to establish an Allied Rapid Reaction Corps (ARRC) based on the new strategic concept. This was a new, more efficient, crisis management function for NATO. However, the ARRC was designed to respond to Article 5 challenges within the NATO area, not to provide security in the East where the new challenges were likely to arise.

Another key area of agreement was a consensus among its members that NATO be placed within a new amalgamated collective security framework of "interlocking institutions." The intent was to use international institutions to assist post-communist democratic and economic transitions in Central and Eastern Europe and to establish a mechanism for early warning, preventive diplomacy, and conflict management as an amalgamated form of collective security. The US and Europe sought to enhance the capacity of institutions to meet the evolving challenges of post–Cold War European security. The primary impetus in this outreach to Central and Eastern Europe came from NATO, which helped its members organize a collective approach to address a rapidly evolving set of security challenges.

The Conference on Security and Cooperation in Europe (CSCE)

Early NATO initiatives to the East focused on strengthening the Conference on Security and Cooperation in Europe as a "Pan European" institution ranging from Vancouver to Vladivostok.[8] Established through the Helsinki Final Act of 1975, the CSCE promoted international norms of the rule of law, non-aggression, and the peaceful settlement of disputes. The original members of the CSCE were thirty-five states from Europe and North America, and the group expanded to fifty-three by 1992.

During the Cold War, the US and its NATO allies emphasized CSCE norms to expose contradictions in the Soviet political system and as part of the general policy of détente. However, they were reluctant to grant the CSCE operational authority as this would have allowed the Soviet Union a veto over matters of direct concern to NATO because CSCE decisions were taken with unanimity. The Soviet Union liked the CSCE's stress on the inviolability of existing borders, which codified the division of Germany and the Soviet incorporation of the Baltic countries into the USSR.

Initially, leaders of the post-communist revolutions in Central and Eastern Europe promoted the CSCE as a forum to raise security concerns and credited the institution with exposing their populations to Western norms and values. For NATO, building a working partnership with the CSCE was a pragmatic means of reaching out to the nascent democracies to their east without expanding formal security guarantees. NATO enlargement was explicitly ruled out. As a senior NATO official commented, "At the London Summit in July of 1990, the decision was that we would establish a friendly relationship, that we would cooperate, and as this has evolved, this has taken more and more concrete forms—but membership is not one of these."[9]

The CSCE heads of state met in Paris in October 1990 and approved the Charter of Paris, emphasizing that: "Our common efforts to consolidate respect for human rights, democracy and the rule of law, to strengthen democracy and the rule of law, to strengthen peace and to promote unity in Europe require a new quality of political dialogue and cooperation and thus development of the structures of the CSCE."[10] The CSCE leaders established a Secretariat in Prague, a Conflict Prevention Center in Vienna, and an Office for Free Elections in Warsaw. Furthermore, the members created a Council of Ministers of Foreign Affairs for political consultation, to make appropriate decisions, and to prepare biennial CSCE summits. A Committee of Senior Officials was established to endow the CSCE with a standing body and a permanent organizational structure.

NATO's engagement with former Warsaw Pact countries via the CSCE accelerated at the June 1991 Copenhagen meeting of the NAC. The foreign ministers declared that NATO's security was linked to that of Central and Eastern Europe and provided further encouragement for the CSCE. However, wanting to ensure that the primary decisions affecting security in Europe were taken in the institution where it had the most influence, the US insisted that the Copenhagen communiqué state that "NATO is the essential forum for consultation among the Allies and the forum for agreement on policies bearing on the security and defense commitments of its members under the Washington Treaty."[11]

Further measures to strengthen the CSCE were taken by its foreign ministers in Berlin on 20 June 1991. At that meeting, agreement on an emergency mechanism for consultation and cooperation on violent conflict in Europe was reached. Such situations were defined as a violation of one of the principles of the Helsinki Final Act or as the result of major disruptions endangering peace, security, or stability. A state with a particular security concern resulting from the actions of another state could request an explanation from that state of its behavior and was entitled to receive a response within forty-eight hours. The foreign ministers agreed to allow twelve or more members to call an emergency meeting of the Committee of Senior Officials in the absence of the violating state should the time limit be breached.

In December 1991, the NATO foreign ministers agreed to exchange information and documents and expressed a desire to make the collective experience of NATO available to the CSCE. NATO offered to support seminars sponsored by the CSCE Conflict Prevention Center on defense conversion and the role of armed forces in democratic societies. The ministers also invited military officials from all CSCE states to attend special courses at the NATO Defense College in Rome and the NATO School in Oberammergau.

NATO's affiliated parliamentary organization, the North Atlantic Assembly (NAA), also sponsored special CSCE interparliamentary conferences on European security and provided staff support for CSCE parliamentary meetings. The North Atlantic Assembly is independent of NATO. To complement the alliance, the NAA began an extensive program of associate membership and funding for these associate members' participation in seminars addressing areas such as democratization, civil-military reform, and broader issues of European security. Under initiatives guided by its Deputy Secretary General Simon Lunn, the NAA played a critical leadership role by exposing postcommunist parliamentarians in Central and Eastern Europe to Western democratic norms and procedures.

Increased diplomatic activity originating from NATO and the NAA enhanced stability in the East by reassuring the new democrats that they had the moral support of the West during a time of uncertainty and rapid change. They also benefited from interacting with Western officials within the multinational setting of NATO. For example, in the NATO military schools, the participants were exposed to principles of civilian control of the armed forces—a key aspect of stable democratization. In the NAA, Central and East European parliamentarians gained practical experience in democratic procedures, which they could then use to educate colleagues in their capitals. High-level exchanges, with military officials from Central and Eastern Europe coming to NATO headquarters and NATO officials traveling to the new democracies of Central and Eastern Europe, helped to raise the awareness of the challenges these countries faced. The result was a growing sense of trust, which quickly eroded Cold War boundaries.

However, in 1991 war erupted from the collapse of Yugoslavia. Europe needed urgent action beyond social activity if NATO and the CSCE were to have any relevance in actual crises. The immediate problem was a CSCE decision-making procedure requiring that all decisions be unanimous. This procedural arrangement in the CSCE made it a useless institution for conflict resolution, as an aggressor could use CSCE procedures to block action against it.

Gathering at Prague in January 1992, the CSCE foreign ministers amended the consensus rule so that in situations where there are clear, gross, and uncorrected violations of CSCE commitments, a majority of member states could act in the absence of the state concerned. Consensus would remain the fundamental decision-making procedure in the CSCE. However, this new approach—called "consensus minus one"—could allow the organization to sanction a member state in violation of CSCE principles.[12] Europe had taken a small step toward rationalizing the institutional capacity to promote collective security.

Meeting in Helsinki in July 1992, CSCE foreign ministers called for the continued strengthening of orderly procedures for conflict prevention and crisis management by seeking the support of other international institutions and organizations, strengthening of the chairman-in-office, appointment of a high commissioner for national minorities, and creation of a Forum for Security Cooperation (FSC) to meet regularly in Vienna. The ministers also established procedures for crisis prevention and management, to include early warning mechanisms (focusing on human rights and the development of democratic institutions), political management (drawing attention to nonviolent measures available for lowering tensions), specific instruments (such as fact-finding missions), and formal peacekeeping operations.[13]

Further steps to build CSCE institutions were made by the CSCE foreign ministers meeting in Stockholm in December 1992, when they established a Commission of Conciliation and Court of Arbitration to examine and rule on disputes. The ministers also created an Office of the CSCE Secretary General. However, despite these institutional advancements, the CSCE did not have the joint planning, training, and infrastructure needed to assume responsibility for peacekeeping, even if a consensus could be attained among the fifty-plus members.

The North Atlantic Cooperation Council

Hoping to promote a more direct relationship with NATO and the democracies of Central and Eastern Europe, NATO created the North Atlantic Cooperation Council (NACC) at the Rome Summit in November 1991. An American initiative, the NACC was a new "institutional relationship of consultation and cooperation on political and security issues" open to all former (and newly independent) members of the Warsaw Pact.[14] The NACC states began extensive consultation on issues including national defense planning, principles and key aspects of strategy, force and command structures, military exercises, democratic concepts of civil-military relations, civil/military coordination of air traffic management, and the conversion of defense production to civilian purposes.[15] Following the collapse of the Soviet Union, the NACC grew to include thirty-eight members. The NACC also served as a forum for sharing information on technological, scientific, and environmental issues and facilitated the dissemination of information about NATO among the NACC countries.

As one senior NATO official suggested, the objective of the NACC was to promote extended security based on assessments of self-interest by the NATO members:

> What we are after is our own security. In the kind of situation in which we live now, the security of any state in Europe is linked to the security of all other states. If there is chaos throughout Europe, if there are local conflicts, if there is ethnic strife, our own security in the long run will suffer. So this is one of those circumstances where [security] is not a zero sum game. Increased security for one does not mean less security for another. Increased security for us means increased security for the rest of Europe. It is in that spirit that the North Atlantic Cooperation Council was set up.[16]

NATO officials stressed that the NACC was a consultative forum and not a decision-making body. The NACC would permit formal and informal exchanges of views and promote a long-term understanding of national and multilateral security concerns. NATO officials initially had to go to considerable length to explain to NACC member state representatives that their participation did not mean membership in NATO. As a result, the NACC failed to meet the security demands of several Central and East European countries. It was also operationally weak as the NACC had a limited budget of $1.5 million in 1993, no secretariat, no formal doctrine, and, most importantly, no security guarantee.

The most important function of the NACC was to provide a multilateral forum for discussion and sharing of information on peacekeeping. The NACC partners created an Ad Hoc Committee on Peacekeeping, which released an extensive report on NATO/NACC peacekeeping planning in June 1993. The report stressed that peacekeeping should be carried out only under the authority of the UN Security Council or the CSCE, on a case-by-case basis, and with the UN or CSCE defining peacekeeping operations, including command relationships, and that peacekeeping requires a clear political objective and a precise mandate.[17] The group sponsored a number of high-level seminars focusing on the peacekeeping experiences of individual participants and on cooperation with other relevant institutions.

The NACC also received detailed studies from NATO's military authorities addressing technical issues of peacekeeping. This included presentations addressing assets and capabilities required for the conduct of peacekeeping operations; the possibility and utility of developing a database of available resources; and the requirement for forces, procedures, and equipment to facilitate cooperation in peacekeeping operations. NATO also developed a paper for the NACC covering theoretical and generic planning issues relating to command-and-control standards and procedures, standard operating procedures, and rules of engagement for peacekeeping operations. The NACC also created its own Ad Hoc Technical Sub-Group to facilitate the development of technical issues affecting peacekeeping missions.

In sharing military experience in the NACC, military-to-military contacts between NATO and the former Warsaw Pact nations grew considerably, to the extent that military relations outpaced political cooperation. Due to French opposition, there was no ministerial-level defense component to the NACC. Thus, one of the most important aspects of democratization, that of civilian control over the military, was missing from the NACC experience.[18] Absent France, however, the remaining NATO countries created an informal Group of Defense Ministers to act as a conduit for requests for assistance from Central and East European countries to the NATO member nations most willing or capable to deal with a particular problem.

Because it was a multilateral forum and continued to operate on a consensus basis, a participating state could create major obstacles within the working agenda of the NACC, thereby limiting its potential. This became clear after a NACC meeting in Istanbul on 10 June 1994. The Russian delegation haggled for five hours over the final communiqué, forcing the NACC to drop any language related to NATO enlargement and CFE deployment levels. The Russian posturing caused a lengthy and embarrassing delay in the release of the NACC final communiqué. A senior NATO diplomat described the NACC session as a "pretty bloody affair, an absolutely Soviet exercise, a disastrous performance by the Russians [that] does not augur well."[19] Another NATO official wondered whether there could ever be another working NACC meeting if this was to be the model for future Russian behavior.[20] After the Istanbul meeting, the NACC stopped issuing a formal communiqué and instead opted for a chairman's summary. This weakened the appeal of the NACC for some non-NATO participants who had seen it as a way to move closer to formal NATO activities, perhaps leading toward membership. As a result the NACC was only a partial success in the process of institutional adaptation.

The Partnership for Peace

By 1993 several Central and Eastern European states felt that only full NATO membership would resolve their perceived security dilemmas, promote stability to attract economic investment and membership in the EU, and provide reassurance for democratic and market reform–oriented political leaders. This view was promoted by three American analysts at the RAND Corporation (Ronald Asmus, Richard Kugler, and F. Stephen Larrabee), who circulated a draft paper in the summer of 1993 calling for NATO to focus on internal and external restructuring—including NATO membership for Hungary, Poland, the Czech Republic, and possibly Slovakia. Failure to do so, they said, would make NATO "like the aging knight replete in splendid armor, impressive to admire until someone one day lifts the visor to discover it is a hollow shell. NATO will go out of area or out of business."[21] Arguing that the challenge in Europe was between forces of integration and forces of disintegration, the authors felt that the alliance could encourage the former by shifting its focus to Article 4 of the NATO treaty to include issues such as peacekeeping, search and rescue, and humanitarian/disaster relief.

Though Washington had previously ruled out any NATO enlargement beyond the united Germany, by mid-1993 there was a growing need for the US to reconsider. Germany had begun quietly but assertively pushing to expand NATO in order to stabilize its eastern border and provide economic stability and reassurance for the growing free markets in the region. Germany proposed Associate Membership in NATO for some Central and East European countries. Defense Minister Volker Rühe in particular argued that Associate Membership could speed full entry into NATO for the Visegrad countries. Though the Germans never suggested as much, it was, in theory, possible that if NATO did not engage the East, Germany might act unilaterally to provide security guarantees to its eastern neighbors—something that both Russia and the West would view as provocative.

Senior officials from the US State Department Policy Planning Staff and National Security Council (NSC) agreed that NATO enlargement could promote stability, the peaceful resolutions of disputes, and democratic reform, in the East. In particular, some officials believed that by integrating new members into the transparent multilateral planning process in NATO, post-Communist reformers would be able to avoid costly national defense build-ups if they had to provide for their own self-help. Such a renationalization of defense in Central and Eastern Europe in and of itself could prove destabilizing to the region. Some advocates also hoped that NATO enlargement might push the EU to open its doors to new members in areas where it might not in the absence of NATO membership coming first. However, the pace and scope of enlargement was hotly debated with serious interagency differences emerging. Supporters advocated a policy of gradual enlargement to show Europe that the US was committed to its security, that Germany was not driving the alliance east, and that NATO was still relevant after the Cold War. Politically, enlargement would also satisfy a number of American ethnic groups of Central and East European origin who were lobbying aggressively for their home countries' inclusion in NATO. This domestic appeal might provide members of Congress, who were becoming increasingly skeptical of funding a US role in Europe, with new justification for supporting NATO. A prolonged debate over NATO enlargement would also shift discussion from whether NATO was needed after the Cold War, to whether or not it should expand. Finally, a major initiative toward NATO would also help President Clinton establish his foreign policy credentials.

National Security Advisor W. Anthony Lake and key State Department figures (including Ambassador to Germany Richard Holbrooke and the US negotiator at the Helsinki CSCE conference, John Kornblum) were convinced of the institutional value of using enlargement to encourage post-communist reform and ease German pressure. A gradual approach to NATO enlargement also fit well into the new US policy of "enlargement and engagement" formulated by Lake and his NSC staff. This approach stressed the importance of international institutions where the US could best direct policy—such as NATO. The goal was to expand the number of democratic nations in the world while engaging troubled areas through partnership where possible and with power if necessary.[22] Nevertheless, as support within the Clinton administration for NATO enlargement grew, senior officials in the Department of Defense, and especially in the Joint Chiefs of Staff, expressed doubts about taking on substantial new military commitments while downsizing US capabilities. Such concerns combined with caution signals from Russia experts from various agencies in the administration to produce an interagency compromise—the Partnership for Peace (PFP).[23]

Within NATO there was shared sentiment that some sort of compromise was necessary that would allow the Eastern nations to go beyond the NACC but stop short of membership. There was no consensus in the NAC that NATO enlargement was a sound policy. As a senior NATO official told the *Washington Post* on 31 August, "Right now, the prevailing wisdom is that bringing in Poland or any other state would be risky and self-defeating for the Alliance as a whole."[24]

On 6 October NATO Secretary General Wörner met with President Clinton and his top foreign policy advisors in Washington and received a briefing on the US plans for partnership with Central and Eastern Europe. The intention was to use prospective NATO membership to maintain momentum for reform in Central and Eastern Europe while buying the alliance time. NATO partnerships would be open to all NACC/CSCE countries and they would gain all of the institutional benefits of NATO—except a security guarantee. Practical security cooperation could be attained through training and exercises in preparation for joint peacekeeping operations.

At a meeting of NATO defense ministers on 20–21 October in Travemünde, Germany, the group reached an informal understanding that new members would be admitted only in the long term; the PFP was endorsed as an alternative. Indeed, it was consensus in NATO not to enlarge—or at least to defer any substantive discussion of the issue. Reflecting concerns that NATO enlargement would unnecessarily isolate Russia and damage democratic reform there, Wörner affirmed that the "Western Alliance would consider the legitimate concerns of Russia" and that "we do not want to isolate Moscow."[25] These comments also reflected an informal response to a confidential letter sent by Russian President Boris Yeltsin on 15 September to NATO Headquarters and to the major NATO countries, outlining strong Russian opposition to enlargement. Yeltsin claimed that enlargement would violate the spirit of the understanding on which Germany was unified and the Cold War ended. As an alternative, Yeltsin proposed a joint NATO–Russian security guarantee for Eastern Europe.

In a speech to the Atlantic Council of the United States on 3 December 1993, US Secretary of Defense Les Aspin identified five key benefits of the PFP:

> First, it does not redivide Europe. . . . Partnership for Peace gives all nations the same chance to take part, but makes the results dependent on the effort of each partner. Second, Partnership for Peace sets up the right incentives. In the old Cold War world, NATO was an alliance created in response to an external threat. In the new, post–Cold War world NATO can be an alliance based on shared values of democracy and the free market. Partnership for Peace rewards those who move in that direction. Third, Partnership for Peace requires that partners make a real contribution. It doesn't just ask what NATO can do for its new partners, it asks what the new partners can do for NATO. . . . Fourth, it keeps NATO at the center of European security concerns and thereby keeps American involvement at the center of Europe. Finally, it puts the question of NATO membership for the partners where it belongs, at the end of the process, rather than at the beginning.[26]

The PFP would, according to Aspin, allow those partners that took full advantage of the program to "pick up NATO's standard operating procedures, habits of cooperation, and routines of consultation."[27]

The PFP compromise was popular in the Department of Defense, whose senior officials felt that the decision not to enlarge NATO had been made. However, this view was not shared by senior NSC officials, some of whom felt that the PFP was designed solely to facilitate NATO enlargement and who bristled at the notion that it should be interpreted as anything other than that.[28] Supporters of NATO enlargement were a minority in the US government;

however, they held key positions of influence and were ultimately able to move the bureaucratic opposition into their favor.[29] Thus, while presented to the NATO allies as a compromise over enlargement, the PFP was largely intended as a means of advancing the consensus process in NATO towards enlargement.

Personally briefed on the PFP by US Secretary of State Warren Christopher, President Yeltsin described the plan as "brilliant." Central and East European countries were not as thrilled, although NATO's promise to keep its door open via the PFP was intended to provided reassurance that they might ultimately attain membership. Despite promises from US Assistant Secretary of State for European and Canadian Affairs Stephen Oxman on 26 October that "we do not want to be perceived or in any way treat others as second-class citizens," some critics felt that PFP did exactly this. Polish officials were especially animated in their rhetoric—disturbed by what they perceived as "Yalta II." Sen. Richard Lugar, an early and leading architect of the case for NATO enlargement, labeled the PFP a "band-aid offered in place of corrective surgery" and as a bureaucratic half-step with a "Russia-first" orientation that would give Moscow a de-facto veto over NATO's future and encourage neo-imperial tendencies in Moscow.[30] Nonetheless, NATO as a whole was largely satisfied and in consensus not to expand at that time or to place a decision to expand on the NAC agenda.

At their meeting in Brussels in January 1994, NATO heads of state approved the PFP and declared: "We expect and would welcome NATO expansion that would reach to democratic states to our East, as part of an evolutionary process, taking into account political and security developments in the whole of Europe."[31] The NATO leaders invited NACC and other CSCE countries that were able and willing to join the PFP, which "will play an important role in the evolutionary process of the expansion of NATO."[32]

The NATO countries would establish "16-plus-1" consultations with permanent offices at NATO Headquarters and at a SHAPE Planning Cell in Mons, Belgium.[33] The "16-plus-1" refers to the collective relationship of all sixteen NATO members with the individual partner country. Consultation would include the right to call a 16-plus-1 PFP meeting "if that partner perceives a direct threat to its territorial integrity, political independence, or security."[34] The heads of state added: "At a pace and scope determined by the capacity and desire of the individual participating states, we will work in concrete ways towards transparency in defense budgeting, promoting democratic control of defense ministries, joint planning, joint military exercises, and creating an ability to operate with NATO forces in such fields as peacekeeping, search and rescue and humanitarian operations, and others as may be agreed."[35]

NATO did not have any historical reason to expect that such an institutional adaptation would succeed. However, given the demand from some Central and

Eastern European countries for membership in NATO, the alliance was in a position to use leverage to link cooperation and consultation with certain behavior from the states that joined the PFP. Therefore, at the Brussels meeting, NATO approved a uniform document for each country to sign when joining the program. Participation was contingent upon adherence by the partner to the "protection and promotion of fundamental freedoms and human rights, and safeguarding of freedom, justice, and peace through democracy [which] are shared values fundamental to the Partnership."[36]

The PFP required NATO partners to cooperate with the Alliance in pursuing the following objectives:

1. Facilitation of transparency in national defense planning and budgeting processes.
2. Ensuring democratic control of defense forces.
3. Maintenance of the capability and readiness to contribute, subject to constitutional considerations, to operations under the authority of the UN and/or the responsibility of the CSCE.
4. The development of cooperative military relations with NATO, for the purpose of joint planning, training, and exercises in order to strengthen their ability to undertake missions in the fields of peacekeeping, search and rescue, humanitarian operations, and others as may subsequently be agreed.
5. The development, over the longer term, of forces that are better able to operate with those of the members of the North Atlantic Alliance.[37]

Each partner would submit an Individual Partnership Program (IPP), identifying ways to work with the alliance and what assets it might contribute to joint planning for peacekeeping and other forms of 16-plus-1 (or multilateral) activity. Partner countries were required to list the steps that had been or would be undertaken to promote transparency in the national defense planning and budgeting processes, and to ensure democratic control of the armed forces. Operationally, the program required an indication of long-range plans, force development goals, and other planning factors that could affect a participant's future involvement in the partnership (such as changes in the structure of the armed forces or the setting up of special peacekeeping units). Partners were required to fund their own PFP activities and share the full burdens of mounting exercises in which they were taking part.

Describing the PFP, a senior advisor to Polish President Lech Walesa invoked memories of Britain's appeasement of Hitler when he complained, "We've gone from Chamberlain's umbrella to Clinton's saxophone."[38] Nevertheless, the PFP grew to include twenty-seven partnerships—none of which was hampered by the size constraints of the NACC or CSCE. This activity involved hundreds of PFP- or "in the spirit of PFP"- related NATO programs.

PFP eventually included major peacekeeping exercises—largely modeled after hypothetical Balkan scenarios and held in NATO and partner country territory.

Those countries who chose to integrate closely with NATO planning were invited to join the partnership Planning and Review Process (PARP) where they can (every two years) exchange data on their defense plans and budgets, and identify areas in which they agree to improve interoperability between their military forces and those of NATO in the fields of peacekeeping, search and rescue, and humanitarian operations (to include areas as specific as communications procedures and refueling capabilities). By 1996, fifteen countries had joined the PARP. To facilitate this conditional opening of the alliance, NATO's committees were expanded in scope to include direct activity in support of the NACC and the PFP.

The PFP struck a creative balance between reassurance of Russia and of the democracies in Central and Eastern Europe. It helped prepare interested partners for NATO's multilateral planning norms—thus lowering the costs of restructuring their militaries and possibly integrating their forces into NATO. Should the political and military situation in Russia or the other former Soviet republics change or other unforeseen events threaten the stability of Central and Eastern Europe, NATO could expand more easily since the states would have had a period of working within NATO's rules and procedures. Several months after the announcement of the PFP, a senior US official asserted that, "should the situation deteriorate in the East and Russia, and it became necessary at some step to draw the line between Eastern and Western . . . the Partnership for Peace would put us in a better position to do that."[39] Absent that worst case, the PFP allowed for considerable flexibility in direct and multilateral relationships among potential partners—including Russia.

The PFP was not without problems and contradictions. Because the PFP was seen by many Central and East European countries as a direct path into NATO, it unintentionally encouraged competition between some partners to meet unspecified NATO criteria at the expense of their own bilateral and multilateral cooperation and dispute settlement. Like the NACC, the PFP emphasized military-to-military cooperation, with the potential to undermine civil-military reform efforts in Central and Eastern Europe.[40] Additionally, the program was commenced with no direct resource allocation from NATO and thus the potential partners were initially disinclined to participate. The US hoped to show that participation in PFP would have visible gains by providing $100 million for fiscal year 1996 for PFP support programs.

Some PFP countries stressed quantity over quality in their programs. For example, of the 232 PFP programs proposed by Hungary in 1995, only four promoted democratic control of the armed forces. These were limited to three information exchanges among experts and one conference.[41] The PFP process also failed to promote transparency, because partners were reluctant to publish their IPPs; only Hungary volunteered to do so. In a worst case, the PFP had the appearance of security enhancement without increasing deterrence capacity for the partner states. A participant could join NATO's peacekeeping planning, but it was unclear how preparation for peacekeeping was relevant to the capability of, for example, the Baltic states to defend their borders against an attack.

NATO and the Balkans

By 1994 the elements of a European security architecture were in place—NATO, the NACC, the PFP, the CSCE, and to a lesser extent the EU and the WEU. The missing ingredient was peace in the former Yugoslavia. In 1992 NATO embarked on a process of building peacekeeping capabilities which could, in theory, aid international institutions that might provide a mandate for engagement in the Balkan crises. In practice, however, there was no consensus on how and when to conduct peacekeeping operations and what was the correct institutional framework for action. What became a debate over institutional arrangements for peacekeeping obscured, clouded, and inhibited the attainment of peace and security in Bosnia-Herzegovina from 1991 through 1995. For all of its adaptation during this period, NATO appeared irrelevant and close to collapse over the Balkan crises.

Institutional Culture and Peacekeeping

At a June 1992 meeting of NATO foreign ministers in Oslo, the US announced that it would contribute manpower to a NATO and CSCE peacekeeping force in the former Yugoslav republics. This reflected a sudden policy shift by the US, which was increasingly concerned that a failure to act in the Balkans might undermine NATO's general credibility. At the Prague CSCE ministerial meeting in January 1992, the German delegation (backed by Italy, the Czech and Slovak Federal Republic, and Poland) had proposed creating standing CSCE peacekeeping forces, but because of opposition from the US, Britain, and France, the proposal had been tabled. However, the idea was kept alive by Dutch Foreign Minister Hans van den Broek, who suggested that NATO should have a peacekeeping role under CSCE auspices. Eventually, this view was accepted—with serious reservation—in Washington.

Addressing the NAC, US Deputy Secretary of State Lawrence Eagleburger stated, "The United States is prepared to make essential contributions, such as lift and logistics, to peacekeeping operations. . . . We also do not exclude providing ground contingents on the same basis as other nations."[42] While the German delegation concurred, the United Kingdom and France were hesitant. Britain was especially distressed that NATO could become "Europe's policeman." In a speech to the Diplomatic and Commonwealth Writers' Association prior to the meeting, British Foreign Secretary Douglas Hurd stated that "neither marines nor parachutists nor new-fashioned Blue Helmets can fight their way to peace among peoples mingled together village by village." Yet he conceded that "NATO must make its resources available when the international community has decided that action needs to be taken."[43] For France, there was an ongoing concern that any overture from NATO to the CSCE would increase the role of the US in Europe. Therefore France (joined by Belgium and Spain) insisted that any peacekeeping request be made to individual governments and not to NATO Headquarters.

Because of the diverse perspectives among key NATO members toward peacekeeping, the Oslo meeting was mostly symbolic. The foreign ministers cautiously stated:

> The Alliance has the capacity to contribute to effective actions by the CSCE in line with its new and increased responsibilities for crisis management and the peaceful settlement of disputes. In this regard, we are prepared to support on a case-by-case basis in accordance with our own procedures, peacekeeping activities under the responsibility of the CSCE, including by making available Alliance resources and expertise.[44]

NATO members were concerned about creating an automatic mechanism for NATO peacekeeping, thus the case-by-case language. They also included a requirement that NATO forces could be made available in response to an official CSCE request addressed to NATO (where consensus was required for a response) and to its individual member states. This procedural mechanism turned the relationship into "interblocking" institutions. A consensus would have to exist in NATO for CSCE peacekeeping. Should a NATO member (all of whom had overlapping membership in the CSCE) oppose peacekeeping, it could discourage or veto an initial CSCE request and still deflect blame for inaction onto that institution. Nevertheless, Secretary General Wörner suggested that peacekeeping could cover "not only transport, other infrastructure facilities, and supplies of military equipment, but also troops if necessary."[45]

While proclaiming the agreement historic, NATO stressed that it did not indicate a commitment to intervene in the Balkan conflict. Thus, the Oslo statement served two essentially symbolic roles. The first was a veiled threat to the warring parties in the former Yugoslavia that mechanisms for the possible use of force were being incorporated by NATO and the CSCE. The second provided continued impetus to the CSCE for its scheduled review conference the following month in Helsinki.

At Helsinki, the CSCE foreign ministers welcomed the NATO initiative, but failed to act.[46] The false promise of NATO/CSCE peacekeeping in the Balkan crisis prompted NATO to look to the UN for an out-of-area mandate in spite of the fact that its own members were largely responsible for blocking action in the CSCE. Because the CSCE had identified itself as a regional organization under Article 8 of the UN Charter at Helsinki, the UN was quick to call on the CSCE for peacekeeping assistance in Bosnia-Herzegovina. A copy of a UN request for CSCE assistance was forwarded to NATO Headquarters, prompting a divisive debate in the alliance as to how to respond to these overlapping institutional requests. Some NATO members felt that in order to get a mandate for planning out-of-area activities, it was necessary to receive a formal request from the CSCE. However, others argued that since the CSCE was now a regional organization under the UN, the request to the CSCE was sufficient to justify NATO planning.[47] In the end, ongoing debates within and among institutions inhibited international efforts to bring peace to the Balkans. NATO was unable to provide peace in Europe's bloodiest conflict since World War II.

The Rise and Fall of the United Nations

Absent a NATO consensus for significant involvement in the Balkans, UN peacekeeping became the only alternative for arranging international efforts to promote peace. At the December 1992 NAC ministerial, NATO signaled that it was prepared to undertake peacekeeping operations under the authority of the UN Security Council and to "respond positively to initiatives that the UN Secretary General might take to seek Alliance assistance in the implementation of UN Security Council Resolutions."[48] However, internal NATO disputes continued to block active consideration of policy options toward attaining peace in the Balkans.

By early 1993, interlocking institutions were becoming, at best, excuses for national inaction and, at worst, obstacles to ending the conflict. In particular, the arms embargo on all parties in the former Yugoslavia imposed by the UN in 1991 and enforced by NATO (and the WEU) maintained an imbalance of power favoring Serb forces (which had inherited most of the military apparatus of the Yugoslav National Army), allowing them to make territorial gains and commit genocide. However, lifting the arms embargo became politically impossible once the UN had deployed peacekeepers on the ground in 1992, because participating states worried that their troops would get caught in increased fighting if more weapons flowed into the region.

Having moved away from the CSCE and toward the UN, NATO could now support UN humanitarian efforts and enforce a no-fly zone over Bosnia-Herzegovina. By 1994 NATO missions in the Balkans included protection of heavy weapons exclusion zones and safe havens for civilian populations.

Operationally, the institutional cultures of NATO and the UN clashed. In response to the initial UN request for assistance in Bosnia-Herzegovina NATO began planning for military operations in the region. For example, military planners studied how to support the provision of humanitarian assistance to alleviate the Serb siege of Sarajevo. NATO planners calculated that, since a peaceful environment did not exist, the UN request to guarantee the delivery of aid in a hostile environment would require up to 100,000 troops. On the other hand, because UN peacekeeping planning traditionally assumes a peaceful environment when forces are deployed, the UN had estimated needing only 2,000 to 4,000 troops.[49]

The US was extremely reluctant to place its armed forces on the ground in Bosnia-Herzegovina. However, in 1993 NATO military officials were instructed by the NAC to begin planning for a force of around 50,000 peacekeepers. Of those, 25,000 would be US personnel made available for deployment into Bosnia-Herzegovina once a peace settlement was reached.

NATO planning included peacekeeping activities such as monitoring ceasefires and withdrawals of forces; supervising disarmament and control of weapons; escorting, controlling, and protecting convoys; creating safe corridors; creating and monitoring buffer zones; providing logistical assistance; and removing hazardous munitions.[50] However, working simultaneously in the UN and NATO political bodies, and with troop commanders on the ground, France successfully blocked formal NATO consideration of command and control arrangements. Paris insisted that military planning remain in the UN and thereby effectively prevented an immediate or substantial NATO role in promoting peace in the region.[51] At this point, 141,000 people had been killed, and 3.5 million refugees had fled the conflict—all in spite of UN and EU negotiated ceasefires and the deployment of some 24,000 UN peacekeepers on the ground.

A New Russian Assertiveness

Just as the US and Europe were bypassing it in Bosnia-Herzegovina, the CSCE reentered the institutional debate in autumn 1993. Russia promoted the CSCE as an alternative to NATO's increasing role and as a way to legitimize Russian peacekeeping or peacemaking in the former Soviet Union. On 30 November Russian Foreign Minister Andrei Kozyrev asked the CSCE to support (especially financially) Russian peacekeeping missions in the former Soviet Union and suggested that the CSCE should take over the political coordination of peacekeeping missions organized by the Commonwealth of Independent States (CIS), NATO, the NACC, and the WEU.[52] The Russian proposal placed NATO members in the difficult position of balancing the strong opposition of the three Baltic countries and Ukraine to the Russian proposal, the reality that NATO would not assume a peacekeeping role in the former Soviet Union, and a desire not to alienate Russia over the expanding role of NATO.

The Baltic countries were particularly concerned about any international recognition of a stronger Russian role in the CIS. However, they were also realistic. For example, Estonia acknowledged that it might be necessary to allow Russia to undertake peacekeeping operations for the CSCE in some parts of the former Soviet Union in some cases. Yet Estonian Foreign Minister Trivimi Velliste was adamant that Russia should be permitted to do so only under strict conditions and only on a case-by-case basis. He stressed that under "no circumstances should Russia be given a broad mandate to be the CSCE force."[53]

Central and East Europeans were especially worried that the Kozyrev proposals were part of a return to traditional Russian nationalism or even neo-imperialism. While Moscow's rhetoric outpaced Russian capabilities, growing public support for extreme nationalists in the December 1993 Russian parliamentary elections fueled this concern.[54]

The CSCE foreign ministers did not endorse the Russian proposal, but agreed to strengthen the CSCE as a pan-European forum for cooperative security and political consultation on the basis of equality. In deference to Russia, they also agreed "to pursue the possibility of enhancing capabilities to apply CSCE crisis management arrangements on a case-by-case basis to situations involving third-party forces when such arrangements are determined to be supportive of CSCE objectives."[55] However, most NATO and Central and East European countries had lost interest in the CSCE. Thus the challenge was to find a creative way to keep Russia facing West, short of granting too much authority to the CSCE. The solution was found in the PFP.

Though President Yeltsin had welcomed the PFP, Russia began using its participation to obstruct NATO enlargement. When Russian Defense Minister Pavel Grachev addressed NATO defense ministers on 25 May 1994, he said that "It wouldn't be correct for Russia to set forth some specific conditions for cooperation or trying to say that we want to occupy a better place, a so-called warmer place under the sun, in the program." However, Grachev was also clear that Russia would request special privileges via an undefined "active mechanism" for consultation with the West over peacekeeping operations, strategic planning, and joint exercises outside of the PFP.[56]

The NATO members agreed to negotiate a "special status" with Russia but strove to avoid any perception that they were granting Russia a sphere of influence in the East or a veto over NATO policy. Nevertheless, at the 10 June NACC meeting, NATO appeared to defer to Russian sensitivities to the point of conferring a de facto veto for Russia within the alliance. Kozyrev announced Russia's intention to join the PFP but insisted on first negotiating a detailed and signed cooperation program that would formalize a relationship based on what Kozyrev called "no mutual vetoes or surprises."[57] Kozyrev expected a formal piece of paper from NATO signaling broad deference toward Russia to prove to hard-liners in Moscow that NATO had given in to Russian demands. At a press conference in Moscow that afternoon, President Yeltsin said with regard to Russia's special status that "NATO has agreed . . .

it is necessary to sign such a protocol—even if some bureaucrats reject that protocol, we will sign it anyway."[58]

In Brussels the NAC took up the prospects of increasing dialogue with Russia. After consultation between NATO Assistant Secretary General Gebhardt von Moltke and Russian Deputy Foreign Minister Vitaly Churkin, the outlines of a deal establishing a special relationship between Russia and NATO was reached. Kozyrev visited NATO headquarters on 22 June and signed the PFP framework document and a joint NATO/Russian declaration. The declaration stressed that NATO and Russia each have an important role in European security and that a cooperative relationship built upon mutual respect and friendship are a key element of European security.

This early move toward a special NATO–Russia relationship was designed to promote dialogue and cooperation in areas where Russia has a unique and important contribution to make, commensurate with its size and role as a nuclear power, through what NATO hoped would be an extensive IPP. This relationship was to be based on the sharing of information on issues regarding political and security-related matters having a European dimension; political consultations, as appropriate, on issues of common concern; and cooperation in a range of security-related areas including, as appropriate, peacekeeping.[59] NATO officials expressed relief at the commitment by Russia to work with NATO, which could pave the way toward close military cooperation in areas of shared interest—especially peacekeeping.

Breakthrough in the Balkans

By 1995 several NATO operations were providing operational support for UN peacekeeping in the Balkans. Operation "Provide Promise" flew humanitarian assistance into Bosnia (totaling several thousand sorties by 1995). Operation "Sharp Guard" was conducted jointly with the WEU to enforce the UN arms embargo against the combatants. Operation "Deny Flight" organized NATO air power to deny military flights by the warring parties over the region. Operation "Able Sentry" was a complementary UN mission that included several hundred US ground forces placed in Macedonia as a "trip-wire" force to deter the spread of the war.

At one level NATO was highly successful in the one mission that it was most well-suited for—it contained the Balkan conflict by preventing its spread into a much wider international war. However, despite the hope that a variety of institutional activities could actually end the war, nearly 250,000 had died by mid-1995. In the fall of 1993, the US sought consensus among its NATO allies for a more robust use of air power against violators of UN resolutions—to include the targeting of transportation facilities, command and control sites, weapons storage depots, and other noncivilian stationary targets.

European countries with troops on the ground rejected this approach. It was also publicly criticized by the UN political representative on the ground in Croatia, Yasuchi Akashi. He insisted that Serb attacks on UN Safe Areas were not sufficient to justify calling in NATO air strikes. Akashi labeled US policy as "somewhat reticent, somewhat afraid, timid and tentative" and insisted that Washington send ground forces to Bosnia-Herzegovina. The comments thoroughly discredited Akashi within the inner circles of the US government and with the Bosnian Muslims as well. US Ambassador to the UN Madeleine Albright complained to UN Secretary General Boutros Boutros-Ghali that Akashi was out of line and that international servants "should remember where their salaries are paid."[60]

After another year of futility, by spring 1995 NATO agreed on a more robust use of air power to support a new ceasefire negotiated by former US President Jimmy Carter. NATO also began preparations for the possible deployment of forces to evacuate UN peacekeepers in the event that they were to be withdrawn. Responding to Serb violations of UN resolutions in May, NATO forces bombed Serb ammunition depots—which resulted in the UN peacekeepers' worst nightmare. Serb forces took several hundred peacekeepers hostage. Some hostages were chained to likely NATO air targets as human shields.

Following the negotiated release of the UN soldiers, Croatia launched successful attacks against Serb-held territory lost in 1991 and Bosnian government forces, massed near Sarajevo, prepared to break the Serb siege of that so-called safe haven. NATO was fundamentally split on its response, with the US quietly encouraging the Bosnian Muslims while the Europeans attempted to maintain neutrality. The essence of the crisis was summarized by a senior French military official on 30 June 1995: "If the Europeans are on one side and the Americans on the other, it would be like an earthquake in the Atlantic alliance."[61] US Secretary of Defense William Perry was even more blunt in his assessment of NATO in the summer of 1995: "Paralyzed into inaction, NATO seemed to be irrelevant in dealing with the Bosnian crisis. . . . It appeared to me that NATO was in the process of unravelling."[62]

In July Bosnian Serbs overran the UN safe havens at Gorazde and Zepa in eastern Bosnia in blatant defiance of NATO and the UN. NATO sought to launch air strikes to protect these cities, but the request was turned down by the UN. Even in the absence of NATO air power, however, the Serb forces became vulnerable. The Serb offensive had borrowed heavily from their forces occupying Muslim territory in western Bosnia, thus creating a power vacuum that allowed Muslim and Croatian forces to make simultaneous gains in western Bosnia and southern Croatia. While Bosnia had been under a series of ceasefires in 1994 and 1995, the Muslim forces had quietly regrouped and rebuilt their forces with outside assistance attained through violations of the

UN arms embargo. This was apparently aided by an informal Clinton Administration decision to permit Iran to export arms to the Muslims.

Recognizing this power shift on the ground, the US launched a major diplomatic initiative in July and August 1995 to bring peace to Bosnia-Herzegovina and restore the credibility of NATO. On 25 July the US attained consensus in the NAC for NATO to prepare for a much more assertive use of air power should a political decision be taken by the NAC to protect UN Safe Areas. According to US officials involved in presenting the US position to the NATO allies, the process was surprisingly easy as the allies were desperate for American guidance. In reality, most of the NATO allies had been hoping for American leadership since 1993.

US determination was heightened by the accidental deaths of Ambassador Robert Frasure, Deputy Assistant Secretary of Defense for Europe and NATO Joseph Kruzel, and Col. S. Nelson Drew on the Mount Igman road outside Sarajevo.[63] While conducting shuttle diplomacy in an effort to end the fighting and establish a cease-fire, their armored personnel carrier slid off a dangerous mountain pass. The three officials were among the most creative thinkers regarding overall US policy toward NATO and were each very respected officials in the US government. Their loss strengthened US and NATO resolve to see the conflict come to an end.

On 28 August Bosnian Serbs shelled Sarajevo, killing thirty-nine civilians. NATO responded with operation "Deliberate Force" in early September. This was a major NATO air operation with narrow political objectives: to end the shelling of Sarajevo, to open the airport and the roads around Sarajevo for safe transit, to remove all Serb heavy weapons from a 12.5-mile radius of Sarajevo, and to deter attacks on other safe havens. The air power combined with Muslim and Croat territorial gains to push the Bosnian Serbs toward a cease fire and a negotiated settlement that would retain Bosnia-Herzegovina as a unitary state based on a 51 to 49 percent division favoring the US–negotiated Muslim and Croat Federation.

Domestic political calculations contributed to the decision by President Clinton to intervene in Bosnia. Congress had been asserting intense pressure on the administration, with bipartisan support, for a unilateral lifting of the arms embargo against the Bosnian Muslims against the wishes of the European NATO allies. The administration argued that such "feel good" measures were endorsed by members of Congress who knew that such a step, taken unilaterally, would probably increase the bloodshed, split NATO, and raise the possibility of US troops being deployed to evacuate UN peacekeepers while entering on the ground to train and supply Bosnian Muslims. Nevertheless, the Republican-led Congress had reached a point of assertiveness to the extent that it was beginning to direct US Bosnia policy and thus President Clinton's political future was linked to an ability to reassert his authority in foreign policy.

Under the tutelage of US Assistant Secretary of State for Europe and Canada Richard Holbrooke, the warring parties met in Dayton, Ohio, in October
and reached an agreement on a peace settlement for Bosnia-Herzegovina
signed on 15 December 1995. The political preconditions for peace were not
entirely due to NATO bombing. There had been dramatic shifts in the balance
of power on the ground, and the Yugoslav patrons of the Bosnian Serbs in
Belgrade needed to gain favor with the West in order to end devastating UN
economic sanctions. However, the accord and the peace it hoped to preserve
depended on NATO and its institutional planning begun in 1993. Without a
rapid deployment of strong and credible peacekeeping forces, the agreement
would likely unravel. Adequate reassurance did not exist for the warring parties in the absence of a credible peacekeeping presence.

NATO's rapid deployment was necessary to reassure the Muslims and
Croats. They feared that the Bosnian Serbs might negotiate a ceasefire only to
regroup in the hope that Serb-led Yugoslavia would intervene and annex Serb
territory in eastern Bosnia in the name of "Greater Serbia." Such Serb actions
might prompt Croatia to annex western Bosnia. At a London dinner reception
earlier in 1995 for Croatian President Franjo Tudjman, the leader of the British
Liberal party Paddy Ashdown asked the Croatian how he viewed Bosnia in
ten years. Tudjman reportedly took his dinner napkin and drew a map of the
region where there was no Bosnia at all, Croatia and Serbia having expanded
and divided the territory. Only NATO could prevent such a possibility. The
plans that the alliance had undertaken since 1993 in the NACC, PFP, and
NATO were quickly put into place through the Bosnia Peace Implementation
Force (IFOR) and its follow-on Bosnia Stabilization Force (SFOR).

Without NATO, the warring parties would not have been sufficiently reassured of their protection while agreeing to end hostilities. A temporary international coalition might have been attainable for peacekeeping, but
establishing such a coalition would have required consolidating a multinational force with infrastructure, logistics, intelligence, and a command and
control structure. Because there was urgency to the peacekeeping deployment,
only NATO had integrated capacity to act. Under the framework of operation
"Joint Endeavor," NATO was able to deploy rapidly some 60,000 troops to
Bosnia-Herzegovina—of which about one-third were Americans.

NATO troops were given a mandate by the UN Security Council to use "all
necessary force" to maintain the integrity of its mission of peace implementation. The specific military tasks of IFOR, as approved by the NAC, were: to
ensure self-defense and freedom of movement; to supervise selective marking
of boundaries and a Zone of Separation (ZOS) between the parties; to monitor
and—if needed—enforce the withdrawal of forces to their respective territories and the establishment of the ZOS; to assume control of the airspace over
Bosnia-Herzegovina and of the movement of military traffic over key ground
routes; to establish Joint Military Commissions to serve as the central bodies

for all parties to the peace agreement; and to assist with the withdrawal of UN forces not transferred to IFOR.[64]

In late 1995, NATO's Crisis Management Organization (CMO) was activated to coordinate Joint Endeavor. This included elements from operations, intelligence, logistics, systems divisions, and liaison elements coming together in one planning cell to streamline and lower the transaction costs of this multilateral military action.[65] NATO demonstrated that after four years of futile institutional activity, it had moved from theory to practice in terms of its post–Cold War role. NATO had become more flexible, could field new and creative command structures, and at the same time could continue to facilitate the use of raw power when necessary. However, NATO had also shown that it could not function in the absence of American leadership.

The Partnership for Peace and Peacekeeping

NATO peacekeeping, which brought together military forces from thirty-three countries, was greatly enhanced by the PFP. Eager to show their willingness to contribute to a NATO operation and (for some) to enhance their prospects for membership in NATO, thirteen of twenty-seven PFP countries joined the NATO forces.[66] The exercises that PFP countries had conducted with NATO paved the way for integration of contingents from PFP countries, adding nearly 10,000 personnel to IFOR. For example, in October 1995 (just prior to IFOR deployment) staff officers from nine NATO/PFP countries participated in operation "Cooperative Light" as a command post exercise simulating the establishment of a buffer zone between two warring parties.

The importance of this contribution was acknowledged by the NATO foreign ministers meeting in Berlin in June 1996:

> Partnership for Peace has become a permanent element of European security cooperation and has demonstrated its value in the current IFOR operation. We are particularly pleased that 12 Partners have joined us in this endeavor, which has benefitted from the experience and interoperability gained in the last two years from the participation of Partner troop contributors in joint PFP exercises and other PFP activities. This first common experience in IFOR charts the course for future security cooperation. We hope to ensure that cooperative relationships developed during the IFOR operation between Allies and Partners continue in the future to enhance the Partnership.[67]

Through IFOR and SFOR the PFP countries gained operational experience in the NATO command structure that could never be attained through exercises and seminars alone. For Hungary, the mission meant a direct increase in its security, as its territory was used as a staging ground for US forces going in and out of Bosnia-Herzegovina. A former Warsaw Pact country now had a NATO base on its soil. More generally, for those countries sharing the risks,

PFP participation in IFOR could only help those partners that sought NATO membership.

The PFP also provided a framework for bringing Russia into Bosnia under a NATO command. Russia had been critical of NATO's Operation Deliberate Force. President Yeltsin even labeled the attack on Serbs as genocide and threatened to withdraw from the PFP if the air attacks did not stop. Eventually conceding that the US initiative was bringing peace to the Bosnians, Russia cosponsored the Dayton talks and agreed to send two thousand troops to Bosnia-Herzegovina under a NATO command with a Russian general serving in the NATO operational planning cell at SHAPE. Operating under NATO command and alongside American troops in the Posevina Corridor (one of the most dangerous areas of operation) would help show Moscow that NATO was not working against Russia. IFOR and SFOR became an inclusive model for NATO–Russian cooperation.

The Bosnian operations strengthened the PFP process. For example, although military command-and-control problems increase proportionally with the number of participants in a multinational operation, the common NATO procedures shared via the PFP had reduced this risk. Moreover, operational challenges highlighted national problems in partner country contributions which might be adjusted for in their PFP programs. As Jeffrey Simon has shown, partners could compensate for weaknesses in their military planning via their IPP and PARP, resource allocation, and future budget plans. For example, the Hungarians, Poles, Czechs, and Romanians each experienced strains and distortions in their defense budgets; found it difficult to stand up their battalions and concluded that it would be necessary to establish pre-standing units for future peace support operations; learned that military officers' language training needed to be improved; and determined that communications equipment and training needed to be changed. For Hungary, the experience showed that it was unprepared to provide transit and host national support for other nations. Hungary also lacked sufficient knowledge about what to do and how to accomplish these tasks, or with whom to liaise and coordinate among the various allied and national military commands and civilian agencies.[68] For these partner countries IFOR and SFOR were a laboratory for deepening interoperability with NATO.

Peace without Security in Bosnia-Herzegovina

NATO completed its major military tasks as mandated by the Dayton accords by the summer of 1996. Warring parties were successfully separated, thereby creating an environment in which the nonmilitary aspects of rebuilding could begin.

The Dayton accords, premised on the hope that a lasting peace would result in the reintegration of a multiethnic Bosnia-Herzegovina, required reconciliation among the parties. Thus freedom of movement, expression, and association guaranteed through free and fair elections was necessary. This responsibility fell on the Organization for Security and Cooperation in Europe (the CSCE was renamed OSCE in December 1994) and on the UN High Commissioner for Refugees (UNHCR).[69] In addition to organizing elections, the OSCE was responsible for arms control and human rights guarantees in Bosnia-Herzegovina.

Responsibility for trying to instill a sense of peace with justice was given to the Hague War Crimes Tribunal, which was established in February 1993. The tribunal was mandated to indict and prosecute war criminals. Other international agencies, including the EU and World Bank, were given the primary task of channeling aid for economic reconstruction and providing administration in some cities. Reconstruction costs were estimated by the World Bank to be $6 billion. Aid programs would be organized by the EU through a conference of donor countries. By summer 1996, only $1.8 billion had been pledged.

Officials from the World Bank saw rebuilding as a particular challenge for international institutions. By summer 1996 there remained up to six million land mines; 80 percent of power generators were damaged or out of operation; 40 percent of bridges had been destroyed; and telecommunications were inoperative in large parts of the country. Additionally, 30 percent of Bosnia-Herzegovina's health facilities, 50 percent of its schools, and 60 percent of its housing had been damaged. Per capita income stood at $500, industrial output was at 5 percent of its prewar levels, and the war had left an overwhelming external debt and arrears, mostly owed to commercial banks and bilateral creditors. In addition to 250,000 dead or missing, 200,000 were wounded, about one-fourth children. There were some two million displaced persons within Bosnia-Herzegovina and about one million outside the territory. Eighty percent of Bosnia's population was dependent upon humanitarian assistance. Central and federal ministries were weak, and low-level political institutions embryonic at best.[70]

Successful implementation of the civilian aspects of the Dayton accords would be essential for lasting security. NATO forces were tasked by the NAC to play a limited but important role in this process. Within its capabilities and resources, and the limits imposed by carrying out its key military tasks, IFOR was mandated to:

1. help to create secure conditions for the conduct by others of non-military tasks associated with the Peace Agreement, including free and fair elections;
2. assist the United Nations High Commissioner for Refugees and other international organizations in their humanitarian missions and assist the movement of these organizations; assist in the observation and prevention of interference with the movement of civilian populations, refugees

and displaced persons, and respond appropriately to deliberate violence
to life and person;
3. assist in the monitoring of the clearance of minefields and obstacles.[71]

In carrying out its basic mission, NATO indirectly contributed to a number
of nonmilitary operations by contributing over four hundred civil affairs personnel to IFOR in support of the Combined Joint Civil-Military Cooperation
(CJCIMIC) program, which united active and reserve civil affairs officers
from around the world. Their specific role was to identify needs and projects
for rebuilding civil infrastructure and institutions and to coordinate with international organizations, nongovernmental organizations, and humanitarian
agencies to obtain the necessary materials, money, and manpower to meet
these needs.[72]

NATO military and civilian representatives worked in conjunction with the
World Bank and a variety of nongovernmental organizations to identify over
two hundred projects for infrastructure reconstruction. NATO also made direct
use of its infrastructure programs to build bridges; repair roads; and provide
staff for similar projects such as power, natural gas, water, and telecommunications in carrying out its deployment mission. In addition, NATO provided
an increased security presence when a cargo of a strategic nature, such as
electrical transformers or hydroelectric turbines and turbine shafts, were trans-
ported over disputed territory.

By March 1996, 80 percent of Bosnia's major roads were open for use. This
was a key NATO contribution to freedom of movement.[73] Large-scale NATO
projects included rebuilding the Sarajevo airport access road and the road
which leads to the primary gas facility outside Sarajevo. Smaller, but symbolic, steps toward reconciliation included NATO assistance transporting
eighty-seven school children on an educational field trip from Tuzla to Zagreb
and arranging for local schools to receive computers as donations from private
voluntary organizations. Computer and public administration expertise was
also made available to the OSCE to help it prepare for the process of electoral
reconciliation.

NATO's role was nonetheless half-hearted when it came to facilitating the
arrest of war criminals and delivery to The Hague for trial. NATO was willing
to arrest such figures if they were to happen upon them—but would not seek
them out. Not wishing to spark confrontations, NATO commanders applied a
strict interpretation of this mandate for the first two years of the mission. Thus
while NATO could provide security as a rapidly deployed peacekeeping force
to help aid the voluntary separation of the warring parties, it was not well
suited for policing or long-term security provision. The serious nature of this
institutional weakness was underscored by Bosnian President Alija Izetbe-
govic, who said in August 1996, "No one can expect us to legalize something
that we have been fighting against and ask us to accept the results of a war

of conquest and genocide. . . . As days go by our doubts and questions are multiplying."[74] With NATO occupying the country, Bosnia-Herzegovina existed in an absence of war, but without lasting security.

Outside of NATO, the other institutions charged with facilitating the civilian elements of long-term peace in Bosnia-Herzegovina remained weak. In November 1996 President Clinton announced what had been in the works for months—that US and NATO forces would remain in Bosnia-Herzegovina in substantial numbers for an additional eighteen months in a follow-on Stabilization Force. Through 1997, SFOR successfully maintained the status quo, but little changed in terms of the civilian implementation of the Dayton accords. Thus NATO's contribution to security was only a partial success. Two years after President Clinton promised that the US and NATO would only be in Bosnia-Herzegovina for twelve months, he announced an additional extension of American force commitments in December 1997. This time, however, the commitment would be indefinite.

NATO and the East: A Mixed Record

After the Cold War, NATO prioritized adaptation of its institutional structures to stabilize the East through the NACC and the Partnership for Peace and by promoting interlocking institutions. However, while focusing on institutional outreach to the East, NATO and other European institutions appeared ineffective in managing a real war in the Balkans.

By 1995 the transatlantic relationship grew so strained that NATO verged on collapse. Indeed, a primary reason for US engagement in Bosnia-Herzegovina was to restore credibility to the alliance. Once put into action, NATO showed its potential, facilitating coalition-building for crisis management as it was critical to implementing the early stages of the Dayton peace agreement. However, the mission only succeeded with American leadership. As President Clinton said on 27 November 1995: "The only force capable of getting this job done is NATO, the powerful, military alliance of democracies that has guaranteed our security for half a century now. . . . And as NATO's leader and the primary broker of the peace agreement the United States must be an essential part of the mission. . . . If we're not there, NATO will not be there."[75]

To ensure that NATO would continue to "be there" both in Europe and Bosnia, NATO subsequently prioritized two new and potentially conflicting institutional processes of external enlargement and internal restructuring.

5

NATO Enlargement

Why NATO Enlargement?

Post–Cold War NATO enlargement was approved, in principle, by NATO's members at the January 1994 Brussels Summit. It was formalized via invitations to Poland, Hungary, and the Czech Republic to negotiate membership at a heads of state summit in Madrid in July 1997. The rationale for NATO enlargement was unclear and the timing of the decision appeared driven by American electoral politics. Moreover, it was not a universally popular policy among the NATO allies.

NATO enlargement was formally intended to promote a security community in Central and Eastern Europe by consolidating democracy and enhancing stability. Informally, the policy appeared designed to extend American influence over Germany and constrain Russian power in Eastern Europe. This stood in direct contradiction to another formal goal of integrating Russia into a new European security framework. As a result, NATO enlargement often caused more questions about the future of European security than it solved. Indeed, the positive or negative impact of NATO enlargement on European security will likely not be known for years.

NATO Enlargement and Russia

While NATO enlargement was conceived, NATO governments initially worried that this mechanism for stabilizing the East might backfire. In particular, the allies were concerned that enlargement could have a negative impact on Russia's foreign and domestic policy. Russian officials, from the most liberal reformers to the most virulent nationalists, had united in opposition to NATO enlargement. President Boris Yeltsin once warned of a flame of war spreading throughout Europe, and his former National Security Advisor Alexander Lebed once predicted World War III if NATO tried to enlarge.[1] Officials from the Russian Ministry of Defense suggested that Russia would establish a new Warsaw Pact–style defense alliance in the former Soviet Union and retarget nuclear weapons at the new NATO members. Pro-Western Russian reformers were bewildered by the enlargement policy. They complained that it was fueling Russian nationalism and undermining their efforts to build a pro-Western democratic Russia.

NATO hoped to assuage Russia's concerns by claiming that enlargement would be open to all interested countries in Europe that met certain criteria—including Russia. The idea of keeping the door to NATO membership rhetorically open to Russia was pushed strongly by the US and Canada. Yet few NATO countries considered full Russian membership an option, as they felt it would radically alter the foundations of NATO from alliance to collective security. The challenge was to find ways to engage Russia while at the same time preventing it from having too much influence in NATO's internal affairs. A policy of enlargement that resulted in a dilution of NATO would be self-defeating for both old and new members. Thus the requirements for admission to NATO would be set high enough that, if it ever applied and qualified for membership, "Russia would be a very different place—a true Western democracy," according to one senior US defense planner.[2] For the many officials in the Department of Defense who preferred the PFP over NATO enlargement, setting high standards for membership would also likely exclude many, if not all, Central and Eastern European states. Indeed, for some US government officials who strongly supported enlargement, the notion of criteria was worrisome because they could be used to delay further a decision on when to enlarge. Pro-enlargement advocates in the US government had reason for concern given that Poland still had serious problems with its civilian control over the armed forces. The Czech and Hungarian militaries were unprepared for membership and public support in these applicants for membership in NATO was low.

Serious differences of opinion among the NATO allies over how to treat Russia also emerged. For example, internal disputes between the US and Germany over how to approach Russia became obvious in September 1994. At a conference in Berlin, German Defense Minister Volker Rühe rejected Russian membership. He stated that it would "blow NATO apart, it would be like the United Nations of Europe, it wouldn't work."[3] At the same meeting, US Secretary of Defense William Perry indicated that he would not rule out Russian membership in NATO, although he did admit that it would not happen in the foreseeable future. Wanting NATO to speak as one voice, the Clinton Administration formulated a dual-track strategy in the autumn of 1994 to accelerate a NATO dialogue over enlargement while accommodating Russian concerns by strengthening the Conference on Security and Cooperation in Europe, which remained Russia's preferred security institution.

The US concluded that NATO should establish a working group to define membership criteria for applicants. The guidelines for the NATO study were elaborated by US Undersecretary of Defense Walter Slocombe in a November

1994 speech to the North Atlantic Assembly's Annual Session in Washington, D.C. According to Slocombe, NATO should only want new members who have "passed beyond ambitions toward the territory of their neighbors, who have accepted the rights of their minorities, and who have established real and working democratic systems."[4] According to a State Department official involved in defining the enlargement criteria, this policy was "not designed to create an obstacle but to begin a process."[5] However, the process supported enlargement while actually making it difficult in practice. US and NATO officials hoped that the study would allow NATO to defer the hard decisions on enlargement by two years—until after the scheduled Russian and American presidential elections.

By proposing to strengthen the organizational capabilities of the CSCE, the US hoped to demonstrate to Russia that there were opportunities for international security cooperation besides NATO. The US also signaled that there had been a change in the traditional American view toward the CSCE. As a senior US official stated on 1 December 1994, the US was

> making clear that NATO will expand, but this is going to be part of a larger European security structure that involves many different institutions—the European Union and in particular the CSCE. . . . We consider, for the United States, NATO still to be the number one organization from our point of view, but we certainly want to increase the role of CSCE. . . . This is a strategy that emphasizes our desire to have an inclusive relationship between NATO and all the Partners for Peace, that when NATO expansion occurs, it's not going to be directed against Russia, but part of the broader policy of integration. CSCE fits into this larger policy as an institution where Russia is a member.[6]

However, when NATO Secretary General Willy Claes met with senior US officials at the State Department in November 1994, the American participants said surprisingly little about the CSCE linkage. NATO officials complained that the US seemed uncertain of its enlargement strategy and policy toward Russia. The US did support a change of name from CSCE to OSCE—the Organization for Security and Cooperation in Europe.[7] Yet Washington appeared to want to create the appearance of a strengthened OSCE without granting it too much authority.

Cooperation or Conflict?

When Russian Foreign Minister Andrei Kozyrev traveled to Brussels in December 1994 to formalize Russia's full PFP participation through its IPP, he declined at the last minute. Kozyrev declared shock and surprise at what he saw as accelerated discussion of NATO expansion in Brussels and elsewhere, even though the US had briefed Russia on its plans for NATO in advance. America's NATO allies were also uncomfortable with the US approach. The

US sought to complete the review of enlargement criteria in the following spring, but this was rejected by key European members as moving too fast.[8]

On 22 November 1994 German NATO Ambassador Hermann von Richthofen cabled his foreign ministry complaining that "the US Administration is moving quickly to expand NATO without consultations on the consequences for the Alliance." He specifically noted the division in NATO over where to start the enlargement, with Greece and Italy favoring Romania, Bulgaria, and possibly Malta, while northern NATO countries wanted to prioritize admission of Poland, Hungary, and the Czech Republic. Von Richthofen asserted that, without a clear sense of mission and strategy "the Alliance is divided and in crisis."[9]

Intra-alliance differences were ignored on 1 December when the NATO foreign ministers announced:

> We expect and would welcome NATO enlargement that would reach to democratic states to our East, as part of an evolutionary process, taking into account political and security developments in the whole of Europe. Enlargement, when it comes, would be part of a broad European security architecture based on true cooperation throughout the whole of Europe. It would threaten no one and would enhance stability and security for all of Europe.[10]

The ministers approved the US proposal for a NATO working group to study the "why" and "how" of enlargement and report to the NAC by the end of the year.

On 5 December President Clinton attended the Budapest CSCE heads of state summit to reinvigorate US goals regarding its multi-institutional approach towards stabilizing the East. He declared:

> We must not allow the Iron Curtain to be replaced by a veil of indifference. We must not consign new democracies to a gray zone. . . . We seek to increase the security of all, to erase the old lines without drawing arbitrary new ones, to bolster emerging democracies and to integrate the nations of Europe into a continent where democracy and free markets know no borders but where every nation's borders are secure.[11]

President Yeltsin, who also attended the meeting, ruffled the public relations aspect of the US plan when he tersely replied:

> A system of blocs, that is to say something we have left behind, is now coming back—the NATO bloc on the one hand—and Russia on the other. . . . Without compromise on this issue between NATO and Russia, there would be no point in continuing a partnership. . . . Otherwise we will go our own ways, and why have a partnership at all?[12]

Yeltsin added that if NATO expands, it risks bringing a "Cold Peace" to Europe. Clinton was described by aides as merely expressing "concern and a state of perplexity about what the Russians were up to."[13] The Georgian leader, and former Soviet Foreign Minister, Eduard Shevardnadze lamented after the meeting that: "The Cold War is over. . . . Beware of the Peace."[14]

Responding to Russian sensitivities and domestic critics who felt that enlargement advocates had not articulated a clear vision for Europe, an effort at defining US strategy was advanced by US Assistant Secretary of State Richard Holbrooke. Writing in *Foreign Affairs* in March 1995, Holbrooke asserted that:

1. The goal remains the defense of the Alliance's vital interests and the promotion of European stability. NATO expansion must strengthen security in the entire region, including nations that are not members. The goal is to promote security in Central Europe by integrating countries that qualify into the stabilizing framework of NATO.
2. The rationale and process for NATO's expansion, once decided, will be transparent, not secret. Both Warsaw and Moscow . . . should have access to all aspects of the alliance's thinking in order to understand that NATO should no longer be considered an anti-Russian alliance.
3. There is no timetable or list of nations that will be invited to join NATO.
4. Each nation will be considered individually, not as part of some grouping.
5. The decisions as to who joins NATO and when will be made exclusively by the Alliance.
6. Although criteria for membership have not been determined, certain fundamental precepts reflected in the original Washington treaty remain as valid as they were in 1949: new members must be democratic, have market economies, be committed to responsible security policies, and be able to contribute to the Alliance.
7. Each new NATO member constitutes for the United States the most solemn of all commitments: a bilateral defense treaty that extends the US security umbrella to a new nation. This requires ratification by two-thirds of the US Senate.[15]

Holbrooke claimed that the US would make more vigorous use of the OSCE's consultative and conflict prevention mechanisms. He conceded, "If the West is to create an enduring and stable security framework for Europe, it must solve the most enduring strategic problem of Europe and integrate the nations of the former Soviet Union, especially Russia, into a stable European security system."[16]

Holbrooke also endorsed a proposal by former National Security Advisor Zbigniew Brzezinski that Moscow should be offered a formal treaty of cooperation with NATO.[17] Holbrooke noted many difficulties in this approach but hinted that the US was not ruling it out: "The US government as well as its major allies have supported development of this important new track in the European security framework."[18] Indeed, in early 1995, Russia had quietly approached officials in Washington indicating that Moscow might accommodate a slow and limited expansion of NATO under certain circumstances. Moscow sought guarantees that the process would not be rushed, that there would be no nuclear weapons stationed on the territories of new members, that Russia could be a member of NATO eventually, and that the end result would be a forum for East–West cooperation on security issues and a NATO–Russia non-aggression pact.[19]

US and NATO officials viewed the Russian position as an important change in diplomatic rhetoric and, prematurely, concluded that Russia was beginning to accommodate NATO enlargement. Actually it was not clear if Russia was seriously altering its stance on NATO enlargement, or if it was using a softer tone to lessen the historical fears of East European countries, which were driving them toward NATO. The US hoped to resolve the conflicts over NATO expansion within the context of a NATO–Russian dialogue. For example, Vice President Al Gore said in Tallinn, Estonia, on 14 March:

> It is important to understand that the process by which NATO expands is a process that must take place at the same time the relationship between NATO and Russia is deepened and clarified. Both processes must take place simultaneously and both processes must take place in full open, public view with no surprises and no sudden movements.[20]

EU foreign ministers meeting in France that same week concluded that NATO might "consider an agreement, treaty or charter between the Atlantic Alliance and Russia in parallel with the enlargement of NATO to show Russia that we are not neglecting it," in the words of French Foreign Minister Alain Juppé, summarizing the EU position. It was necessary in order to "find something to reassure Russia," Juppé declared.[21] British Foreign Secretary Douglas Hurd stressed that while Russia could not veto NATO policy, such an agreement would be based on the principle of no vetoes and no surprises. Nonetheless, during the meeting European differences emerged over what form a special NATO–Russia accord would take. For example, France supported a formal NATO–Russia treaty while Germany pushed for a less formal charter that would not require ratification by all members and would be less legally binding.

Actually, the Western allies had misread the Russian position on enlargement. On or around 15 March Yeltsin sent a directive to Kozyrev admonishing him for being weak on NATO and ordering a harder line from the foreign ministry. Five days later in Paris, Kozyrev said of NATO enlargement: "Why rush things if we run the risk of creating new lines of division?"[22] US Secretary of State Warren Christopher asserted that Kozyrev seemed to believe that "there had been some change in the position of the United States or NATO, that we were going at a different pace than before. . . . That is not correct."[23]

In Geneva on 23 March Warren Christopher delivered a personal letter from President Clinton that outlined the US position on NATO enlargement. In response, Kozyrev declared, "The honeymoon has come to an end."[24]

Bringing Russia In

Following a meeting in Moscow with US Secretary of Defense Perry on 3 April, Russian Defense Minister Pavel Grachev linked Russian continued commitment to the CFE treaty to NATO expansion, and warned, "Countermeasures could be taken. . . . We might create necessary military groups in the most threatening directions and set up closer cooperation with other CIS countries."[25] The speaker of the upper house of the Russian parliament told Perry that parliament was unlikely to ratify the START II treaty—which would reduce the number of nuclear weapons capable of reaching the United States—if NATO expanded.[26] Russia's first Deputy Defense Minister Andrei Kokoshin was quoted in the Russian press asserting that enlargement would put at risk the "semi-demilitarized zone which has now emerged in Central and Eastern Europe" and that "it is necessary to abandon the false impression that NATO expansion is inevitable and unavoidable."[27]

Russia's increasing perceptions of a threat from NATO were heightened by a series of public statements from Visegrad and NATO countries suggesting that the process of expansion was accelerating. On 3 April Czech President Vaclav Havel asserted, "There are a number of indications that we are seeing a new momentum on the subject of future membership of the new democracies in the North Atlantic alliance. . . . One year ago, NATO membership did not seem likely."[28] The next day President Lech Walesa intensified pressure on NATO when he told the BBC that, as during World War II, Poland was being "let down by the West" and that Russia threatened European security. One day later Polish Prime Minister Jozer Oleksy told reporters, when departing Warsaw to visit NATO headquarters, that in the debate over NATO expansion, "Russia has no significance. . . . Poland defines its own aims and goals. . . . Other countries can have their opinions on the subject, but they cannot have any influence." In Brussels, Oleksy told NATO officials that, "Our answer to the question when NATO should open up to new members is—as soon as possible."[29]

On 14 April Robert Hunter, the US ambassador to NATO, said in Prague that the decision to expand NATO "is made, now it's just a matter of doing it right." Confirming what had been agreed to privately among the allies, he said that NATO rules would be applied strictly to each new member and that each would have to join and contribute to the NATO integrated military command structure. "An ally is an ally is an ally. . . . You join the Alliance and you do what allies do. . . . If necessary, countries joining NATO will accept deployment on their territory of whatever is required for security," he added.[30]

Despite the accelerated rhetoric over enlargement, NATO's internal timetable had not changed. American officials thus sought to clarify the situation primarily to alleviate Russian perceptions. On 24 April Secretary of State Christopher said: "The process of NATO expansion has proceeded on precisely the same timetable that we decided on last December. . . . This timetable has not been altered because of other events since that time. . . . It is a deliberate timetable." He added that "NATO is not a social club. . . . Any decision on enlargement will be taken with great care and deliberation and precision."[31] NATO Secretary General Claes insisted: "The European security architecture is not possible without Russia. . . . It is not possible to give an answer on the timing of expansion."[32] Nonetheless, the following week, Russian Foreign Minister Kozyrev warned that if NATO were to expand, nationalists could devour him and that he would have to write his memoirs "from the Gulag."[33]

At a Moscow meeting between presidents Clinton and Yeltsin in May 1995 (commemorating the fiftieth anniversary of the end of World War II), the US signaled to Russia that it could be a member of NATO and that Washington would give written assurances to that effect as well as on the nondeployment of nuclear weapons on the new members' territory.[34] The US worked tirelessly to get Yeltsin to commit fully to the PFP. Eventually, Yeltsin promised to join the PFP and to negotiate a special NATO–Russia dialogue. On NATO expansion, President Clinton said that:

> I made it clear that I thought that anything done with NATO had to meet two criteria. Number one, it must advance the interests of all the Partners for Peace, the security interests of all of them, including Russia. And number two, it must advance the long-term goal of the United States which I have articulated from the beginning of my presidency, of an integrated Europe, which I believe is very important, and I think Russia shares both of those objectives.[35]

Assurances by Clinton may not have been enough for the Russians. As Sergei Karagonov, a Yeltsin advisor, said on 11 May, "You cannot build up a special relationship with Russia when you are talking about enlargement at the same time."[36] To this Andrei Androsov, head of the Russian Foreign Ministry's NATO Department added: "We need NATO to change its attitude from expansion to real partnership. . . . If the same treatment continues, I fear cooperation will be affected."[37]

At a 30–31 May North Atlantic Council ministerial meeting, NATO restated its goals and intention to enlarge. The ministers also supported Russia's decision to participate in the PFP and build a special NATO–Russia relationship. Invited to address the NATO leaders, Kozyrev insisted:

Russia's position regarding NATO expansion has remained unchanged. We continue to believe that it does not meet either the interests of Russia's national security or the interest of European security as a whole. Furthermore, the hasty resolution of the issue may threaten the establishment of truly mutually advantageous and constructive relations between Russia and NATO and the usefulness of Russia's involvement in the PFP. It will not create greater stability and security either. . . . We suggest to halt and think rather than act hastily and blindly.[38]

In a formal letter to the NAC, Kozyrev was more blunt: "A decision about the enlargement of NATO to the East would create for Russia the need for a corresponding correction of its attitude toward the Partnership for Peace."[39] After the ministerial, NATO officials quietly asserted that, following the completion of the enlargement study, the issue would be placed on the back burner. "Something like this has to be driven through and there is not much drive in NATO at the moment," said one NATO official.[40] Indeed, within NATO it seemed somewhat dubious to be proceeding with enlargement at a time when Bosnia was undermining the very credibility and viability of the alliance itself.

Some American officials, nonetheless, sought to continue momentum toward enlargement. US Deputy Secretary of State Strobe Talbott, who had initially opposed the policy, reversed himself and advocated a broad rationale for NATO enlargement.[41] According to Talbott, candidates for NATO membership should be judged according to the strength of their democratic institutions and their ability to meet the obligations of membership. The process would be transparent, open, and ongoing. NATO enlargement would promote reform in post-communist Europe through respect for democracy and international norms of behavior and explicit preconditions for membership. NATO would be a force for the rule of law both within Europe's new democracies and among them.[42]

Talbott maintained that NATO enlargement would have a positive impact on domestic politics within potential member states and help to grow democracy in post-communist Europe. Each new member would have full civilian control by establishing parliamentary oversight over military affairs and by appointing civilians to senior defense positions. The policy would promote conflict—or dispute—resolution by making convincing progress in resolving disputes with neighbors peacefully and show that candidates are committed to multiethnic democracy. Finally, stability would be promoted via the extension of NATO's classic mission—as a hedge against a resurgent Russian threat.

The NATO Enlargement Study

In September 1995 NATO completed its enlargement study explaining the "how" and "why" of enlargement—but not the "who" and "when" nor airing potential negative consequences. Indeed, the strategic rationale and military criteria of NATO enlargement were never publicly articulated. NATO viewed the policy as:

1. Encouraging and supporting democratic reforms, including civilian and democratic control over the military;
2. Fostering in new members of the Alliance the patterns and habits of cooperation, consultation and consensus building which characterize relations among current Allies;
3. Promoting good-neighbourly relations, which would benefit all countries in the Euro-Atlantic area, both members and non-members of NATO;
4. Emphasizing common defense and extending its benefits and increasing transparency in defense planning and military budgets, thereby reducing the likelihood of instability that might be engendered by an exclusively national approach to defense policies;
5. Reinforcing the tendency toward integration and cooperation in Europe based on shared democratic values and thereby curbing the countervailing tendency towards disintegration along ethnic and territorial lines;
6. Strengthening the Alliance's ability to contribute to European and international security, including through peacekeeping activities under the responsibility of the OSCE and peacekeeping operations under the authority of the UN Security Council as well as other new missions;
7. Strengthening and broadening the Trans-Atlantic relationship.[43]

New members must conform to the "purposes and principles of the Charter of the United Nations, and the safeguarding of the freedom, common heritage and civilization of all Alliance members and their people, founded on the principles of democracy, individual liberty and the rule of law."[44]

According to NATO, enlargement seeks to avoid drawing new divisions in Europe after the Cold War. In this context, the enlargement study stressed that: "A stronger NATO–Russia relationship should form another cornerstone of a new, inclusive and comprehensive security structure in Europe. . . . This further development of the NATO–Russia relationship, and its possible eventual formalization, should take place in rough parallel with NATO's own enlargement, with the goal of further strengthening stability and security in Europe."[45] NATO–Russia relations would reflect Russia's significance in European security and be based on reciprocity, mutual respect, and confidence, and no surprise decisions by either side which could affect the interests of the other.[46]

While acknowledging that there are benefits from stationing allied troops on a new member's territory, the study underscored that the redeployment of existing Allied forces from current locations or pre-positioning of equipment would be expensive and potentially provocative. Thus the presence of allied conventional forces on a new member's territory might take a variety of forms in terms of exercises, dual basing of air assets, or the prepositioning of equipment and material. Nonetheless, for new members, the peacetime stationing of other allied forces on their territory should be neither a condition of membership nor foreclosed as an option. New members should be prepared in principle for such an event, but there would be no immediate necessity for allied forces to be stationed on new member territory.

The collective defense principles of Article 5 of the North Atlantic treaty would be applied to all new members—including nuclear defense planning and deterrence. However, the study also concluded that "there is no a priori requirement for the stationing of nuclear weapons on the territory of new members" and that there is no need to change current NATO posture under existing circumstances. New members would choose to accept the military consequences of membership not only in principle, but also in practice, if the strategic environment were to change. NATO walked a fine line by assuring that it would not invite states solely as consumers of security, while at the same time seeking to allay Russian fears. The end result, however, would be a policy of bringing in new members without a full security guarantee based on the stationing of credible deterrent forces. The deterrent value behind NATO enlargement would be a promise to consider reinforcement and intervention—not an immediate security guarantee.

Toward Enlargement

Some partner countries welcomed NATO's discussion of the modalities of enlargement and eleven submitted formal applications by early 1997. Polish officials were skeptical and claimed that NATO was buying time with delaying tactics because of Russian opposition and American indecisiveness. These concerns were heightened by NATO's formal acceptance of the enlargement study in December 1995, which began a year-long consideration of the implications of enlargement, via briefings to interested parties and an invitation for countries to signal their intention to apply for NATO membership. The best thing that Polish Deputy Foreign Minister Andrzej Towpik could say about the study was: "I am happy with this document for three reasons, it is on time, . . . it is a very substantial document, and it takes the discussion into a new stage."[47]

During the first week of October 1995, NATO officials confirmed that the alliance would put enlargement "on the back burner" until after presidential elections in Russia, scheduled for June and July 1996.[48] Senior American officials were reported to have advised the NATO allies to be "dull and boring" on enlargement.[49]

However, the US had finally attained a higher degree of internal consensus to move NATO toward enlargement. By March 1996, senior US officials indicated that, at a NATO heads of state meeting in 1997, "two, possibly three, states" would be invited to initiate negotiations toward joining NATO.[50] The message to Moscow was firm—NATO will enlarge, it will do so on its own terms, and Russia should take advantage of the opportunity to build a special NATO–Russia relationship. This view was put forward strongly to the Central and East European aspirants to NATO in a March 1996 speech by US Secretary of State Warren Christopher in Prague. He suggested that a failure by Moscow to take advantage of the special relationship with NATO would be similar to the rejection of the Marshall Plan of the late 1940s and that only Russia could isolate itself.[51]

In March 1996, newly appointed Russian Foreign Minister Yevgenii Primakov took full control over Russia's strategy toward NATO enlargement. Primakov had been the head of the Russian foreign intelligence services and was schooled in Soviet foreign policy strategies. He was brought in primarily to appeal to nationalists and communists, who then dominated the Russian parliament. Primakov was also given the foreign minister portfolio in part because of the Western-oriented Kozyrev's failure to convince the West to accommodate Russian opposition to NATO enlargement.

Primakov sustained Russia's strong opposition to NATO enlargement but shifted tactics. He suggested that Russia might be open to a deal on enlargement, if new members agreed not to station nuclear weapons on their territory and if they only join NATO's political structures, without military integration. Previously, Primakov and his staff at the Russian foreign intelligence services had determined that Moscow's hostile tone opposing NATO enlargement was accelerating the drive by Central Europeans toward NATO. Primakov concluded that the best way to slow enlargement was to make friendly initiatives to the West which might impact the NATO consensus by splitting the US from its European allies.

Russia hoped to take the steam out of the enlargement process as Western countries entered into more serious discussions about the consequences and costs of the policy. This approach stemmed largely from a confidential report prepared in April and May 1995 for President Yeltsin by senior Russian officials. The report, titled "Russia and NATO: Thesis of the Council for Foreign and Defense Policy," was chaired by Yeltsin advisor Sergei Karagonov. The report recommended that the Russian government not accept NATO enlargement as inevitable, and that an active and reasonable policy might enable deferment or even cancellation of NATO's enlargement plans. The report rejected seeking compensation for NATO enlargement as signaling consent.[52]

The Russian study also rejected costly countermeasures to enlargement that would undermine Russian economic reform. The report noted that supporters of enlargement were a minority in the West but that they had come to occupy key decision-making positions in the Clinton administration. The study concluded that as enlargement becomes a closer reality and its economic, military, political, and cohesion-related costs become more obvious, the numbers of opponents of enlargement might grow, with their opposition getting stronger. The group suggested that Russia could encourage this perspective by prompting such debate in political and academic circles in NATO countries, first of all in the United States. The study concluded: "We should not act against the West; instead, we should help it to avoid making a mistake dangerous for everyone, first of all for the West itself." Finally, the group advised that Russia tone down its rhetoric and stress cooperation—thereby denying the West a threat-based rationale for enlarging the alliance.

This tactical shift in Russian strategy regarding NATO enlargement was accepted by the Yeltsin government. Yeltsin began to lobby individual NATO members against enlargement. He hoped to at least stall the policy beyond the 1996 Russian presidential election. Yeltsin personally appealed several times by telephone to German Chancellor Helmut Kohl to stop, or stall, the drive toward enlargement in the run-up to the June presidential election. Kohl responded sympathetically to Yeltsin's appeal. He urged NATO to be more sensitive to Russian security concerns at a gathering of NATO specialists in Munich in February 1996. Kohl's shift was tactical, as his support for NATO enlargement never wavered. However, it did suggest that Germany was increasingly worried about the impact that NATO was having on Russia. Nevertheless, at the same meeting, US Secretary of Defense Perry asserted that: "NATO enlargement is inevitable and if NATO enlargement is a carrot encouraging reforms, then we cannot keep that carrot continually out of reach."[53]

Endorsing this perspective, and hoping to appeal to voters of East European origins, President Clinton used his one foreign policy speech of the 1996 general election to set a timetable for NATO enlargement after wavering on the policy for nearly four years. NATO enlargement was to be completed by NATO's fiftieth anniversary in April 1999. Having demonstrated caution about NATO enlargement, President Clinton finally chose to advance the policy in unambiguous terms and thus set NATO on an irreversible track towards enlargement. The only difference between Clinton and his opponent Sen. Robert Dole was over who would enlarge NATO faster—with Dole promising to enlarge NATO one year sooner. Domestic political calculations were a critical factor leading to a hard commitment from the US to expand NATO. There are some 23 million Americans who trace their heritage to Eastern Europe, including over 9 million Poles. As there are a dozen states where these groups constitute more than 5 percent of the electorate, taking a firm position in favor of NATO enlargement was a no-lose bipartisan political decision at the time.[54]

Potential problems with the policy were not aired by the president and he was ambiguous about the costs. At no point was any explanation offered as to why NATO enlargement was deemed a bad idea in 1993 but a good one in

1996. Strategic and military implications were left to be addressed at a later time. Unaware that his microphone was turned on at the Madrid Summit in July 1997, Canadian Prime Minister Jean Chretien complained that the US had no strategic vision for Europe and that America's two year campaign to enlarge NATO was "done for short-term political reasons, to win elections."[55] Indeed, the lack of a clear consensus on the rationale for enlargement was symbolized by the fact that at this stage NATO could only agree that "one or more" countries would be invited to negotiate membership in NATO. Indeed, serious differences would emerge within NATO as the US decided that it would endorse only the three invited countries. The majority of its allies wanted Romania and Slovenia invited as well. For its part, Turkey threatened to block NATO enlargement if it was not given a clear perspective toward membership in the EU.

As NATO accelerated toward its announcement of initial candidates for membership in 1997, NATO undertook serious efforts to decrease Russian opposition by offering a formal NATO–Russia charter. The results were codified in the NATO–Russia Founding Act on Mutual Relations, Cooperation and Security between NATO and the Russian Federation, completed in May 1997. This agreement culminated efforts to build a special NATO–Russia relationship and created a variety of consultative mechanisms to provide Russia with what is termed "a voice, but not a veto," within NATO.

In attaining Russia's agreement, NATO made a number of concessions to ease Moscow's concerns over enlargement. This included agreeing not to permanently station large deployments of current member troops and conventional forces on new member territories, not to deploy nuclear weapons or nuclear weapons infrastructure on the territory of new members, and to create a special NATO–Russia Permanent Joint Council (PJC) for consultation. US and NATO officials claimed that this would not damage the consensus process in NATO if interests diverged with Russia.

Nevertheless, the allies, at sixteen or nineteen, would have to come to a consensus on every issue on the PJC agenda. Because it is in the consensus process where the actual NATO veto lies, Russia may have an opportunity to exercise a de facto veto in alliance decision-making. In a crisis, the entire consensus process may freeze the institution and make it ineffectual if serious Russian interests are divergent with those of the alliance. Additionally, NATO has formally declared its plans for further enlargements through an "open-door" policy that would continue the process of expanding to interested and qualified countries. If not carefully managed, these developments may fundamentally shift NATO's rationale away from a traditional alliance into a new form of general European collective security architecture in which shared national interests—for example between France and Russia—emerge within the NATO framework. Henry Kissinger, an early public supporter of NATO enlargement, concluded of this new institutional arrangement that, "Had I known the price of NATO enlargement would be the gross dilution of NATO, I might have urged other means to achieve the objective."[56]

The Great Debate

NATO enlargement created deep divisions among scholars and policymakers drawing from either realist or institutionalist traditions of international relations.[57] However, enlargement supporters were in the minority and scholars almost universally opposed the policy. As John Lewis Gaddis suggested, if there is one area in which "my normally contentious colleagues seem to be in uncharacteristic agreement: it is that the NATO expansion initiative is ill-conceived, ill-timed, and above all ill-suited to the realities of the post–Cold War world. . . . Indeed I can recall no other moment, in my own experience as a practicing historian, at which there was within our community greater unanimity against, which is to say less support for, an official foreign policy proposition."[58] As one senior State Department official conceded, enlargement is not popular among academics, and the US and NATO have not done a very good job of explaining what it is about.[59] Another administration official was more blunt complaining that "there is a very adverse trend in the conventional wisdom on the part of the thoughtful elite."[60] Ultimately, there would be two degrees of success for NATO enlargement: Senate and allied parliamentary ratification, and enhancing European security. The true measure of NATO enlargement's success will be whether or not it strengthens, or dilutes, the transatlantic relationship.

Realist Arguments in Support of NATO Enlargement

Realists favoring NATO enlargement generally drew from a balance of power analysis. This suggests that moving the Cold War line farther east will increase security in Europe because Russia remains a threat. Such balancing would, in theory, also lessen the chance that a united Germany will find itself in security competition with Russia. Some realists also asserted that Russia may return to its Great Power status and pursue traditional imperialist behavior. Thus, it would be best to enlarge NATO rapidly, while Russia is incapable of mounting a major preventive response. This would assure NATO's future as an anti-Russian collective defense alliance. Moreover, expanding NATO to include a group of willing countries with sizable military assets would add to the West's resources, defray some of the deepening cuts in defense spending among NATO countries, and open up new arms markets for current NATO member states. Perhaps most importantly, NATO expansion would be an important tool of sustaining US primacy over Europe and ensure that no peer competitors arise that might challenge American power in the region.

Peter Rodman endorsed NATO enlargement in such geostrategic terms, suggesting that, "The only potential great power security problem in Central Europe is the lengthening shadow of Russian strength, and NATO has the job of counterbalancing it."[61] Henry Kissinger concluded that without NATO enlargement, Central and Eastern Europe would again become a vacuum in which German and Russian security competition will develop.[62] Similarly, Zbigniew Brzezinski suggested that while NATO enlargement should not be viewed as hostile toward Russia, it should replace the strategic vacuum in Central and Eastern Europe.[63] Columnist William Safire endorsed NATO enlargement because Russia is "authoritarian at heart and expansionist by habit. The time to push the protective line eastward is now, while Russia is weak and preoccupied with its own revival, and not later, when such a move would be an insufferable provocation to a superpower."[64] Moreover, as Jonathan Eyal maintained, delaying enlargement until Moscow does something to warrant a threat could provoke or escalate crises, and thus it is preferable to enlarge during a time of peace.[65]

Some realists acknowledged that NATO enlargement would draw new lines in Europe, but that this would increase general security. Enlarging NATO to include Poland, in particular, would settle the question of the eastern frontier of Germany and remove a major historical reason for German aspirations in the East. As Conor Cruise O'Brien speculated: "A new wave of national pride—perhaps early in the new century—might cause Germany to resent its subordinate position within a NATO perceived as dominated . . . by the United States, France, and Britain. Germany might then withdraw from NATO . . . and set up its own system of alliances in Central Europe."[66] Kissinger added that if the Visegrad states' requests to join NATO are rejected and the states bordering Germany are refused protection, "Germany will sooner or later seek to achieve its security by national efforts, encountering on the way a Russia pursuing the same policy from its side."[67]

Stephen Pelz maintained that inclusion of the Visegrad countries into NATO would permanently settle Germany's eastern frontier, bind Germany in the West, and reassure both the West and Russia as to Germany's growing economic and political power. Pelz suggested that this would provide a clear and defensible line between the West and the disputes to the East. A new buffer zone would be comprised of Finland, the Baltics, Belarus, and Ukraine, whose security would be respected by Russia and the West if guaranteed in a treaty.[68] This approach would purposefully draw lines between East and West and recognize spheres of influence which already exist informally. Such a "Yalta II" would bring clarity and predictability to European security.

A similar argument was expressed by Karsten Voigt, the German Social Democratic party foreign policy spokesman, who asserted that, left alone, "the countries of Central and Eastern Europe could fall victim yet again to the rivalries and tensions that have plagued the region from time immemorial;

only through integration can we ensure that the 'old game' of competing spheres of influence does not return."[69] One German official noted that "insofar as the Germans like happy neighbors, they also think that the presence of the United States is an insuring element, a stabilizing component to prevent our neighbors from perceiving that something might happen. . . . This is what you objectively call a stabilizing factor. . . . So it has not only to do with an outside threat, it's an internal balancing element inside the European security structure as such."[70]

Realist support for NATO enlargement also drew on alliance theory. Some Central and East European countries may naturally want to associate with the winning side in the Cold War. By joining NATO, they hope to reap the benefits of the West's relative gains by sharing the spoils of victory.[71] If NATO rejected requests for membership, these countries might, in theory, engage in their own destabilizing balancing behavior—by forming regional alliances, establishing bilateral security guarantees with countries from within NATO, or pursuing expensive and provocative self-help national military buildups.[72]

Realist Arguments against NATO Enlargement

Some realists pointed to the absence of balancing alliances among the Visegrad countries or the Baltics as evidence that they do not really feel threatened. Looking at the distribution of power and capabilities, some opponents stressed the dissolution of the Russian armed forces, Russia's dismal military performance in Chechnya, and the fact that there would be considerable warning time of a renewed Russian threat to Central and Eastern Europe. To enlarge NATO in the absence of a threat could cause renewed security competition among states not included in NATO or provoke Russia to respond by reintegrating parts of the former Soviet Union as a defensive act. Rather than promoting stability, NATO enlargement would thus create instability which does not currently exist. Placed within the context of the rise and decline of great powers, this relative gain by the West could prompt hegemonic war in the worst case. Some realists added that NATO is the wrong institution for consolidating democracy. With the US reducing its commitments abroad, the security guarantee would be weak for new members. Alternatively, the EU would be better suited for meeting new security challenges.

Michael Brown stressed that the countries of Central and Eastern Europe need membership in the EU, not in NATO. He noted that if the Central and Eastern European countries were really threatened, they would be increasing their defense capabilities. In reality, Poland, the Czech Republic, and Hungary had been reducing military conscription and their mechanized and infantry forces. Only Poland credibly sought to enhance the capabilities of its armed forces in the context of a fifteen-year force modernization program. Moreover, despite the suggestion of a "security vacuum" in Central and Eastern Europe, the German government eventually urged NATO to move slowly on enlargement and to signal restraint toward Russia.[73] There is no evidence that Germany ever considered advancing its security interests toward the East in any manner other than in the context of NATO. Thus Brown concluded that NATO should expand only in the event of serious Russian threats toward the West.

To Michael Mandelbaum, who was perhaps the most consistent and articulate of the opponents to the policy, NATO enlargement represented a significant shift in the European balance of power likely to damage the West's relations with Russia and undermine the existing security regime in Europe. Among his more cogent arguments, Mandelbaum asserted that Europe already had a functional security architecture in the shape of the CFE and START agreements, which might be seriously undermined by enlargement.[74] Mandelbaum noted, "the [Visegrad] countries under active consideration are precisely those best placed to make a successful transition to democracy and free markets without NATO membership."[75]

Theoretically, if Russian behavior really does require a neo-containment response by NATO, it makes little sense to expand NATO only to the Visegrad countries and thereby create a buffer zone open to Russian interference. If NATO is to be a neo-containment mechanism, then it should include Ukraine and expand right up to Russia's borders.[76] However, even in this event, some realist approaches would see NATO enlargement as self-defeating for the West. Richard K. Betts warned that: "Under realist norms, the West should leave Ukraine to its fate—tragic for the Ukrainians, but safer for everyone else."[77]

Realists also had reservations about NATO enlargement based on skepticism that institutions can promote security. In this view, NATO enlargement clouds a more concrete debate over whether NATO should be maintained at all. Such realists conclude that NATO is needed as an insurance policy against a new Russian threat but that enlargement may bring about that threat in a self-fulfilling prophecy. Thus not only do institutions not cause peace, but well-meaning institutionalists are promoting policies that may decrease security. In this vein, George Kennan wrote: "it never pays . . . for one great power to take advantage of the momentary weakness or distraction of another great power in order to force upon it concessions it would never would have accepted in normal circumstances. . . . Over the long run, it almost always revenges itself." To Kennan, NATO enlargement is "in the highest degree deplorable."[78]

Former National Security Council official Philip Zelikow suggested that NATO enlargement can do little to promote reform or resolve interstate conflicts because NATO is a state-dominated institution and merely a tool of the member states. As Zelikow saw it, "NATO membership for Poland seems to confer few tangible benefits to Poland or to current NATO members that cannot be achieved through the Partnership for Peace."[79] He further maintained,

"Citing other analogies, such as 'NATO membership helped stabilize democracy and stem authoritarian backsliding in Portugal, Spain, Greece and Turkey,' neither elaborates a chain of logic or applies that reasoning to, say, Poland or Hungary."[80] Similarly, Owen Harries stressed that even the idea that a "western" community can be expanded is based on a false premise. Arguing that the West's identity was based largely on the threat from the East, the cohesiveness of the West will disintegrate after the Cold War.[81]

Fred Iklé, former undersecretary of defense in the Reagan administration, noted that for five years before joining NATO, Greece and Turkey received considerable American economic assistance, which aided their transition, and that no such aid is likely to come to Europe's East. He also observed that if "Slovakia is a vacuum, why not Slovenia; if Slovenia, why not Macedonia, Moldova or Belarus?"[82] Iklé co-chaired a commission with Yeltsin adviser Sergei Karagonov, which included a number of senior American and Russian national security specialists who recommended against NATO enlargement. They concluded that the US and Russia share common security interests and that their defense policies should be harmonized. "Any eastward expansion of NATO that would exclude Russia would be detrimental to the harmonization of US and Russian defense policies," the study concluded.[83]

Charles L. Glaser stressed national interest in security cooperation and maintained that NATO has an important role to play in the future of Europe as currently constituted. NATO is thought to remain the best mechanism for dealing with three major challenges to contemporary European security: resurgent Russia, war in the East, and improbable conflict in the Western community. There remains a strong case for realigning NATO—not as an expanded collective security mechanism, but rather as a low-cost insurance policy.[84] The continued American military presence in Germany should decrease any German desire to pursue nationalist foreign policy objectives, but the same policy would not necessarily be duplicated for countries such as Ukraine. Thus Glaser made a case for revamping NATO rather than expanding it into some new form of collective security organization.

These theoretical concerns entered the public US policy debate in the summer of 1995 when US Sen. Sam Nunn announced strong opposition to NATO enlargement. Nunn asserted that no one had explained the "why, or at least why now" of enlargement. Nunn argued that NATO enlargement would undermine reformers in Moscow and, because of Russia's conventional weakness, Russia eventually would be forced to respond by deploying nuclear weapons—thereby undermining security for all Europeans. Nunn was concerned that enlargement was creating the worst possible scenario of decreased US military capabilities and increased political commitments. The senator charged that the policy was promoting a false promise of security similar to that offered by the League of Nations before World War II. According to Nunn:

NATO is fundamentally a military alliance. If you denigrate the military side of it, then it becomes a political and psychological alliance, which is something very different. . . . The last thing we need is a repeat of what happened before World War II, when commitments were made that were not backed up by military capabilities and intentions.[85]

Nunn suggested that enlargement should be dependent upon a country first qualifying for EU membership and that it be linked to Russian behavior. If Russia were to make aggressive moves against other states, violate arms control accords, or if democracy should collapse, then NATO enlargement would be justified.

Institutionalist Arguments in Support of NATO Enlargement

Institutionalists supporting NATO enlargement dominated the policy decision-making process. They explicitly rejected realist arguments for the policy and maintained that the goal is to promote a united Europe and spread democracy and stability. As NATO Secretary General Javier Solana suggested:

What we are expanding is a European, indeed Atlantic, civic space. I deliberately include our military arrangements into this definition of "civic space." The post-war experience in Western Europe suggests that political and economic progress and security integration are closely linked. Once their security is taken care of, countries can devote themselves with more confidence to their longer-term evolution. And a responsible military, firmly embedded in our democratic societies and under civil control, is part and parcel of that civic space, as are military structures that are transparent, defensive, and multinational.[86]

Some observers particularly felt that, once in NATO, new members would not nationalize defense policies in the pursuit of self-help because they would attain an important psychological reassurance. William Odom asserted that the best argument for NATO's expansion

is found in its inception: the concern of its proponents with internal political and economic affairs in Western Europe. While their national motives were at odds—Germany seeking early independence, France seeking to prevent a new German military threat—leaders in both countries realized that a US military presence within an Atlantic alliance structure would create the security and political context for economic recovery and the building of new international relations. To play its role the United States had not only to be a military hegemon; it also had to bring its political ideology to Europe. A purely realist American approach to NATO would have failed.[87]

Ronald Asmus, Richard Kugler, and F. Stephen Larrabee added:

East-Central Europe's democrats well understand that democracy will succeed only if their states belong to a secure European and Western political, economic, and military community. The West too previously understood this link—as demonstrated with the case of West Germany. That nation might never have become a stable Western democracy had it not been accepted into NATO's fold. Similarly, NATO membership helped stabilize democracy and stem authoritarian backsliding in Portugal, Spain, Greece and Turkey.[88]

Among the advocates of NATO enlargement, this trio of RAND analysts had considerable influence on US policy. Asmus was appointed deputy assistant secretary of State responsible for NATO enlargement and Kugler was hired full-time by the Department of Defense in 1997.

Jamie P. Shea, NATO's spokesman, suggested that NATO enlargement should come before EU membership for the Visegrad countries, based on NATO's founding principles, which created "a climate of confidence and stability which allowed governments not to overspend on weapons or to shut themselves off from their neighbors, but to use their scarce resources for infrastructure renewal, for education, and for social reform."[89] Though NATO may incorporate instability by enlarging, Shea maintained that it faces a dilemma of either taking in these countries or dealing with them from the outside. One way or another, these crises will affect NATO and are more easily managed within the institution. Thus Shea argued, "If one is not actively spreading security, one is increasing one's own vulnerability to insecurity. . . . The situation cannot be frozen in a timeless balance of calculable forces."[90] Shea stressed that the most important guarantee granted in NATO is reassurance and that NATO has always been

> seen as providing political reassurance, and if push came to shove, the Americans would provide air support and logistics. It was the Korean War which produced US ground troops in Western Europe, not the Washington Treaty. NATO's security guarantee has always been much more a question of day-to-day cooperation, joint exercises, and military integration than of binding obligations. The credible guarantee has been the practice of 'doing' security together, not the legal document.[91]

For addressing Russia and Ukraine, Shea stressed the importance of the PFP, where "facile notions like a 'security vacuum' only disguise the large-scale military cooperation that is already taking place and that will give Central and East European countries special consultative rights vis-à-vis NATO through the PFP. . . . This will convey a special responsibility, if not a binding security guarantee. . . . This is no minor privilege."[92]

Some analysts concluded that the solution to potential security competition caused by one institution (NATO) can be offset by another institution (the OSCE or EU). The dual-track strategy of strengthening the OSCE and institutionalizing a special relationship between NATO and Russia is a case in point. Senior Baltic officials note that in January 1996, Ronald Asmus circulated a paper among officials in the three Baltic countries advancing a multi-institutional solution to the inevitable sense of loss that will result from the Baltic states being left out of NATO. Resolving this issue would be central to NATO enlargement, for, as Asmus wrote, "If mishandled, the Baltic issue has the potential to develop into the proverbial train wreck which could potentially derail NATO enlargement as well as poison the West's relations with Russia."[93]

Asmus noted that, rightly or wrongly, many in the West do not see the Baltic states as an area of vital strategic interest. Moving NATO into the Baltics would be nearly impossible for several reasons: it would be completely unacceptable to Moscow; there are problems involving Russian minorities in some Baltic countries; the Baltics are largely indefensible in the absence of a credible deterrent; and the Russian enclave of Kaliningrad being encircled would further add to Russia's heightened concerns over enlargement. Indeed, outside of Denmark, the Baltics had no strong advocate for their membership within NATO. Asmus therefore proposed a creative multi-institutional strategy to resolve the Baltic security dilemma.

First, the three Baltic countries should institutionalize defense cooperation among themselves. Second, involvement of the Nordic countries aiding and assisting efforts by the Baltic countries to increase their security via a wide range of cooperative programs should accelerate. The third (and central) pillar of the strategy would be coordination of NATO and EU enlargement policies so that "the EU flag would go up in Estonia at the same time that the NATO flag goes up in Warsaw."[94] Fourth, the process of NATO enlargement should be clearly open-ended. Finally, further institutional efforts should be made to modify Moscow's concerns over NATO enlargement by including Russia in the emerging web of institutional security cooperation wherever possible, and the West should look for ways to encourage constructive Russian–Baltic security interaction.

Because the Asmus proposal advocated an "Estonia first" policy, the proposal had the unintended adverse short-term effect of stalling Baltic cooperation because of the exclusion of Latvia and Lithuania. The proposal was ultimately viewed by some senior Baltic officials as trying to deal with the Baltic problem at the expense of their prospects for joining NATO. As a result, all three Baltic countries jointly and specifically informally rejected this institutional proposal of managing their security dilemma.

Some advocates of NATO enlargement have shown that the process of using linkage with membership to promote political reform in candidate countries has had a positive influence on stability in the region. However, point setting criteria that are too strict would fail to reward those states who have made progress. For example, Jeffrey Simon maintained that setting the criteria for civil–military relations too high may be an obstacle that is impossible to overcome. Effective civilian control over the armed forces includes constitutional provisions for a clearly defined division of authority between the president and government over the running of the military in both peace and war. Civilian control requires parliamentary oversight of the military via effective control over the defense budget, with a civilian defense ministry in control over the general staff and military commanders, and a general restoration of the prestige of post-communist militaries. If NATO required all of these as prerequisites for membership, Poland, Hungary, and the Czech Republic would not qualify. Subsequently they would not be rewarded for the considerable steps they have made since 1989.[95] Eventually some countries would have to be admitted so that the process of opening NATO is seen as genuine.

Some observers saw the enlargement process as actually shaping a more positive and Western-oriented Russian foreign policy. Adrian Karatnycky suggested that the diplomacy of NATO enlargement was having a positive impact on Russian behavior by focusing Moscow on its relations with the West and constraining its capacity to do damage in its near abroad. He noted that after NATO deferred enlargement in 1994, "Russia proceeded with a barrage of aggressive behavior in neighboring republics, threatened Ukraine with economic blackmail, acted as a bully at international forums, wooed Iran and Iraq, tried to topple Azerbaijan's president and launched a war against Chechnya."[96] "If properly and carefully implemented in ways that reassure the Russian public," Karatnycky wrote, "the process of NATO's eastward expansion can have a salutary effect on Russia's fundamental internal debate over its foreign and defense policies."

There were also some backers of NATO enlargement sympathetic to arguments that democracies do not go to war with each other and thus NATO should promote a club of democratic states.[97] For example, Harlan Cleveland suggested that NATO should become such a "Club of Democracies."[98] Allen Sens maintained that the West's own values are at stake and enlargement would "stand as a testament to the strength of Western commitment to its own principles. . . . To refuse to extend NATO membership to peaceful, democratic countries asking for admittance, especially when such membership has been openly suggested by Alliance leaders, would be an affront to those principles."[99]

For proponents of collective security, NATO's enlargement may be likened to creating a collective security institution like the League of Nations. A new European collective security institution involving the US from the beginning might provide a workable case for collective security. In this context, NATO should enlarge quickly and include Russia. For example, former CIA director William Colby chaired a panel arguing for rapid expansion of NATO to include Russia on the premise of collective security.[100]

Other observers supported an expansion of NATO as a means of lowering the risk of war between aspirants and thus spreading a security community.

For example, in August 1996 Hungary and Romania successfully completed a treaty (signed on 15 September 1996) that would lower bilateral tensions over Transylvania. This region had been a source of distrust between the two countries because of the sizable minority Hungarian population there. NATO had identified settlement of such outstanding regional disputes as a criterion for entrance into the alliance. Thus, four years of delay over the Hungarian-Romanian treaty had hindered both countries' quests for NATO membership. Pressure on these two countries from American and NATO representatives linking their cooperation with membership in NATO eventually had a positive impact moving them toward the treaty. However, US Ambassador to NATO Robert Hunter may have overstated its importance when he proclaimed in Budapest on 28 August: "It is now impossible for Hungary and Romania to go to war."[101] Moreover, the decision to invite Hungary to join NATO, while leaving Romania out, appears to have weakened this important rationale for NATO enlargement.

Finally, some supporters concluded that NATO enlargement became necessary after NATO committed to it—first in 1994 and then again in late 1996.[102] Having said repeatedly that it would enlarge, NATO's failure to do so would have seriously reduced its credibility, damaged the transatlantic relationship, and harmed US prestige around the world. Others argued that perhaps NATO should enlarge politically but not militarily. Using Denmark and Norway, or France and Spain, as a model, NATO could bring in new members without provocative military deployments or integration into the NATO military command structures.[103] While NATO has formally ruled out any such "second-class" status for new members, they are actually coming into the alliance on a largely political basis.

Institutionalist Arguments Against NATO Enlargement

The institutionalist case against NATO enlargement, interestingly, shared many of the concerns raised by the realists. However, some institutionalists were particularly concerned about the impact of the decision on consensus in NATO. As former Deputy Undersecretary of State Arnold L. Horelick suggested, NATO enlargement "displays the same kind of logic that leads a couple in a deeply troubled marriage to forgo marital therapy and have a new baby instead."[104] Horelick maintained that NATO enlargement would make "governance matters worse."[105] In this view, NATO enlargement risks decreasing NATO's efficiency and as a result reduces its capacity to organize effective coalitions for crisis management. Rather than decreasing the transaction costs of security provision, NATO enlargement would raise them in terms of diplomatic time and energy spent on bargaining over coalition building.

This view was shared by Charles A. Kupchan, who asserted that enlargement would destroy consensus and turn NATO into a talk shop.[106] Kupchan agreed that NATO was an important institution promoting stable relations among its members during the Cold War, but he was skeptical about whether this could be duplicated for new members. He too believed that disparate interests would collide among the member states and dilute NATO. As an alternative, Kupchan called for the creation of an "Atlantic Union" that would subsume the EU and NATO. The Atlantic Union would replace NATO's emphasis on territorial defense with a broad mandate to preserve peace in the Atlantic area via collective security. Such a move would not be based on an anti-Russian premise nor would it ask electorates in the West to extend new defense commitments. Kupchan explained:

> The elimination of NATO's Article V guarantee would weaken the alliance's deterrent power, but as long as Russia continues to pose no danger to Western or Central Europe, the tradeoff makes sense. Western Europe enjoys a deep and stable peace that would not be shaken by a more relaxed American commitment, especially if US troops stay put on the continent. Indeed, although officials on both sides of the Atlantic are reluctant to admit it, the absence of a common threat has already eroded the credibility of Article V. By explicitly recognizing this change and seeking to include Russia in a new Europe, the Atlantic Union promises to make a pan-European community of democracies a reality, not just rhetoric to placate Moscow as Poland enters a NATO that everyone knows will never go further East.[107]

Kupchan concluded: "By sacrificing depth for breadth, the Atlantic Union promises to lock-in the most profound transformation of our century: the creation of a community of North Atlantic democracies among which war has become unthinkable."[108]

From an institutionalist perspective, NATO enlargement was most effective while the states seeking to join were still outside the alliance. Once in NATO, there was no guarantee that states would continue to adhere to institutional norms and procedures. Thus the strength of NATO's socialization process lay in the *idea* of NATO enlargement rather than the actual implementation of the policy. In this view, the Partnership for Peace was the critical mechanism for socializing states and shaping the security environment in the East. By taking the three main PFP countries out of that process, that program will likely be undermined and lose its legitimacy for those countries not invited to join NATO. Thus the decision to enlarge NATO was reasonable, but premature. As former EU chief Jacque Delors complained, the US was "overhasty" in pushing for NATO enlargement, which was "a premature initiative which was badly timed."[109]

Also, by emphasizing the military aspects of reform, the wrong aspects of post-communist transitions may be prioritized in some Central and East European countries. Instead of working toward currency reform, for example, a state might be tempted to purchase expensive F-16 fighter planes to show their commitment to NATO. In 1996, the Czech Republic sought to purchase six F-16s from the US in order to enhance its quest for NATO membership. At a cost of $25 million per airplane, six F-16s would take up one-fifth of the entire Czech defense budget. Furthermore, if the Czech Republic were to replace its outdated Soviet-made MiG-21s one-for-one, it would require twenty-four, not six, fighters.

The Clinton administration privately urged Czech and Hungarian officials to increase defense spending so that they would be contributors to and not merely consumers of security. For example, the Hungarian defense budget in 1997 was about 1.3 percent of GNP; the most basic standards of NATO military integration would likely require an increase to 2.2 percent. In June 1997, the International Monetary Fund's managing director personally warned US Treasury Secretary Robert E. Rubin that increased defense spending in new NATO members could negatively impact the IMF's engagement with them. Yet the Czech Republic and Hungary continued to press for expensive purchases of F-16 or F-18 fighter jets, seeking $8 billion in jets. This exceeded the combined annual defense budgets of all three invited countries.[110]

Finally, enlargement may enhance political and economic reform in a new NATO member but hinder it in a state left out. States such as Romania or Estonia, which have done nearly everything that had been asked of them to meet enlargement criteria, are left out of NATO because of their history and geographic location.[111] Inclusion of Hungary and not Romania could push Romania into a defensive arms race out of historical fear of Hungary and the issue of Hungarian minorities living in Transylvania. In Russia, the most liberal and pro-Western of Russian political leaders remained bewildered at the policy, which they view as playing directly into the hands of nationalist and antidemocratic forces.

The Implications of NATO Enlargement

NATO enlargement was a well-intended but risky strategy of promoting stability in the East. It is risky because it may dilute NATO and transform it into a new form of general collective security architecture for Europe. In this context, Russia's opposition to the policy is not the critical issue. Indeed, the bigger issue may be the consequence of having to bargain over the policy in a way that may have created an informal Russian veto in the NATO consensus process. Once the decision was made to enlarge NATO, some sort of accommodation with Russia was necessary or the West risked redividing Europe and perhaps even prompting a new Cold War. Some key US NATO allies would not have allowed enlargement to go forward without an accommodation with Russia. However, now that Russia has been granted a voice in NATO affairs, there is no mechanism for constraining it from negatively influencing NATO's consensus process. Knowing when to dissolve partnership with Russia is as important as when to work with Moscow. Any decision to break relations with Russia could be seriously damaging to alliance cohesion.

Russia's concerns, however, about an additional round of enlargement to include the Baltic countries, should be taken seriously. No matter how it is packaged, NATO enlargement moves the military responsibility of the US and Germany—Moscow's two twentieth-century enemies—closer to Russia's borders. Though not intended as such, enlargement challenges Russia's pride, serves as a bruising reminder that Moscow was on the losing side of the Cold War, and leaves even moderate Russians feeling that they are being punished for the sins of their Soviet forefathers. If enlargement includes the three Baltic countries, it is not unreasonable to expect that Moscow would deploy its dilapidated nuclear forces, with weakened command and control capabilities, targeted at new NATO members. Additionally, Russia may take steps to destabilize states on its Western periphery, including Belarus and Ukraine in an effort to create a new Russian-led alliance. In sum, if handled poorly, NATO enlargement risks decreasing security for nearly everyone involved.

Most significantly, NATO enlargement could damage the transatlantic relationship on which European security is currently dependent through a growing paradox of international and domestic dynamics affecting the US. Within Europe there is an increasing frustration with what is perceived as efforts by the US to dominate NATO decision-making and enhance America's position in the world. Indeed, a policy of NATO enlargement designed to prioritize NATO over European alternatives, in the view of some, is explicitly intended to sustain US dominance over Europe. Particularly bristling at comments by US Secretary of State Madeleine K. Albright that the US is the "indispensable power," some European leaders have sought to reduce US political dominance.

The dilemma of behaving as a unipolar power is that primacy often promotes balancing. Ironically, rather than Russia balancing NATO enlargement with a new defense pact of its own, it is seeking new partnerships with countries from within NATO. By strengthening its bilateral relations with countries in NATO, and particularly with France and Germany, Russia appears to be pursuing a policy of coalition-building against US influence within NATO, rather than outside of it. Thus while NATO language may define the institutional norms and rules of the organization, states are continuing to behave in ways that enhance their perceived national interests.

At the same time, domestic politics may further decrease the ability of the US to sustain its new extended security commitments in Europe. In particular, the US Congress may balk at paying the costs of an ongoing enlargement process and insist that current allies share the major burden. The RAND Corporation forecast initial NATO enlargement costs at $20–110 billion and the US Congressional Budget Office estimated costs between $61–125 billion.

Officially, the US assumed costs of $27–35 billion dollars over a ten-to-twelve–year period would be paid by new members and current European members as part of their own force modernization programs. The US would pay about 7 to 10 percent.

The wide range in estimates reflects varying options for NATO's institutional role in Europe. For example, the RAND estimates (which the US study closely mirrored) assessed three military scenarios for NATO enlargement to include Poland, Hungary, and the Czech Republic. A limited military enlargement based on existing self-defense support in the new members would cost $20 billion—of which 55 percent would be paid by new members, 33 percent by all of NATO, and 12 percent by the key members (US, Germany, Britain, and France). A strategy that would help prepare new members for joint power projection (such as IFOR and SFOR operations) would cost $42 billion, of which 25 percent would be paid by new members, 25 percent by the full NATO, and 50 percent by the key members. Finally, a full forward presence based on a containment model would cost $110 billion, of which 20 percent would be paid by new members, 25 percent by the full NATO, and 55 percent by the key members.[112]

Because NATO has committed to further enlargements, it is impossible to know what the real costs of NATO enlargement will ultimately be. Fiscal constraints in the US and Western Europe are likely to mean that the bulk of costs will be carried by new members and thus either break their budgets for economic reform or result in second class NATO membership, possibly leading to a hollow and irrelevant NATO role.[113] US senators supporting NATO enlargement would have no idea what the budgetary implications of their vote to enlarge NATO were. Getting the estimates wrong in the first round of NATO enlargement would do serious damage to the credibility of the idea that NATO's door remains open to further enlargements. However, this contradicted a short-term effort by the US and NATO to downplay the costs of NATO enlargement to ensure parliamentary ratification.

The cost dynamic was made even more problematic by French President Jacques Chirac who, speaking at the Madrid summit, announced that France did not intend to spend any additional money on NATO enlargement. Through 1997 the European allies argued that the US was pushing a high cost assessment of NATO enlargement primarily to justify arms sales to new member states whereas the Americans were looking largely at costs in terms of what would be needed to keep Article V of the NATO treaty credible. The Europeans made it clear to the US that they did not intend to pay for NATO enlargement—not even by modernizing their own forces to help facilitate reinforcement of new members if they were threatened. For many European countries, particularly in the southern region, which never had much enthusiasm for enlargement, it was bad enough that NATO was expanding—let alone that the Europeans were being told to pay the primary costs.

In October 1997, US Secretary of Defense William Cohen told the Senate Appropriations Committee that estimated enlargement costs would be lower than anticipated. Because the initial US cost study assumed four invited countries and the infrastructure of the new members was found to be in better shape than expected, the direct costs of NATO enlargement would only be $1.3 billion over ten years. This was a figure that was reduced from $5 billion in a spring 1997 NATO study, while the initial US cost study assumed direct enlargement costs of $9–12 billion.

Direct enlargement costs are the specific costs of integrating into common NATO programs such as air defense and headquarters facilities. They exclude the costs of making the new members' militaries compatible with western standards. There is reason to question the finding that new members' militaries were in better shape than expected. NATO had been working with them on their territory since 1994 in one form or another—which led to the initial cost estimate of $27–35 billion by the US. Since there were no substantive changes in the new member countries between the February 1997 US study and the official NATO report, the claim that the US or NATO did not know the state of infrastructure in these countries was problematic. Actually, it signaled a concession by the US to its allies over a formal NATO cost study which had been delayed over a split between the US and all of its allies who wanted the lowest possible cost figures.

Acceptance of the European proposal was a dramatic shift for American diplomats. In May 1997, a US official in Brussels commented that, "We've laid it on the line about costs to our allies. They're low-balling the cost and that's not acceptable."[114] However, the remaining costs of elevating new members to a mature capability level would still require additional funding on a bilateral level. For example, Polish officials indicated they will require up to $2 billion in credits to purchase multipurpose aircraft. This is not an assessed cost of enlargement and such assistance would shift the cost burden from new member countries to those providing assistance. The RAND Corporation estimated that to equip five divisions and ten air wings already in NATO so that they could rapidly reinforce the three new members in a crisis and to stockpile in the new countries supplies and ammunition for the reenforcement's use would cost $22 billion.

The direct costs of NATO enlargement will be low. However, the indirect bilateral costs of making new members able to work with NATO militaries may eventually be higher than anticipated for the US because it is the only country in NATO who views expenditure as necessary. For this reason, a US General Accounting Office audit of NATO enlargement costs concluded that the US estimates were "quite speculative."[115] This left Washington with dubious alternatives—force the primary costs onto the fragile budgets of the new members; pay nothing for enlargement and thus contribute to a military dilution of NATO; or pay for all of it through bilateral assistance and thus risk alienating the US congress over burdensharing in NATO.

Political support for NATO enlargement among US Senate and House members was bipartisan, but also soft and contradictory. For example, while approving nonbinding legislation to enlarge NATO, Congress passed formal legislation cutting the routine US payment for NATO infrastructure from $229 million to $86 million in 1995. While signalling support for expanded US security commitments, the US Congress has been reducing NATO's capabilities to help meet them.

The US needed leadership and education in a Congress that was increasingly losing its institutional memory and reducing its willingness to fund commitments abroad. In a time when the spirit of the Vandenberg Resolution would have benefited the overall transatlantic relationship, the person sitting in Vandenberg's chair in the Senate Foreign Relations Committee was the most committed isolationist in the US Senate, Jesse Helms.[116] Helms declared his support for NATO enlargement only with serious conditions, including: that no limitations be placed on the number of NATO troops or type of weapons to be deployed in the new member states; an explicit rejection of Russian efforts to establish a nuclear-free zone in Central Europe; that NATO deliberations on key issues such as arms control, strategic doctrine and further alliance expansion be off-limits to Russia; emphasis on the development of a NATO anti-ballistic missile defense system to defend Europe; and a rejection of all efforts to tie NATO decisions to UN Security Council approval.

Uninformed and contradictory American public opinion is also a constraint on NATO enlargement. According to a detailed study by the Chicago Council on Foreign Relations, 24 percent of the US public supported NATO membership for the Czech Republic, Poland, and Hungary in 1995. However, when the issue of sending troops to resist a Russian invasion of Poland was raised, 50 percent of the public was opposed and only 32 percent in favor.[117] If Americans are not willing to equate Warsaw with Wichita, Prague with Pittsburgh, or Budapest with Boston, then NATO cannot afford the loss of credibility that would come in the event of some (unlikely) attack on Poland or any other new member.

By 1997, another poll showed that 60 percent of the American public supported NATO membership for Central European nations. However, only 10 percent could name one of the countries that had been invited to join.[118] In the US, little effort by the Clinton administration went into educating the American public at large as to the implications of NATO enlargement. Instead, the administration built momentum towards Senate ratification by targeting specific interest groups which could lobby for Senate support. For example,

American arms contractors spent $51 million on lobbyists and campaign contributions to advance ratification of NATO enlargement.[119] At times it appeared that the administration sought to keep the Senate discussion as low key as possible to avoid any large scale public debate over the implications of enlargement. The failure of US leaders to develop a strong and sustainable popular consensus for NATO enlargement was a missed opportunity to generate a renewed and vibrant public commitment to the transatlantic relationship.

Even in Germany, whose leaders precipitated NATO enlargement in 1993, public support for NATO enlargement is very soft. According to the United States Information Agency, in 1996, 61 percent of Germans felt that NATO enlargement would benefit European security. By 1997, this number was down to 38 percent. If voting in a referendum to approve Polish membership, Germans were 51 percent against Poland's joining NATO when asked: "Keeping in mind that our country must defend any NATO member that comes under attack, please tell me how you would vote if there was a referendum tomorrow on including Poland in NATO."[120]

An additional dilemma for NATO's enlargement policy is that, while increasing stability is the formal goal, Poland, Hungary, and the Czech Republic were attractive candidates primarily because they were not threatened.[121] However, the Baltic countries are potentially threatened. As some critics of NATO enlargement note, any enlargement that does not include the Baltic countries consigns them to a gray area of Russian influence, but an invitation to the Baltic countries to join would likely destabilize all of Europe. This possibility raised serious concerns in Finland and Sweden, whose leaders quietly questioned how NATO's enlargement increases security in the Baltic region. When Ukraine and Kaliningrad are added to the geostrategic setting, NATO could face a potentially explosive situation in the region. In this context, it is reasonable to question whether such potential instability right at Polish borders—which currently does not exist—would be in Warsaw's interests or that of any other NATO member.

On 14 May 1996 Russian Defense Minister Grachev warned that Poland and Lithuania's "early entry into NATO would create definite difficulties for Russia in relation to the Kaliningrad region. . . . We would not want to be cut off from the special defensive district of Kaliningrad by NATO states."[122] Grachev added that Baltic membership in NATO might prompt Russia to create defensive alliances with its former Soviet allies and that Moscow could not rule out preemptive military action by its armed forces against states determined to join NATO.[123] The same day that Grachev spoke, a Polish public opinion poll showed that 47 percent of Poles believed that an alliance between Russia and Belarus was a danger to their country's interests. Because one of several factors accelerating Russian–Belarussian strategic cooperation was Poland's quest for NATO membership, there appeared be a serious contradiction between what Poland wanted from NATO and the security and stability that it thought it was getting.

Perhaps most dangerous, however, is that NATO enlargement will be conducted without a strong security guarantee for new members. NATO will rely on a reinforcement strategy to defend a new member such as Poland. However, the strategy is weighted with serious dilemmas. First, any decision to reinforce Poland in the event of a border crisis with Belarus (for example) is inevitably going to raise concerns in Russia that the conditions on which it accepted NATO enlargement are being violated. Second, such a decision would be as likely to divide as to unite NATO, leading to delay, obfuscation, and fraction within the alliance. Third, Germany's security will remain defined by events in Poland. Absent NATO consensus to reinforce Poland, Germany might, in theory, be just as likely to act unilaterally to advance its interests as without NATO enlargement. Thus NATO enlargement does not necessarily solve the potential problem of relative German power in Europe. Fourth, as Germany sees its security defined by events in Poland, Warsaw will see its security affected by events in Lithuania, Belarus, and Ukraine. Outside of NATO, Poland was a buffer that prevented the US from having to extend its deterrence line into the former Soviet Union. Inside NATO, Poland increases the prospects for US military engagement in what used to be the Soviet Union.[124]

There are many legitimate reasons to have serious concerns about the potential impact of NATO enlargement, as both realists and institutionalists opposed to enlargement warn. Perhaps most disturbing about the policy is that it was decided on before the strategic rationale and military implications were considered. For example, in a high-level Clinton administration meeting in 1994 to discuss NATO enlargement, Gen. Wesley Clark of the Joint Chiefs of Staff reportedly asserted that there were "some issues we need to discuss." Assistant Secretary of State Holbrooke responded: "That sounds like insubordination to me. Either you are on the President's program, or you are not."[125]

There is, however, a historical rationale to ensuring that European states need not worry about possible security competition between Germany and Russia over Polish territory. Whether NATO enlargement will effectively do that remains to be seen. NATO enlargement will hopefully enhance NATO's traditional mission by keeping the Americans in, the Russians out, and the Germans constrained. By permanently settling the border between Germany and its eastern neighbors, NATO enlargement may promote reassurance in an area where uncertainty has led to catastrophic war in Europe. NATO enlargement would not fundamentally hedge against a Russian threat, but rather, be a hedge between Russia and Germany.

The success or failure of NATO enlargement to enhance security will rest on the capacity of its members to adapt NATO's institutional form to the post–Cold War security environment. As Czech President Havel suggested in

1995: "The expansion of NATO should be preceded by something even more important, that is a new formulation of its own meaning, mission, and identity."[126] This means implementing a major internal restructuring of NATO based on a new burdensharing arrangement in which Europeans assume primary responsibility for their own security. However, the trends are in the other direction for both current and new European members of NATO. NATO enlargement may, or may not, succeed in stabilizing parts of the East, which is a critical security challenge in Europe. Ultimately, for NATO to have any usefulness beyond enlargement, it must now prioritize its founding task of facilitating a more balanced security institution.

6

Restructuring Transatlantic Relations

Institutional Realignment

As NATO members contemplated enlargement, they embarked simultaneously on an internal adaptation to make NATO better reflect changing dynamics in the transatlantic relationship. The end of the Soviet challenge, a perceived decline in US interest in Europe, and a growing potential for European members of NATO to assume greater responsibility for their own security were the major events prompting US and European leaders to seek more balanced transatlantic security relations. The process often took the form of competition between the US and some of its European allies, who wanted a European Security and Defense Identity (ESDI) to be created outside NATO and thus give Europe more freedom of action in international affairs. However, this option was constrained by the Cold War legacy of European military dependence on the US and NATO.

Absent credible European capabilities or a political willingness to spend resources on an independent ESDI, an accord was reached in 1996 that the ESDI would be formed within NATO. This institutional realignment was dramatized by a gradual return by France toward NATO military planning. Yet at the same time, the failure of Europe to assume responsibility for its own security affairs was dramatically symbolized in its collective unwillingness to retain forces in Bosnia-Herzegovina without US troops involved on the ground.

Competing National Views

The Maastricht Treaty on European Union, completed in 1991, sought to create a Common Foreign and Security Policy (CFSP) via an ESDI built through a revitalized Western European Union (WEU). The European Union members agreed that a community of 350 million citizens with two nuclear powers should be able to exert influence in security matters and take more responsibility for their own affairs after the Cold War.

However, the leading European states split over the form the ESDI would take: Britain wanted it subordinated to NATO, France wanted it fully independent of NATO, and Germany sought to reconcile both views.[1] France was especially adamant in its support for an independent ESDI. Paris hoped to propel European integration and confine Germany within an institutional framework that France could dominate. France also worried that the US presence in post–Cold War Europe would decline and that Washington could no longer be relied on. Among the smaller European states, Portugal, the Netherlands, and Denmark supported the British view. The remaining continental powers were, to varying degrees, sympathetic to the French position. Italy was sensitive to both views.

Early signals from Washington heightened European concern about the US commitment to Europe. The administration of President George Bush began dramatically cutting US forces stationed in Europe and insisted that the Europeans take responsibility for burdensharing and management of the Balkan crisis, while simultaneously opposing an ESDI.[2] Some Clinton Administration officials suggest that Bush likely let the Europeans take the lead in the Balkans because he was confident that efforts toward the ESDI would collapse there and thus ensure the continued primacy of NATO.[3] This was a common view of Washington's intentions among European and many American officials at NATO headquarters in 1992. European concerns were heightened when Canada announced on 5 February 1992 that it would withdraw its standing forces in Europe because of overstretched commitments and costs.

The Clinton administration sent early signals that reinforced Europe's concerns about America's dependability. In May 1993 a senior State Department official said that economic priorities would shape US foreign policy and that the US would define the extent of its commitments commensurate to its economic interests. He hinted at a coming shift in attention from Europe to Latin America and Asia.[4] Secretary of State Warren Christopher mused that the US had been too Eurocentric in its foreign policy priorities.[5] In 1994, Secretary of Defense Les Aspin suggested in an annual report: "For their part, US allies must be sensitive to the linkages between a sustained US commitment to their security on the one hand, and their actions in such areas as trade policy, technology transfer, and participation in multinational security operations on the other."[6] Also in 1994, the US House of Representatives approved a proposal rejected by the Senate calling for Europe to reimburse 75 percent of the total costs of stationing US troops in Europe. The proposal would have provided for the withdrawal of US troops if Europe did not agree.

Ongoing divisions between the US and its allies over the Balkans, especially American reluctance to commit ground troops there, further added to Europe's concerns. For France, this split was a clear indication of the need for

Europe to have an independent capability for handling crises. As French Foreign Minister Alain Juppé said in November 1994, "The conflict in Bosnia has shown the necessity to move beyond NATO and American guarantees to build a credible European defense that could back up our common foreign policy interests."[7] Conversely, in the US view, the futility of European efforts reinforced the view that an ESDI was unworkable.

Despite Europe's frustration with the US, an independent ESDI would be redundant to NATO, expensive, and possibly harmful to European integration if EU members became worried about supranational intrusions into their national security. It might also damage the transatlantic relationship, on which European security still depended, if not carefully managed. Thus the EU approach to building the ESDI took two conflicting forms: promoting a gain for the EU while strengthening the transatlantic relationship by demonstrating operational burdensharing. Reconciling the desire to go independent from NATO and strengthen NATO at the same time would eventually prove insurmountable.

The Limits of European Union

The Bush administration sent strong signals in 1991 that European support for an ESDI created at NATO's expense would be met with firm US resistance. For example, at the November 1991 NATO heads of state meeting in Rome, French President François Mitterand questioned the emphasis on NATO, characterizing the alliance as "a good one, but it is not a Holy Alliance." President Bush was terse in his response: "If you have something else in mind, if you want to go your own way, if you don't need us any longer—say so."[8] In compromise language, the Rome Summit endorsed the cost-effective use of alliance resources and concluded: "Integrated and multinational European structures, as they are further developed in the context of an emerging European defense identity, will also increasingly have a similarly important role to play in enhancing the Allies' ability to work together in the common defense."[9]

During the preparations for the Rome meeting, the ESDI language was the most contentious issue in the discussion of NATO's new strategic concept. Some members viewed the language as carte blanche support for an ESDI. NATO officials noted that its placement, at the very end of the communiqué, showed the priority NATO put on the ESDI. Moreover, the consensus language was clear—an ESDI would have to strengthen NATO.[10]

While NATO prepared for the Rome Summit, Europe was engaged in a parallel process, drafting the Treaty on European Union to be signed at Maastricht, the Netherlands, in December. The European leaders endowed the EU with a Common Foreign and Security Policy based on an evolutionary construction of an ESDI. There was consensus among the Europeans on the need for an ESDI. Unable to speak or act with one voice during the 1990–91 Persian Gulf War, Europe had proven unable to protect its own vital interests without the US.[11] Thus many of the countries gathered at Maastricht believed it was necessary to build a European capability for defense and power projection. Nevertheless, disputes between the Europeans over the form of an ESDI and its relationship to NATO hindered the goal.

In December 1990 France and Germany proposed a formal relationship between the EU and WEU. The WEU would "in time become part of Political Union."[12]

The Franco-German initiative would have signaled a major increase in the WEU profile. The WEU had been dormant since the mid-1950s. In October 1984 it was reactivated to signal burdensharing intentions among the Europeans and to enhance movement toward the 1986 Single European Act, which established the framework for political and economic union in Europe to take place in 1992. Operationally, the WEU was limited to minesweeping activities during the Iran–Iraq war. During the 1991–92 Persian Gulf crisis, the WEU coordinated European efforts to enforce a naval embargo against Iraq and it performed minesweeping duties. Shortly after its reactivation, Portugal and Spain joined the WEU.

The US responded to the Franco-German proposal with a terse diplomatic démarche delivered to WEU members signaling strong US opposition. The US insisted that all decisions to commit an ESDI to out-of-area activity involve consultation with the US; there should be no WEU integrated command structure duplicating that of NATO; and there should be no "backdoor" security commitment to Central and Eastern Europe via WEU enlargement that implicitly extended the American commitment to NATO.

A compromise was broached by Britain and Italy on 4 October endorsing an ESDI as embodied in the WEU which would be subordinated to NATO. The Anglo-Italian initiative would have reserved the WEU for out-of-area operations, with NATO retaining sole responsibility for security within the European area. Such mission-based burdensharing would be attained via a European Reaction Force consisting of forces separate from the NATO structure. However, on 14 October France and Germany responded by insisting that the EU have clear ties to the WEU, that the EU promote an independent European armaments agency, and that Europe develop military units that would be solely allocated to the WEU.[13]

The Maastricht Treaty reflected a compromise between these competing views. The EU members agreed: "The common foreign and security policy shall include all questions related to the security of the European Union, including the eventual framing of a common defense policy, which might in time lead to a common defense."[14] The Maastricht accord did not create a formal tie between the EU and WEU. Instead, it identified the WEU as an integral part of the development of the union and as its defense component. Non-WEU members of the EU were invited to join or become observers. European members of NATO not belonging to the WEU were offered the same opportunity.

In keeping the WEU informally linked to the EU, the problem of neutral countries such as Ireland using veto authority over WEU activity was avoided. Similarly Denmark, which is an EU member in NATO, but is not in the WEU, could not obstruct its development. In 1992, Greece joined the WEU. Iceland, Norway, and Turkey have since become associate members and Denmark, Austria, Sweden, and Ireland are observers.

The EU members agreed that they may request the WEU to implement decisions made and actions desired by the EU that have defense implications.[15] In a separate statement, the nine WEU ministers at Maastricht affirmed the need for a genuine ESDI and a greater European responsibility on defense matters. Formally, the WEU would be the defense arm of the EU and at the same time strengthen the European pillar of NATO.[16] EU members hoped that the WEU might develop through an evolutionary process, beginning with a loose contribution to the development of the EU, complementary to NATO, and eventually leading to a common EU defense.

The Franco-German Corps

The Maastricht compromise produced a disparity between the EU's foreign policy aspirations and its organized military capabilities. To compensate, German Chancellor Kohl and French President Mitterand announced the creation of a Franco-German Corps on 21 May 1992.[17] The Eurocorps, as it became known, enlarged an existing Franco-German brigade to a corps-level unit of 35,000 troops. France and Germany hoped to use the Eurocorps to enable the WEU to act in accordance with the directives of the EU by aiding in the defense of NATO territory, assisting in peacekeeping activities outside the NATO area, and assisting in humanitarian operations.[18]

Operationally, the corps is composed of the French 1st Armored Division based in Germany, and the German 10th *Panzergrenadier* Division, which wears a dual hat with NATO, meaning that it is available to both the Eurocorps and NATO for planning and operational purposes. The forces are largely stationed in Germany, with headquarters in Strasbourg, France. In peacetime the forces remain national with the only standing multinational activity taking place at the staff level in Strasbourg.

Initially, France hoped that Germany would assign specific forces to be solely Eurocorps assets. However, Germany insisted that the Eurocorps be transparent and complementary to NATO command structures. Wanting the Eurocorps to provide momentum toward the ESDI, France was left with little choice but to accept the German position regarding NATO.

American and NATO planners were especially concerned that the Euro-corps could contribute to instability and uncertainty in a crisis if command and control relationships were unclear. Adhering to NATO's concerns, Germany and France signed an agreement with SACEUR on 22 December 1992 to place the Eurocorps under NATO command in the event of a crisis. According to one published account, the details of the agreement between NATO and the Eurocorps consist of several parts: the Eurocorps would be assigned to NATO command during crises and NATO–run peacekeeping operations; and in peacetime, when the Eurocorps was not under NATO command, NATO's command would have the right to review its operations so as to determine its compatibility with NATO's planning, training, and doctrine.[19] France was thus integrating its military with Germany outside of NATO, but at the same time allowing its assets to be available to NATO in a crisis. While rhetorically France was moving away from NATO in advancing the ESDI, in practice Paris was actually moving closer to Allied military planning. Indeed, this was a point quietly reinforced by German military officials who hoped to convince NATO, and the US, of the value of the Eurocorps.

Belgium, Luxembourg, and Spain subsequently joined the Eurocorps, which became operational on 30 November 1995. However, because the Euro-corps took three years to become operational, it was not a credible effort to deal with the immediate conflict in the Balkans. The EU participants were using action on the ESDI as a guise for crisis management. As Peter Schmidt wrote, "France and Germany tend to agree much more on institution building than on hard-core security policies."[20] The Franco-German corps did symbolize a fundamental reconciliation and unprecedented cooperation between these two historical enemies.[21] However, the popular refrain in NATO circles that the Eurocorps was little more than a "parade army" continues to ring true.

The Western European Union

The WEU faced constraints similar to those of the Eurocorps, though its members hoped to give it a greater operational role. Meeting at Petersberg near Bonn on 19 June 1992, the WEU leadership agreed that while contributing to NATO's common defense in accordance with Article 5 of the Washington Treaty, "military units of WEU member states acting under the authority of WEU could be employed for humanitarian and rescue tasks; peacekeeping tasks; tasks of combat forces in crisis management, including peacemaking."[22] However, the WEU also endorsed a proposal forwarded by British Minister of Defense Malcom Rifkind, which ensured that the WEU would not create its own independent military command structure. The WEU tasked its military officials to identify a variety of assets (such as the Eurocorps, the new British-Dutch amphibious force, or the Multinational Airmobile Division) that could be made available on a case-by-case basis. This proposal was designed to avoid overlap between WEU and NATO member state commitments. As with the Eurocorps, institutional limitations of the WEU forced France to compromise and reevaluate its security priorities.

Politically, the WEU kept apace of changing institutional dynamics by reaching out to Central and Eastern Europe. Like NATO, the WEU was reluctant to expand a formal security guarantee. The Petersberg Declaration created a "Forum for Consultation" to bring interested countries from the former Warsaw Pact into a dialogue with WEU countries.

Meeting in Luxembourg on 9 May 1994, the WEU foreign ministers invited nine Central and East European countries to join the WEU as "Associate Partners." The WEU then had four levels of participation: Members, Associate Members, Associate Partners, and Observers. The new Associate Partners were Poland, Hungary, the Czech Republic, Slovakia, Bulgaria, Romania, Lithuania, Latvia, and Estonia. Associate Partners had no security guarantee and could not veto decisions taken by the WEU. They could attend alternative weekly sessions of the WEU ambassadors in Brussels, where they might raise security concerns. Associate Partners could also contribute troops to WEU peacekeeping missions. The Associate Partners proposal was intended to limit WEU outreach to those Central and East Europeans most likely to qualify for EU membership. Some in the WEU hoped that this limited approach could be more effective than NATO's PFP—in spite of the fact that the WEU had a limited operational capacity.

The WEU's outreach to the East was not a major problem for the US so long as it did not lead to a backdoor security guarantee in which the US would have to intervene in a crisis, drawn in by the non–NATO commitments of one of its allies. It was also not particularly objectionable to the Russians who saw the WEU as an inoffensive substitute for a NATO role in the East. On 1 December 1994 Foreign Minister Kozyrev praised the WEU, saying that it "should take care of the unity of Europe."[23] Central and Eastern European countries welcomed WEU initiatives but also complained that they were being given a "take it, or leave it" proposal from the West that would further defer NATO membership.

By 1995 the WEU had not become a credible institution for organizing significant military operations. Recognizing its continued weakness, the WEU foreign ministers met in Lisbon on 15 May 1995 and took modest steps toward strengthening its operational role. At Lisbon, the WEU established a politico-military group to support the WEU Council, and created Situation and Intelligence Centers. Additionally, the ministers accepted an Anglo-Italian proposal to advance planning for a WEU intervention force in humanitarian crises, but they failed to agree on procedures for financing such operations. The WEU also approved a White Paper, which assessed security threats including unresolved border disputes, terrorism, organized crime, migration, and proliferation of nuclear weapons and ballistic missiles. Absent from the assessment was the sort of conflict immediately challenging European security—the Balkans.

The WEU is a security institution without a military infrastructure. Like NATO, peacetime forces which might be made available to the WEU—including the Eurocorps—remain national. However, unlike NATO, the WEU has no peacetime supreme commander, no peacetime military headquarters, and no standing command and control structure. Without infrastructure, training, and major exercises, the WEU has no capability to project power or promote stability in the event of a crisis threatening its member states. Moreover, the absence of sufficient satellite, transportation, and other logistical capabilities, common language and compatible communication arrangements; the incorporation of standardized and interoperational equipment; or integrated assessments of exact location of equipment available to the WEU made the institution fundamentally weak.

The limits of WEU satellite and intelligence capabilities were exposed in the fall of 1994 when the US announced it would no longer share intelligence with its European allies enforcing a naval arms embargo of the Balkans. Responding to the US announcement, the president of the WEU Assembly, Sir Dudley Smith, stated: "The US dominates the NATO command structure in the Adriatic area and the withdrawal of US ships and aircraft would make a mockery of the embargo operations. . . . This example also proves just how much Europe needs to be autonomous where intelligence gathering, satellite reconnaissance and logistical support are concerned."[24] A week later, Smith qualified his remarks to stress that it is "vital not to weaken NATO because of its essential role in maintaining peace in Europe. . . . Any such weakening cannot be allowed to happen."[25]

An ESDI standing alone against a revitalized Russian challenge at current force levels would prove a destabilizing imbalance. At the conventional level, the relationship between Russia and the combined French, German, and British forces is 4:1 for heavy tanks, 1.5:1 for light tanks, 2:1 for armored vehicles, 3.75:1 for towed or self-propelled guns, 7:1 for multiple-warhead rocket launchers, and 2.6:1 for combat aircraft.[26] Building a credible independent ESDI from scratch would thus prove very expensive. The lowest level of independent military capability is estimated to cost $27 billion over twenty-five years and would still require the aid of US systems to make it function. The highest level of independent ESDI activity would cost $95 billion over twenty-five years. The higher level would be more effective but still not equal the capabilities available in the existing framework in NATO.[27]

Another constraint is the general inability of the European countries to form a Europe-wide military-industrial base. Article 223 of the EU's founding Treaty of Rome excluded the production of and trade in arms, munitions, and war materiel from the normal rules of the common market when essential security interests are involved; thus, rather than integrating the European arms industry, states have continued to buy nationally. The EU and WEU have sought to identify areas of potential cooperation by incorporating the Independent European Programme Group (IEPG) into the WEU and renaming it the Western European Armaments Group (WEAG). Also within the WEU, the Political Division has created an Armaments Secretariat.

In October 1993 France and Germany announced plans for the creation of a joint armaments agency to focus on procurement for the Eurocorps, but with the possibly of future expansion. The purpose of the armaments agency is to integrate national armaments responsibilities to the extent possible in terms of organization, administration, and implementation of projects.[28]

Assuming these high costs and military responsibilities would be very difficult given the steep decline in European defense spending. By 1994, six of the sixteen NATO countries had reduced defense spending as a percentage of GNP to below 2 percent: Belgium, 1.8; Denmark, 1.9; Germany, 1.8; Luxembourg, 1.1; Portugal, 1.6; and Canada, 1.7. Two other countries were just over 2 percent: Italy at 2.1 and the Netherlands at 2.2.[29] The average of European NATO had dropped from 3.6 (1980–84 average) to 2.5 percent of GNP in 1994.

As former NATO Secretary General Willy Claes said in a speech to the North Atlantic Assembly in November 1994, "It is obvious that the sharp decline in most European defense budgets makes it inconceivable that Europe could create its own integrated military organization alongside the one in NATO—and it would be a useless waste of money anyway."[30] In an April 1996 speech in Washington, D.C., German Defense Minister Volker Rühe said: "we would be fools if we did not take advantage of the fact that we already have a solid and functioning Alliance with enormous capabilities. . . . We do not have to start from scratch."[31]

Habits of political and military cooperation and practices in NATO had evolved over a forty-five–year period. Even then, mobilizing NATO for the use of force in Bosnia-Herzegovina proved extremely difficult. Recreating that same institutional culture within the WEU—in the absence of a threat and in the presence of an existing alternative in NATO—would require a convergence of national interests which Europe was far from attaining. Even in NATO, capabilities were being limited by a 60 percent cut in infrastructure spending between 1991 and 1995.

Combined Joint Task Forces

The failure of the US and Europe to deal with the early years of the Balkan crisis prompted the US to formulate a proposal to realign NATO's operational functions in late 1993. Washington recognized that NATO could not survive if its sole military purpose was to deal with Article 5 missions. Indeed, there might be occasions when the US might decline to participate directly in a non–Article 5 NATO mission. The Clinton administration thus recommended a reorganization of NATO command structures based on Combined Joint Task Forces (CJTF) that would permit the creation of an ESDI that was separable but not separate from NATO.

A CJTF is a multinational, multiservice, task-tailored force consisting of NATO and possibly non–NATO forces. Capable of rapid deployment to conduct limited-duration peace operations beyond alliance borders, these forces would be under the control of either NATO's integrated military structure or the Western European Union.[32] Drawing on a practiced US tradition of combining assets from the three services of the armed forces, CJTF would open up multinational command and control outside of the traditional NATO structures. In NATO terminology, "coalitions of the willing" could use assets from the NATO command structure once a political consensus was reached in the NAC. This would, in theory, lower the transaction costs of international security cooperation.

The US had made a major policy shift in its endorsement of the ESDI. As Secretary of Defense Les Aspin said in advance of the 1994 Brussels Summit:

> The European allies have had a long desire . . . for a capacity for military action for missions such as peacekeeping, humanitarian relief and other things that could be undertaken without American participation. They had the desire to have a European pillar to the NATO Alliance. In fact, we don't object to that.[33]

Addressing the NAC, President Clinton said: "We support your effort to refurbish the Western European Union so that it will assume a more vigorous role in keeping Europe secure. . . . While NATO must remain the linchpin of our security, all these efforts will show our people and our legislatures a renewed purpose in European institutions and a better balance of responsibilities within the transatlantic community."[34]

NATO endorsed the strengthening of the European pillar through the WEU and stated that NATO's organization and resources would be adjusted to facilitate this:

> We therefore stand ready to make collective assets of the Alliance available, on the basis of consultations in the North Atlantic Council, for WEU operations undertaken by the European Allies in pursuit of their Common Foreign and Security Policy. We support the development of separable but not separate capabilities which could respond to European requirements and contribute to Alliance security.[35]

The NATO leaders directed the NAC and the NATO military authorities to study the development and adaptation of NATO's political and military structures and procedures for alliance missions, including peacekeeping, and to improve cooperation with the WEU to reflect the emerging ESDI.

The bridge between NATO and the ESDI/WEU would be the CJTF. Since 1991 NATO had recognized the need for smaller, more mobile and more rapidly deployed forces via the Allied Rapid Reaction Corps (ARRC). However, the ARRC was designed for Article 5 (collective defense) contingencies. As the crisis in Bosnia had shown, NATO could be most effective by using its Article 4 consultative functions as a framework for organizing non–Article 5 operations. For Article 4 operations to succeed within the context of a shared NATO/WEU operational framework, it would be necessary to lower the transaction costs of building coalitions for peace by institutionalizing command and control arrangements that could be readily adapted to the specific needs of each operation.

As Charles Barry observes, the unique aspect of the CJTF is an unprecedented development in military doctrine. The CJTF will

> institutionalize the task force concept, a command and control arrangement normally employed for crisis response by ad hoc coalitions. In fact, deploying CJTFs is intended to become the primary *modus operandi* of NATO in peacetime. Task forces are formed rapidly, employed for specific short-term contingencies, and then disbanded. With the CJTF concept, NATO's military hopes to invent a unique, hybrid capability that combines the best attributes of both coalition and alliance forces: that is, rapid crisis response by highly ready multinational forces, backed by political terms of reference, standardized procedures, regular exercises and in-place infrastructure.[36]

As Stanley Sloan concludes, CJTFs would give NATO flexibility to respond to new missions in or around Europe, facilitate the dual use of some NATO command structures for NATO and/or WEU operations, and permit PFP countries to integrate into NATO–run operations.[37] This would be done by establishing multinational, tri-service headquarters, based on deployable self-contained elements in NATO common structures, but adapted further, whenever necessary, to incorporate forces from nations in and outside NATO that are not currently within the integrated military command.

Through the CJTF, full contributions by all NATO members to a NAC–mandated or WEU–run military operation would not be necessary. Coalitions of the willing could engage in peacekeeping or other nontraditional activities while benefiting from existing NATO structures—including areas such as logistics, airlift, and airborne surveillance. Thus states with the most immediate interests in solving a particular security challenge could take the lead with the support and, if necessary, assistance of its NATO allies. The Clinton administration saw CJTFs as a means of enhancing the PFP by using NATO commands to integrate Central and East European countries that might participate in non–Article 5 NATO or WEU operations. Washington also hoped that, through the CJTF, France might be brought closer to NATO military planning. Most important for the US, CJTFs would be a pragmatic means of ensuring that NATO remains the core security institution in Europe while Europeans assume greater responsibility for their own security.[38]

Obstacles to Implementing the CJTF Concept

The CJTF proposal was given a high profile alongside the PFP/NATO enlargement decisions taken at the 1994 Brussels Summit. However, failed attempts to implement the CJTF initiative demonstrated that the underlying tensions that had blocked the restructuring of transatlantic security had not gone away. As Simon Lunn, deputy secretary general of the North Atlantic Assembly, asserted: "The general perception that the [Brussels] Summit reconciled differing attitudes among the Allies towards an ESDI did not happen. Unfortunately, that obstacles to creating a workable ESDI have been removed is far from true."[39] Though it initially appeared that a major compromise on the ESDI had been reached, the CJTF quickly stalled.

NATO and WEU military officials were able to complete planning early. However, without political guidance, military planning could only proceed so far. By March 1994, SACEUR completed a draft operational concept for CJTF command and control. On 28 June, the WEU sent NATO a detailed analysis of operational requirements for a CJTF. Follow-on studies were presented to the NATO Military Committee in September 1994. Political differences on the WEU role emerged over defining the support role of NATO commanders in WEU-led CJTF operations, the potential for the WEU to select its own headquarters (including national commands or in the Eurocorps headquarters) to function as a CJTF, and the WEU's access to NATO assets.[40]

The US was particularly concerned that NATO's infrastructure for Article 5 missions remain intact and that no duplication take place. Additionally, the US worried that while formulated under an Article 4 mission such as humanitarian relief, natural disasters, or peacekeeping, a CJTF could come under attack and possibly involve Article 5 of the NATO treaty. Washington wanted assurances that CJTFs, especially those used by the WEU, would not drag the US into conflicts where it had no desire or interests in intervening. Moreover, for nearly a year France insisted on a separate command structure for non–Article 5 NATO missions, particularly those which do not involve existing allied command structures. The French position raised serious questions about the continued relevance of the NATO integrated military command and why the US should remain a part of it, given that Article 4 missions were those most likely to be carried out by NATO or the ESDI.

Also, because it did not participate in NATO military planning, France sought to increase political oversight of CJTFs. In the US view, CJTFs, once mandated by the NAC, would answer directly to the immediate field com-mander, with command support from SACEUR. Increasing political oversight over CJTFs was viewed by the US (and the Joint Chiefs of Staff in particular) as an unwarranted intrusion on the ability to carry out effective military opera-tions. France also wanted one form of CJTF to be "national"—meaning that a state acting alone could take on an independent mission with NATO assets or possibly head up a multilateral operation with its own command structures but drawing from NATO assets. This was rejected by Washington as a danger-ous infringement on multinational military planning.

The US sent conflicting signals in its endorsement of the ESDI because it found it difficult to reconcile a strategic desire for primacy in Europe and domestic political pressures for operational/financial burdensharing. Since the debacle of US involvement in Somalia in 1993, the US military and Congress were insisting that the US maintain clear command and control of its opera-tions and assets. Moreover, the political leverage that the US has in Europe stems primarily from its actual troop presence. The absence of direct US involvement in a military operation led by the WEU would make it very diffi-cult for the US to wield influence over its allies, as the Bosnian experience prior to IFOR and SFOR showed. France was also divided. Much of the French posturing toward CJTF was related to forthcoming presidential elec-tions in 1995 and neo-Gaullist pressures to ensure France's distance from NATO. This political concern about the rapprochement to NATO was reflected in the fact that most of the problems with CJTF were raised by the Ministry of Foreign Affairs rather than the Ministry of Defense.

By summer 1995, with the West floundering in Bosnia and the future of the CJTFs unresolved, some NATO planners expressed exasperation that pros-pects for making CJTFs operational were slim. As one senior NATO planner complained, "France insists on a special relationship and will likely continue to use the threat of its veto power to prevent such NATO operations from proceeding, if France's direct participation is not required."[41] Some military planners at the Supreme Allied Command Atlantic (SACLANT) gave up on CJTFs and proposed reforming NATO command structures based on func-tional responsibilities and new subcommands to coordinate regional opera-tions.[42] These planners proposed a NATO realignment that would redesign existing commands to allow NATO to act outside its geographical boundaries and even conduct offensive operations to meet future threats such as a ballistic missile attack on a member state or a Persian Gulf–style crisis.[43]

American representatives at SHAPE also expressed reservations about com-mand and control in the event of a deal on CJTF. SHAPE stressed that non–Article 5 CJTF activity could become a large-scale operation requiring NATO to have complete command and control. This position left some Europeans feeling that SHAPE, and its American SACEUR, was insisting on a veto over any European operation not involving the US.[44] By 1996, the NATO Military

Committee had nonetheless agreed to six main principles which CJTF must meet: preserve the integrated military structure; provide for separable but not separate forces in support of the ESDI; maintain a single command structure for Article 5 and non–Article 5 missions; retain the role of the Military Committee in advising and transmitting strategic guidance from the NAC to NATO Military Authorities (including the Chairman of the NATO Military Committee, SACEUR, and SACLANT); avoid ad hoc participation in NATO bodies; and preserve the ability of major NATO Commands to do timely contingency planning.[45]

Bringing the ESDI into NATO

Several factors contributed to a resolution of the disputes over CJTF and led to a transatlantic deal codified at the Berlin meeting of NATO foreign ministers in June 1996. NATO officials were increasingly concerned that the one-year time limit for the IFOR mission in Bosnia could bring about renewed war after its scheduled withdrawal in December 1996. Some initially argued that it was important that IFOR meet its one-year commitment so that the conduct of future Article 4 missions would not be impeded. The US and its allies thus needed a means of reducing the US presence in Bosnia while keeping a meaningful force in place—possibly via a CJTF.

CJTFs were in fact used in IFOR, though they were not formally placed within the conceptual debate in NATO over the ESDI. In order to accommodate force contributions and staff from non–NATO and non-European countries, the Allied Southern Command (AFSOUTH) in Naples had been transformed into a CJTF headquarters. However, the European members insisted that without a US role after IFOR, they would also leave Bosnia-Herzegovina. As one senior European diplomat commented on 26 February 1996:

> IFOR will not be extended. We are now starting to discuss what, if anything, will replace it. European troops on the ground without any US involvement is not a good idea. But we're aware of the dangers of a vacuum. . . . If Combined Joint Task Forces opened up—and we are aiming for an agreement in Berlin . . . I would expect that to play a role.[46]

A senior French official stressed: "The need to do something quickly for the European pillar of NATO because of a possible premature American departure from Bosnia is plausible. . . . But we do not want to discuss that idea publicly."[47]

After a visit to Washington in early May, EU External Affairs Commissioner Hans van den Broek indicated that he had found "widespread support" for the need for Europe to be prepared for a new responsibility in Bosnia after IFOR. Angered by van den Broek's comments, French Foreign Minister Hervé de Charette said: "It was irresponsible for people to talk of IFOR being replaced by the WEU. . . . Everyone should stick to his job . . . then the cows will take care of themselves."[48] Another European official said, "The exit strategy is complete lunacy, it is hindering the long-term success of the mission."[49] In the view of many Europeans, with their forces accounting for two-thirds of the IFOR ground forces, burdensharing in NATO had arrived and the US had to continue its role if the Europeans were to stay past December 1996. In the European perspective, it was the US that was not living up to its share of the burden.

In late February 1996, Assistant Secretary of State for US and Canada John Kornblum and the Director of the European Directorate at the US National Security Council, Alexander Vershbow, traveled to Paris to broker a deal on CJTF. The agreement reinforced the principle that future European peacekeeping operations could draw on NATO force structures, equipment, and logistical support, even if US forces were not involved. France acknowledged that the ESDI must occur within NATO, and the US accepted the possibility that NATO assets could be used for WEU operations in which the US would not participate.[50] Any WEU command arrangement would have to meet NATO standards, use equipment completely compatible with that of the alliance, and receive the prior approval of the NAC.

This Franco-American rapprochement paved the way for NATO to make the CJTF concept operational. Europe had not entirely reassured the US that they would not use NATO assets in a way that might draw the US into military conflicts that it did not have interests in. However, a stress on procedures in the NAC mandating the establishment and use of a CJTF headquarters would allow the US to exert influence over this possibility. Moreover, the continued weakness of the WEU meant that it was unlikely that the US would allow it to act alone if the challenge were serious. As one US official participating in the Paris talks asserted: "There's not going to be a separate WEU. . . . There'll be one defense pot organized around NATO, with forces separable from NATO if the Europeans want to do something."[51] For the short term, it was not necessary for the US to decide how far it might allow CJTF to go into WEU control. Indeed, US officials noted that it was difficult to imagine any situation serious enough to involve NATO assets in which the US would not lead.

The Berlin Accord: Political Guidance for CJTF

Meeting at Berlin on 3 June 1996, the NATO foreign ministers approved the CJTF compromise. Endorsing the development of the ESDI within NATO, the ministers welcomed the completion of the CJTF concept, directed the Military Committee to make recommendations for its implementation, and established a Policy Coordination Group (PCG) to link political oversight from the NAC to the viewpoints developed in the Military Committee.[52]

NATO established three principles to guide its adaptation: performing its traditional mission of collective defense and adopting flexible and agreed procedures to undertake new roles in changing circumstances; preserving the transatlantic link; and the development of the ESDI within NATO.

NATO stressed the need to be able to mount non–Article 5 operations based on one integrated command structure that could perform multiple functions in a cost-effective manner. What had traditionally been ad hoc task force arrangements would be institutionalized via CJTF headquarters "nuclei" permanently placed in selected NATO headquarters. The CJTF command nuclei would be the minimum personnel necessary around which a complete headquarters could be built, once the NAC had approved a NATO or non–NATO CJTF operation. The nuclei would provide the basic elements of necessary military experts for the implementation of multinational, multiservice military functions. To avoid duplication and reduce costs, nuclei command personnel would be dual-hatted to the parent institution (NATO or WEU).

Once a CJTF had been approved by the NAC, the CJTF nuclei would be reinforced with "modules," which are additional staff elements to be assigned based on the particular political and military needs at the time. CJTF headquarters would have to meet a number of basic requirements: support the main objectives of the NATO transformation process, including responding to new missions; be adaptable for new members and nonmembers alike; provide support for the WEU's operational needs; ensure that collective defense requirements can take priority if they arise; preserve both the transatlantic nature of NATO and a single integrated military structure; and incur minimum added costs.[53]

The ESDI would develop within NATO, via full implementation of the CJTF concept, grounded on "sound military principles and supported by appropriate military planning. . . . This would permit the creation of militarily coherent and effective forces capable of operating under the political control and strategic direction of the WEU."[54] NATO committed to prepare, within a transparent and complementary process, for WEU–led operations, including planning and exercising of command elements and forces.[55] NATO endorsed the development of the ESDI within NATO by "conducting at the request of and in coordination with the WEU, military planning and exercises for illustrative WEU missions identified by the WEU."[56] The release of NATO assets and capabilities for WEU–led operations would be authorized by the NAC. The NAC would be informed of the use of NATO assets through monitoring, with the advice of the NATO Military Authorities and through regular consultations with the WEU Council.[57]

The Berlin accord left a number of key issues unsettled for NATO, including ensuring that CJTF development complements any revision of NATO's command structure, taking account of the WEU via full development of "separable but not separate" capabilities, providing for the possible involvement of non–NATO nations in a CJTF, and maximizing cost-effectiveness and avoiding duplication. Additionally, considerable demands may be placed on CJTFs, as they may need to be able to deploy at short notice, move at short notice, and take advantage of the most technologically sophisticated military systems.[58] Specific deployment strategies, the sharing of communications and intelligence, specifications for deployment time, and which of NATO's existing Major Subordinate Commands would become CJTF headquarters also remained to be settled by NATO military planners.

Most importantly, the planning and conduct of exercises utilizing CJTFs would help move the concept from theory to reality, incorporate lessons from IFOR, and help identify areas for further development. As Charles Barry notes, formulating a substantial program of CJTF exercises is essential to its success. Regular CJTF exercises, such as the large annual maneuvers that NATO undertook during the Cold War, will "gradually yield a valuable reservoir of staffs, units and service members experienced in new operations and procedures for NATO." This is especially important, as it is "one thing to develop contingency plans, operational concepts and doctrine for one nation; it is quite another to harmonize the rapid deployment of forces by 16 or more nations."[59]

In mid-1996 the theoretical debate over ESDI took on a sense of practical urgency because of NATO planning for a post–IFOR peacekeeping force in Bosnia-Herzegovina. While the military tasks provided for by NATO were very successful, the civilian side of the Dayton accords lagged, and a substantial NATO military presence was required to maintain the fragile peace. Having committed to a one-year mission in IFOR, the US was under considerable pressure to find a functional alternative through which it could reduce its commitment. A follow-on force might be a perfect opportunity for the Europeans to take responsibility for their own affairs, backed by an American reassurance force in a nearby country such as Hungary or Croatia.

In theory, the US could be out of Bosnia-Herzegovina and the Europeans would implement an ESDI under a NATO command via a CJTF—after all, why have an ESDI if it can not be effectively used? This plan was popular among US military planners, but alliance diplomats could not reconcile the pressure from European members of NATO who were unwilling to take this responsibility and who thus insisted that "we went in as allies, we go out as allies." The same debate continued throughout 1997 to no avail. The US was unable to leave its allies to manage their own security affairs. Thus, in December 1997 President Clinton agreed to extend the US presence in Bosnia-Herzegovina indefinitely.

France Moves to NATO

An important impetus for completion of planning for the CJTF concept was the return of France toward NATO military structures. The Balkan crisis forced France into a gradual return toward NATO military planning, out of concern that it would be left out of alliance decisions that could impact its forces there. Bosnia had also shown the futility of an independent ESDI, and thus a deal with NATO that preserved the principle of the ESDI was in France's interest. The high costs of building an independent ESDI also collided with France's commitment to the EU and its European Monetary Union (EMU), which required strict fiscal programs in a climate of 12-percent national unemployment. As part of its fiscal belt-tightening, French President Jacques Chirac (elected in May 1995) introduced dramatic armed forces reductions and an end to conscription to complement a gradual but conditional return to NATO. The French rapprochement had two basic conditions: that NATO will continue to adapt its internal structures and that the ESDI should be visible and operational.[60] Contradictory institutional commitments and the political economy of European security had forced France to do what the Soviet threat could not—return Paris toward NATO military planning.

France's movement toward NATO military structures began in 1993 with the agreement to place the Eurocorps under a NATO command in the event of an emergency. In September 1994, French Minister of Defense François Leotard participated in a meeting of NATO defense ministers in Seville, Spain. This was the first visit by a French minister of defense to a NATO meeting since 1966. To accommodate French sensitivities, the meeting was labelled an "informal" discussion. French officials from the Ministry of Defense insisted that Leotard's attendance was not a change in doctrine. Rather, they intended to participate on a case-by-case basis to coordinate activities in the Balkans and to discuss Mediterranean security.

Leotard had played a leading role in moving France closer to NATO. In December 1993 he had requested that his government allow him to attend the NATO defense ministerial at Travemünde, Germany, where the PFP and CJTF proposals were initially debated. However, President Mitterand vetoed his participation. Similarly, when the French chief of staff sought to attend a meeting of the NATO Military Committee in April 1994, Mitterand again refused. Nevertheless, at the Brussels NATO summit in 1994, France had informed its allies that it would attend NATO military meetings where issues that might affect French forces were on the agenda. At the time, however, there was no indication that France would cross the line of reintegration into the military command structure. During his presidential campaign in 1995 Chirac indicated that he was prepared to seek closer ties to NATO and take these early initiatives a step further. By summer 1995, he had made a firm commitment to deepen France's NATO ties.[61]

In September 1995 France hosted the first NATO military exercise on French territory since 1966. The exercise included sixty aircraft and one thousand personnel in a four-day Tactical Air Meet over eastern France, with headquarters at a French air base in Toul. The exercise was designed to reflect

NATO air strikes in Bosnia focusing on suppressing enemy air defense systems, practicing air-to-air refueling and electronic warfare, and coordinating different aircraft types with ground air defenses.

Chirac next moved to strengthen ties with Britain. On 31 October Chirac and British Prime Minister John Major initiated a "global partnership," committing both sides to exchange classified nuclear weapons data with a long-term objective of coordinating nuclear policy and doctrine. Chirac and Major also agreed to pursue joint development and procurement of military equipment and to increase joint training. The respective naval chiefs were instructed to draft a letter of intent to promote naval cooperation by intensifying an existing program of military exchanges. They also initiated a Franco-British Euro Air Group at the headquarters of the Royal Air Force Strike Command. Chirac described the Air Group as a "symbol of a new credible European defense that must be based on a strong transatlantic relationship."[62]

On 5 December 1995 French Foreign Minister de Charette announced that in order to strengthen French–NATO cooperation in Bosnia and aid the development of the European pillar of NATO, "France has decided to become more involved in NATO's various organizational bodies."[63] Though the extent of its long-term participation remained uncertain, France immediately took its seat on the NATO Defense Planning Committee and the Military Committee. NATO officials were elated with de Charette's announcement, as it meant a status in NATO similar to that of Spain.

On 16 January 1996 the French ambassador to NATO told his counterparts that Defense Minister Charles Millon would now take part in formal meetings of the Defense Planning Committee. Participation would be limited to matters where the integrated military structure was not raised. However, the French chief of staff would return to the Military Committee. Millon indicated that France was considering closer relations with SHAPE and SACEUR and that it was willing to discuss nuclear policy. France would also participate fully in the NATO Defense College and in the NATO Situation Center.[64]

The announcement effectively acknowledged NATO's central role in Europe and the need to reconsider the institutional basis of the ESDI. As one French security expert said to the *New York Times:* "The fact is that, militarily, we have depended on NATO and our margin of independence has been negligible. . . . But our margin of political influence on NATO was also negligible before today. . . . This was absurd."[65]

When President Chirac traveled to Washington in early February 1996 he told a joint session of Congress that the activity of US and European troops in Bosnia-Herzegovina signaled "the need for the Alliance to adapt itself to a universe that is no longer that in which it was born."[66] The Franco-American compromise on implementing the CJTF concept indicated the sincerity of France's position and the profound nature of the change underlying French NATO policy. As a North Atlantic Assembly report concluded, beyond practical reasons related to military planning in Bosnia, "there is a bottom line: France's will to engage in a real renovation of the Atlantic Alliance, including the development of a true European pillar. . . . What is new is that France has declared its will that this European pillar must be built from within NATO, a stand that has been essential in clarifying France's position and giving reassurance to Americans and other Allies who had expressed concern on French intentions."[67]

Chirac's plan to restructure and reduce the French armed forces was central to the change in Paris's view toward NATO. As part of its commitment to attain EMU by the year 2000, France needed to reduce its $59.3 billion budget deficit. The EMU requirements in the Maastricht Treaty require states to have budget deficits below 3 percent of GDP, the public ratio of debt to GDP to be less than 60 percent, and inflation to be no higher than 1.5 percent above the average of the three lowest-inflation countries in the EU. By 1996 France had to maintain its budget deficit of 3.7 percent, debt of 56.9 percent GDP, and 1.3 percent inflation.[68] With high unemployment and the country occasionally paralyzed by strikes protesting government spending cuts, reducing the size of the French military was a partial solution.[69]

Thus on 22 February Chirac announced sweeping reductions in the French armed forces, to be accompanied by a new strategic doctrine, which would save an estimated $1.2 billion a year. Spending on defense research and equipment would be cut by 18 percent annually—about $37 billion from 1997 to 2002. This was $4 billion less than had been established in 1994. Total defense spending would amount to about 3.1 percent of GDP, which was a 2-percent reduction from 1994. This figure included military pensions, so it was actually higher than the real figures spent on military capabilities.[70]

In July 1996 Chirac announced a streamlining of the armed forces, beginning with a disbanding of thirty-eight regiments; closing barracks, army hospitals and airbases; and retiring one of the two French aircraft carriers. Central to Chirac's overall plan was a decision to end conscription and move to volunteer armed forces. With France's national defense capabilities being reduced to help meet its obligations to the EU, Paris had little choice but to advance its national security interests by pooling its defense resources with its allies in NATO while negotiating the best deal it could get for its gradual return to NATO.

In November 1997, the French National Assembly passed its 1998 defense budget that sharply cut procurement expenses and delayed a number of arms programs. The budget for 1998 stood at $30.8 billion and was a 2.1 percent reduction from 1997 defense spending. Overall weapons procurement production was cut by 9 percent to $13 billion.

Under Chirac's defense plans, France intends to reduce its total armed forces from 573,000 to 437,000 (from 400,000 to 250,000 when paramilitary forces are excluded) while retaining the capacity for rapid deployment of some 50,000–60,000 troops abroad. Some of its European allies worried that France would rely more heavily on its nuclear deterrent—a view hardened during France's undersea nuclear testing in the Pacific in 1995–96. With an eye toward reassuring Germany in particular, Chirac announced that fifteen short-range Hades missile launchers, which could strike only targets in Germany, would be eliminated. Additionally, Chirac stressed that France's contribution (15,000 troops) to the Eurocorps would not be affected by the reductions. However, some German officials predicted that French troops in Germany would likely drop to around 3,000.[71]

The US endorsement of the ESDI made this rapprochement toward NATO more palatable for Paris. NATO made the political economy of European integration easier to manage for France. There was, however, some internal opposition to Chirac's plans. There will likely be a ten-year process of retiring all of the Gaullist, anti–NATO military officials in France. Some French officials wanted the Inter-Governmental Conference (IGC) review of the Maastricht Treaty in 1996 to promote the formation of a standing European army. For example, President Chirac's former Prime Minister Alain Juppé proposed an integrated European army of 350,000 that would be subordinated to the EU for rapid deployments.

However, the victory of the Socialist party in the spring 1997 French parliamentary elections contributed further to the demand to cut defense investments. The Socialists returned to a more traditional Gaullist foreign policy and thereby froze NATO integration. However, they also promised to create more jobs and provide increased government social spending. Those resources will have to come from somewhere, and thus French defense investment is likely to continue to decline. As a result, France's trend toward a low-cost reengagement with NATO is likely to continue—as will its ongoing dependence on the US for major military operations.

In American military circles there was considerable skepticism of France's ambitions. Some felt France returned to NATO so that it could have the greatest impact on European security—especially when the US chose not to lead in a CJTF. For example, during the Bosnian crisis of summer 1995, while the US was reformulating its policy toward the Balkans, France was able to exercise considerable influence over NATO affairs. Thus the ESDI could open the way for France to work within NATO to limit the US role in Europe.

This view was strengthened when France began insisting in late 1996 on a European general heading NATO's Southern Command (AFSOUTH) as a condition of its reintegration into NATO military planning. If enacted, this would have effectively eliminated the US from a land-based major command in Europe. Command structure reform (reducing from 65 to 20 commands) would have left two regional European commands, and the central region already to be rotated among Europeans. France suggested that refusal by the US to hand over the AFSOUTH command, which includes responsibility for the

US 6th Fleet (when placed under a NATO command), would cause Paris to
halt its return to NATO—a threat which was carried out through 1997 and
caused considerable resentment between Paris and Washington.

The AFSOUTH dispute led to an ineffective exchange of personal letters
between presidents Chirac and Clinton. Each outlined nonnegotiable positions. In his letter, Chirac termed the handing over of NATO's Southern Command from an American to a European an issue of "capital importance" in a
hand-written note attached to his official signature. The best NATO's diplomats could hope for was to "kick the ball down the road" a few years so that
more urgent issues could be addressed in NATO. By the end of 1996, Franco-
American relations had deteriorated to the point that the French foreign minister walked out on his colleagues' round of farewell speeches in honor of retiring US Secretary of State Warren Christopher during the December 1996 NAC
ministerial.

This snub was initially reported in the press as describing the French minister walking out on a toast by the NATO secretary general. According to NATO
officials, it actually took place within the NAC as the NATO foreign ministers
were giving farewell praises to secretary Christopher on his last official visit
to NATO. French officials insist that there was never any sign of disrespect,
but rather that the minister simply had a previously arranged press conference
for which he departed as scheduled. Nevertheless, reflective of the animosity
that US and French officials had for each other at this time, American aides
to Christopher leaked their description of the event to the press as an intentional show of disrespect for Christopher and by implication, the US.
Whether it was an intentional snub or not, the departure of the French minister
was considered by many of his colleagues to be unfortunate and at least ill-
timed.[72]

The pro–NATO change in French foreign policy was nonetheless substantial. France's desire for a rapprochement toward NATO appears serious—in
spite of the political bargaining over its role in the command structure. In fact,
France had little choice but to move closer to NATO because of its commitments to another institution—the EU and its EMU. As one high level European official observed:

> The European Union will not within the foreseeable future develop into an inde-
> pendent, credible defense alliance. Therefore the U.S. contribution as a guarantor
> of European security remains vitally important. Europe's own security policy
> interests may best be ensured within a NATO framework in cooperation with the
> United States. Without NATO Europe cannot be stabilized: this has been seen in
> Bosnia.[73]

Weary after four years of futility in Bosnia-Herzegovina, and unable to construct an independent ESDI, France and its supporters in the EU were forced

to change national security priorities, thus confirming NATO's influence at the core of European security. However, at the same time, the unwillingness of France and other European allies to assume operational responsibility in Bosnia-Herzegovina also symbolized the growing dependence of Europe on the US.

Rebuilding NATO

The institutional approaches toward restructuring the transatlantic relationship had little relevance to meeting immediate security challenges. Crises in the Balkans reduced the US and its European allies to "making it up as we go along," as one US official described the process.[74] CJTF was a major institutional adaptation, which could prevent future Bosnia-style conflicts from getting out of hand. Yet the CJTF is a means to an end—the broader objective being the sustainability of the transatlantic relationship. If agreement could not be reached for over four years on crises in Europe's own backyard in the Balkans, diverging interests over Iran, Iraq, Cuba, terrorism, and international trade might pull Europe and North America apart.

The internal fabric of NATO is challenged by the possibility of war between Greece and Turkey, Mediterranean members' concerns about North Africa and the rise of Muslim fundamentalism, and North European worries over the Baltic countries and environmental issues. These diverging interests are likely to increase, absent the Soviet threat, as its members continue to seek to define a "new NATO." Ironically, the new members, which have given NATO a degree of a sense of mission, do not seek to join a "new NATO" but rather the "old NATO" of collective defense. Because they share a different threat perception, regarding Russia, than the old NATO members, they are likely to seek to reorient NATO's command structure to address their perceived threats. As a result, there is likely to be a growing north–south and east–west strategic disconnect within the alliance.

As key strategic thinkers such as Charles Barry, Simon Serfaty, and Stanley Sloan have maintained for some time, for NATO to enhance European security in the twenty-first century, it must attain a functional new transatlantic bargain that makes the US commitment to European security sustainable.[75] Implementation of the CJTF/ESDI concept is the best means to this end—perhaps implemented in long-term peacekeeping in Bosnia-Herzegovina. Successful internal adaptation of NATO will demonstrate that preparing and training for Article 4–style missions will become the primary peacetime function of NATO. The US can thus be reassured about burdensharing and the European goal of implementing the ESDI can be attained.

This is not to say that making NATO a pool from which allies draw to support coalitions of the willing will always work. The states that are undertaking a mission will have to get the political support of the NAC. Nevertheless, once NAC support for the use of NATO assets is attained, intervention can be done rapidly and effectively. NATO will lower the transaction costs of coalition building and thus make security easier to attain than in NATO's absence. Thus NATO has a potential to play a critical institutional role in European security—but only if its members choose to make its institutional characteristics work.

The main physical change in NATO will be a restructuring of its regional and subregional command headquarters, which will be adapted to accommodate CJTF planning. If nonmembers can contribute to CJTF planning for Article 4 missions, they should be able to join these standing headquarters via the PFP, thereby contributing to community-building by lowering the distinction between members and nonmembers of NATO. Regional integrated headquarters will allow rapid and effective responses to crises when states choose to use them. As PFP countries and new members work within the CJTF framework, and Article 4 missions come to be the main focus of peacetime NATO activity, the debate over whether a state should actually join NATO or not may lose its intensity.

Decision-making in NATO vis-à-vis the ESDI will remain largely unchanged—a consensus must still exist in the NAC. However, consensus need not necessarily mean a commitment by all countries to participate in an operation. The principles and norms present in NATO will be enhanced, because in order to use NATO assets via a CJTF, a state must meet the approval of all the members of the NAC. A state in gross violation of NATO principles and norms might form an international coalition for a particular objective outside NATO; however, it would not be easy to do because such a violator will not be able to draw from standing NATO assets. The remaining member states, and likely PFP countries too, would have an advantage by drawing from NATO's standing military organizational structures. As a result, NATO can play a critical role in identifying defection from international cooperation and in punishing serious violators of international norms if necessary.

Absent a credible threat, NATO's future hinges on its internal restructuring. If it does not have the capacity for this sort of fundamental change after the Cold War, NATO may well go the way of most alliances and dissolve in the absence of a threat. NATO has shown a serious potential internal adaptation—particularly through its planning for CJTF and by supporting an enhanced WEU. However, ESDI remains a concept that has yet to be implemented in action—as the Bosnia-Herzegovina experience has shown. If the member states can agree to re-balance the alliance, then NATO will have an important role to play in the future of European security. NATO can facilitate coalitions arranged through the CJTFs led by states with the most immediate interests at stake, while being supported as needed by their NATO allies.

7

NATO and the Future of European Security

The New NATO

NATO is not a panacea, and its relevance to the future of European security is not guaranteed. Nevertheless, NATO is at the center of efforts to provide international organization to Europe. Indeed, there is often too much political focus on NATO, which has become overburdened, understaffed, and underfinanced. US, European, and NATO officials responsible for shaping European security policy have little opportunity to consider the broader strategic aspects of NATO's survival as they focus on hour-to-hour management problems. Expectations of what NATO can do to ensure security in Europe may have been inappropriately heightened as a result.

The transformation of NATO's tasks has not been matched by an enhancement in its organizational capacity. NATO officials in Brussels have thus grown very concerned about the manageability of the institution. Worries about institutional gridlock and bureaucratic redundancy were prevalent by 1998. NATO Secretary General Javier Solana concludes, "If this pace continues, it is hard to predict what NATO will be like just three years from now."[1] As one NATO official warned, NATO's outreach to the East is

> getting as bad as the OSCE. . . . It takes a full minute for the minister from Uzbekistan or somewhere far away just to say how pleased he is to be here and how much importance his government attaches to partnership with NATO. . . . How does that improve anyone's security?[2]

The transatlantic relationship, which provides the anchor that makes NATO work, is in danger if NATO becomes diluted to the point of institutional irrelevance and military futility. Both NATO enlargement and an inability to balance leadership in crisis management may also contribute to an erosion of the transatlantic relationship. A weakened transatlantic relationship would decrease European security in the future.

The Transatlantic Relationship

Politically, the transatlantic relationship is important to European security because of the promise of stable democratic societies working together to promote common interests. Democracy itself does not necessarily cause peace in international relations. Fragile democracies that have not fully developed respect for minority rights or peaceful resolution of disputes may experience high instability and even civil war that can become internationalized. Democracies suffering economic catastrophes can also fall into nationalism and/or dictatorship with expansionist goals. Nevertheless, democracy is, in the long term, the most stable system of government because of its basis on popular legitimacy and the rule of law. Moreover, open societies can enhance transparency in military planning and the possibility of misunderstood state behavior leading to insecurity can be reduced. Thus the democratic members of NATO have a unique responsibility and opportunity to serve as models of international cooperation in military planning, so that the possibility of uncertainty leading to instability in international relations is lowered.

Economically, the US and Europe are deeply interdependent, with about $1.5 trillion in annual shared economic activities. Europe has more of the gross world product than any other region, with 35 percent at market exchange rates and 27 percent at purchasing power parity exchange rates. In the early 1990s, Europe was America's second-largest customer, with 31 percent of US exports of goods and services, and America's second-largest supplier, providing 29 percent of US imports of goods and services. Europe provided the US with relatively balanced trade, with a $7 billion US merchandise trade deficit compared to $115 billion for Asia. Nearly 50 percent of US direct investment abroad is in Europe, and over 60 percent of foreign direct investment in the US comes from Europe (about $260 billion). This provides an important source of capital to offset the low national savings rate in the US. These investment flows account for nearly 7 percent of all jobs in the US and 5 percent in Europe. Some 3 million American citizens are employed in the US by European-owned businesses, and 1.5 million Americans are supported by goods and services that the US exports to Europe. Combined, the US–European trade relationship accounts for about 14 million jobs on both sides of the Atlantic. Culturally too, the US remains strongly connected to Europe. According to the 1990 US census, some 142.5 million Americans (56.9 percent) have sole or primary European ancestry or ethnic origins.[3]

Despite these shared interests, the greatest challenge to European security in the twenty-first century will be the maintenance of the institutionalized security cooperation developed between the US and Europe since World War

II. US interventions in Iraq, Haiti, and Bosnia-Herzegovina have shown that Americans will tolerate post–Cold War international engagement. However, their willingness to come to the aid of others with sufficient means to act on their own can be tested only so often. Americans might perceive that wealthy Europeans have strong governmental safety nets attained underneath the American security blanket. Yet these same allies are often working against the US in trouble spots around the world.

Leaders in the US and Europe have expressed concern about growing trends toward American isolationism. In March 1995 President Bill Clinton warned a bipartisan audience at the Nixon Center in Washington, D.C.:

> The new isolationists are wrong. They would have us face the future alone. Their approach would weaken this country, and we must not let the ripple of isolationism that has been generated build into a tidal wave.[4]

Addressing a joint session of the US Congress in February 1996, French President Jacques Chirac lectured the members on the benefits of foreign aid and chastised them for deep cuts in US aid programs. The speech was poorly attended by members, and many seats were filled with congressional research assistants and pages.

The declining interest in foreign affairs in the US Congress may show in direct correlation between the lowering of its institutional memory toward NATO and the retirement of senators Bill Bradley, William Cohen, Robert Dole, Howell Heflin, Nancy Kassebaum, and Sam Nunn. This diminution of internationalist members of congress especially worried German Chancellor Helmut Kohl. While in Berlin on 18 June 1996 receiving an award from the Atlantic Bridge Group for fostering ties between Germany and the US, Kohl said that the fall 1996 US elections would see "a series of senators and members of Congress drop out who know Germany and Europe and are bound to us in a special way. . . . I do not for now see that the 'old guard' of senators and congressmen is being replaced with successors who approach Europe and Germany with the same intensity."[5]

Balancing the transatlantic relationship is critical to keeping the US–European security partnership vibrant in the future. Indeed, it is a founding task of NATO that remains unfulfilled. For example, in two crises requiring international military action—Bosnia-Herzegovina and the 1997 Albanian internal collapse—NATO and the WEU were each unable to attain consensus for action. In the case of Bosnia-Herzegovina, the Europeans could not organize effectively without the US. In Albania, Italy formed and led a coalition of the willing but without assistance from the international institutions that are supposed to facilitate such security cooperation. Neither NATO nor the WEU was capable of gaining consensus for action in regional crises. If NATO and the ESDI are unable to facilitate the use of coalitions of the willing when conflict breaks out, then they will be of little value to the future of European security.

A new burdensharing arrangement in the context of NATO may require a leap of faith on the part of the US and its European allies—and it will require European members of NATO to spend more money on defense. Trends are in the opposite direction as Europeans are not increasing defense spending or adequately modernizing their armed forces. The end result may be a transformed NATO that is becoming more politically complicated and militarily dysfunctional. The decline in European defense investment impedes the ability of Europeans to participate in power projection missions by modernizing their forces. Indeed, the WEU could probably not sustain any long-term deployment of more than one division or three brigades. Increasingly, the armed forces of the European members of NATO can barely communicate with the modern and high-tech US armed forces. The chairman of NATO's Military Committee, General Klaus Naumann, complains that: "The United States is moving with unparalleled velocity toward the kind of high-tech military equipment that has no match in Europe. I am beginning to worry that one day we will wake up and find that our armies can no longer work well together."[6] By 1998, NATO could mobilize only 2 percent of its overall combat potential in twelve hours—a decline from 70 percent at the end of the Cold War.

It is increasingly necessary for both the US and its European allies to reconcile their short- and long-term security interests. If anything has been gained from nearly fifty years of cooperation in NATO, then now is the time to take practical steps to balance the transatlantic relationship in order to meet the major challenges to European security.

Stability in the East

NATO enlargement will likely complicate and raise the transaction costs of NATO's adaptation as new members integrate and compete for influence within NATO. NATO did effectively link enlargement with principles by adapting its membership rules from restricted to conditionally open, which shaped foreign and domestic policy among aspiring NATO members to the east. Indeed, the institutional linkage strategies which required states to meet certain criteria for membership were the most successful aspect of NATO enlargement. Unfortunately, that linkage had relevance only when these countries were outside NATO. Once members, there is no independent regulative function in NATO that will guarantee their compliance absent direct American pressure. The Greek and Turkish cases demonstrate this NATO dilemma only too clearly.

For NATO enlargement to succeed, it must have strategic value. By including Poland, NATO can serve as a hedge between Russia and Germany. If Germany has no ambitions outside its territory, as its behavior since unification confirms, then it should not have problems with this expansion of internal containment. Additionally, stabilizing the region between Russia and Germany is a rationale for NATO enlargement that Moscow should support as Russia shares this interest. The US also has a long-term interest in promoting such regional stability in the East. America has lost too many soldiers this century to wars prompted by security competition over the region between Germany and Russia. The US did not spend trillions of dollars winning the Cold War only to see Europe destabilized in international security competition emerging from another period of apparent European tranquility.

For NATO enlargement to have full strategic value, it will have to enlarge again to include Romania, and probably Slovenia. Threats, ranging from instability in the Balkan region to the proliferation of weapons of mass destruction capacity in the Middle East or North Africa, make a strong case for Romanian membership. A scenario in which the Saudi or Iraqi government were to collapse and be replaced by a fundamentalist, pro-Iranian regime would immediately shift US strategic priorities to the oil-rich Caspian Sea region—leading to security competition among the US, Iran, and Russia. In such a conflict, Romania's membership in NATO would provide a critical base for US operations by assisting extended deterrence and supporting force projection. Given uncertain trends in Turkey's political development, Romania could become critical to the security of the alliance's southern rim. For its part, Slovenia, when combined with Romania, would help to establish a hedge around the unstable areas of the former Yugoslavia and help contain any future instability there. Slovenia would also serve as a land-bridge to Hungary which currently shares no border with another NATO member.

It is important that a democratic Russia feel at ease with NATO enlargement. Enlarging NATO as an explicitly anti-Russian act, in the absence of Russian behavior that merits such a response, would have been a tragic mistake. By building upon the NATO–Russia cooperation that has developed in IFOR and SFOR in the Balkans, NATO can continue to show that its members hope to integrate, and not isolate, Russia. The NATO–Russia partnership can define this process. However, unless there is a mutual gain from such a relationship, it will have little relevance and Russia may seek to negatively influence NATO's consensus process. Some NATO members tend to view consultation with Russia as informing Moscow of what NATO is doing, while Russia views consultation as a right to veto alliance activity. Squaring the circle of integrating Russia while preventing it from gaining too much influence over NATO affairs will be one of the most fundamental challenges to NATO's relationship to security outcomes in the next century.

Stressing its institutional rather than strategic value, NATO has chosen to enlarge in a manner that is likely to dilute its overall military effectiveness and political cohesion. NATO has agreed to a number of self-imposed restraints regarding its plans for new members. As a result, new members will neither contribute much to NATO nor receive much from it. There are risks to this method of implementing NATO enlargement.

First, by agreeing not to deploy permanently stationed conventional or nuclear forces on new NATO members' territory, NATO will not provide a credible Article 5 guarantee for new member states. NATO is agreeing to consult on perhaps fighting a war on new members' territory, but not to deter an attack on members' borders. Should a new member be threatened, a decision by NATO to reinforce would inevitably escalate any existing conflict and divide the alliance. Age-old questions of whether the West will go to war for the East, as it failed to do at the outbreak of World War II, are likely to persist, with or without NATO enlargement. Without a credible security guarantee to new members, NATO enlargement risks a serious diminution of the principles underlying its Article 5 treaty commitment.

Second, the NATO–Russia Permanent Joint Council may provide Russia with an opportunity to exercise a de facto veto over NATO policy. While NATO will formally agree to a unified policy before coming to the PJC, it is in the consensus process where the NATO "veto" lies. Russia's presence at NATO will enhance its capacity to make NATO decision-making more reflective of Russia's interests by lobbying NATO members directly. As a result, NATO enlargement risks transforming NATO from a well-organized collective defense alliance into a new general European collective security institution.

Third, NATO enlargement will require new members to increase their defense budgets to modernize their militaries to integrate with NATO. The cost of financing membership will come at the expense of other domestic programs and may hinder long-term economic growth and political development in new members. A failure by leaders in the Czech Republic and Hungary, in particular, to inform their publics as to the obligations that NATO entails for its economy and international commitments could haunt reform politicians in any future crisis that places demands on new NATO members.

Finally, if NATO enlargement is perceived by Russia and some NATO allies, such as France, as a tool of strengthening American power over them, it may produce balancing behavior. The risk to NATO is that balancing behavior organized against the US will likely occur within the ever-expanding institution rather than be organized externally against the collective NATO allies. Increasingly, the US has found itself a minority in NATO decision-making processes, for example over what countries should be new members of NATO or who should pay the costs of enlargement. Generally, because it is the most important power and is what makes NATO function in a crisis, the US gets what it wants. However, it must tread carefully in managing relations with its allies and partners to ensure that historical sensitivities among members do not lead to institutional dynamics that make NATO ineffective for managing the demands of its member states. If not carefully managed, state competition within NATO could damage the ability to act in a crisis and, over time, damage the transatlantic relationship.

More broadly, to reduce the potential for misunderstanding in the East, NATO should be clear on what enlargement can do for new members. NATO can provide an institutional forum for political consultation and military planning. However, NATO alone cannot build democracy. As one senior European diplomat notes,

> If NATO is changing a military destiny once based on geography to a defense of common values, then where do we draw the limits? Will we all agree on which values to fight for? And just how far do we go to defend them?[7]

Other institutions—particularly the European Union—must take primary responsibility for building the substructure that lends to stable democratic societies throughout Central and Eastern Europe. NATO should play a complementary role promoting democracy and stability in Europe. However, the PFP and not NATO enlargement per se would most effectively serve that end.

PFP aided nonmembers of NATO in four important ways. First, it opened NATO structures from which participants could gain technical expertise to help them enhance national security as they saw fit. Second, PFP helped states promote stability in their immediate regions. Integrated into CJTFs, PFP participants could more effectively address nontraditional challenges, such as environmental catastrophes, natural disasters, and humanitarian crises. Third, at a general European level, PFP contributed to stability in the case of IFOR and SFOR. Fourth, as the PFP countries participated in other NATO programs and planning, they could socialize and learn from NATO traditions. Given the critical importance of the PFP, NATO members must be willing to ensure that enlargement corresponds to an increase in PFP funding and activities. By enlarging, NATO will spread its area of responsibility to border on some very unstable regions. A broadened and enhanced PFP can help ease this dilemma.

However, its enlargement might undermine the capacity for NATO to respond effectively to these new challenges. First, NATO enlargement undermines the Partnership for Peace. By bringing the three main political drivers of the PFP into NATO as members, there might be little rationale for sustained national support for PFP in the remaining aspirants if they do not feel it will lead to NATO membership. NATO has responded with a so-called "enhanced Partnership for Peace" and by replacing the North Atlantic Cooperation Council with a new Euro-Atlantic Partnership Council (EAPC). However, absent substantial resources allocated to engage the countries in Eastern Europe most in need of assistance, the enhanced PFP may lose its value as a community-building tool. At the outset, the EAPC did little more than serve as a name change for the NACC. If NATO is going to spend considerable resources on three new members that are not threatened and are stable, then its members should devote equal, if not more, money to programs that enhance the security of countries that are potentially threatened, are unstable, and were left off NATO's invitee list.

Second, enlargement may undermine consensus on managing out-of-area crises such as Bosnia-Herzegovina. While the three new members did contribute to the Balkan peace missions in IFOR/SFOR, they did so primarily to advance their case for NATO membership. It is yet to be seen whether, once they are in NATO, the new members will support such missions in the future. The new members want the "old NATO" of collective defense—not the "new NATO" of enhanced European responsibility and crisis management. As a result, there is potential for a divergence of interests between old and new allies. This may become particularly evident in conflicting agendas vis-à-vis Russia.

Finally, NATO enlargement will complicate the internal adaptation essential to NATO's survival. New members will want increased attention paid to NATO's central region, while the challenges facing current members lie to the south. New members cannot necessarily be counted on to approve missions that distract military planning from their own regional priorities in Central Europe. Ironically, NATO enlargement will force the bureaucratic energy of its military planners to prepare to defend Central Europe, which is not threatened, at the expense of a complete focus on areas where stability is challenged—in NATO's southern region.

The success or failure of NATO enlargement to stabilize the East will be crucial to the future of NATO's credibility, but not necessarily to NATO's survival. If NATO enlargement stabilizes some countries or regions in Europe at the expense of others, or if new divisions are drawn, the policy will have failed. Alternatively, if enlargement goes too far, by including former Soviet republics, NATO will have become a collective security organization similar to the League of Nations or the OSCE. Indeed, the NATO–Russia PJC may have already done that. Either way, NATO appears to be here to stay—though in the coming decades states may begin to question which collective security institution to keep: NATO or the OSCE. It is possible that through creative consensus building a pragmatic division of labor can be achieved between Europe's multiple institutions. Absent that, NATO's dilution may seriously inhibit the primary institutional way that it can enhance security in Europe: helping states organize for regional crisis management.

Crisis Management

NATO's early efforts at crisis management focused more on prevention than on resolution by promoting mutual gain in European security through the amalgamated collective security of interlocking institutions. As bloodshed grew in the Balkans, the multiple institutions tasked by states to resolve the conflict—the EU, CSCE/OSCE, UN, WEU, and NATO—all failed to convince the combatants to end war. Even genocide could not mobilize NATO or other institutions to respond effectively. Without shared national interests or independent capabilities, institutions promoted a false sense of security, as Europe witnessed its worst violence since World War II. Paralyzed by the diverging interests of its member states, NATO was on the brink of collapse by mid-1995. NATO could not exist in a vacuum, and if it was to have any relevance after the Cold War, it would have to play a role in resolving the Balkan crisis. By late 1995, a combination of power and diplomacy caused a cease-fire in Bosnia-Herzegovina. This led to a stable, albeit weak, peace—and allowed NATO to show its institutional value for the future of European security. NATO's institutional attributes enhanced the peace in two key ways.

First, NATO planning substantially lowered the transaction costs of forming and maintaining a peacekeeping coalition to facilitate the agreed separation of the Croats, Muslims, and Serbs. The Dayton accords, reached during the autumn of 1995, depended on a rapid deployment of peacekeeping forces—which only NATO could adequately supply. This immediate intervention was possible because of two years of institutional planning in NATO. NATO was essential to the reassurance that each party needed to commit to peace. By organizing 60,000 troops for IFOR, NATO demonstrated that it had evolved to become more flexible and adaptive in its missions. NATO could field new and creative command structures and facilitate the use of power. While still fundamentally an instrument of states, NATO made the implementation of a collective decision easier to attain than it would have been in the absence of the institution.

Second, through the NACC and the PFP information exchanges, NATO integrated nonmember countries into its military planning for peacekeeping operations based on Article 4 consultation. A better understanding of the capabilities available for multinational peacekeeping lowered the transaction costs of planning and reduced the danger that command and control confusion could harm this multinational coalition. NATO's coordination of IFOR included 10,000 personnel from PFP countries. The provision of non–NATO forces was politically significant, as domestic constraints limited the amount of forces the US was willing to commit to Balkan security. NATO's new institutional characteristics thus helped make it possible for its leading member to provide only one-third of the forces. Additionally, IFOR and SFOR would feed back on the PFP process. Operational experience helped partners better define their own national security needs.

NATO's capacity to help Bosnia-Herzegovina move from a situation of peace to one of lasting security was, nevertheless, seriously limited. The removal of NATO from the region would once again expose the weakness of other institutions such as the EU, WEU, and OSCE. Thus the scheduled end of IFOR and SFOR sustained discussion over how to best maintain peace in the Balkans. At the core of this debate were disputes over the relevance of institutions in aiding reconciliation versus the less ideal, but perhaps more stable, partition of Bosnia-Herzegovina along ethnic lines.

The most important lesson of NATO's contribution to peace in the Balkans was that NATO was successful only when the US was fully engaged. NATO could exchange information and facilitate multinational planning for peace-keeping, but this could be implemented only with US leadership. In practice, NATO had changed very little. Europeans remained dependent on the US for political leadership and military effectiveness in a crisis. Eventually, this security dependence could drive the US away from Europe and thereby damage the insurance that the American presence provides against Great Power security competition. The US is the critical variable on which NATO's credibility is founded. For Europe to sustain that relationship they will have to organize effectively for crisis management so that the US does not have to engage repeatedly in institutional rescue missions to save NATO—as in Bosnia-Herzegovina.

Conclusion

Institutions like NATO play an important role in European security. They reflect the ongoing desire of humankind to build a better world and to live in peace. However, this study shows the value of using realist international relations theory to test exactly what institutions can, and cannot, do to impact security outcomes. NATO is still needed because Europe has yet to evolve into a situation of guaranteed peace. Ultimately, the ideal of European security is to create the conditions in which an international organization like NATO is no longer necessary. However, as that day is far beyond the horizon, NATO will likely survive. Whether and how its survival increases, or decreases, European security will be one of the most important issues affecting international politics of the twenty-first century.

Notes

Chapter 1

1. Interview with a senior NATO official, Brussels, March 1992.

2. See Robert O. Keohane, *International Institutions and State Power* (Boulder, CO: Westview Press, 1989), 3–5; and Stephen D. Krasner, "Structural Causes and Regime Consequences: Regimes as Intervening Variables," in *International Regimes*, ed. Stephen D. Krasner (Ithaca, NY: Cornell University Press, 1983), 1–5.

3. See Hans J. Morgenthau, *Politics among Nations*, 3d ed. (New York: Knopf, 1978), 5–12; Kenneth N. Waltz, *Theory of International Politics* (Reading, MA: Addison-Wesley Publishing Company, 1978); Robert G. Gilpin, "The Richness of the Tradition of Political Realism," in *Neorealism and Its Critics*, ed. Robert O. Keohane (New York: Columbia University Press, 1986), 304–305; David Baldwin, *Paradoxes of Power* (New York: Basil Blackwell, 1989); and Joseph S. Nye, Jr., *The Changing Nature of American Power* (New York: Basic Books, 1990).

4. See George F. Kennan, *American Diplomacy, 1900–1950* (Chicago: University of Chicago Press, 1951), 95–103; and John J. Mearsheimer, "The False Promise of International Institutions," in *The Perils of Anarchy: Contemporary Realism and International Security*, ed. Michael E. Brown, Sean M. Lynn-Jones, and Steven E. Miller (Cambridge: MIT Press, 1995), 332–376.

5. Mearsheimer, "The False Promise," 337.

6. Joseph M. Grieco, "Anarchy and the Limits of Cooperation: A Realist Critique of the Newest Liberal Institutionalism," in *Neorealism and Neoliberalism: The Contemporary Debate*, ed. David Baldwin (New York: Columbia University Press, 1993), 128–129.

7. Charles A. Kupchan and Clifford A. Kupchan, "A New Concert for Europe," in Graham Allison and Gregory F. Treverton, ed., *Rethinking America's Security* (New York: W. W. Norton, 1993), 250.

8. Restricted institutions limit membership to a small group of states that have some particular set of interests in common, or those which have specified standards of domestic political structures within states. Conditionally open institutions are accessible in principle to states that are willing to accept a set of prescribed commitments. Open institutions are universal and accessible to all states with the exception of those whose policies represent gross violations of specified institutional norms. Robert O.

Keohane, "The Analysis of International Regimes," *Regime Theory and International Relations*, ed. Volker Rittberger (Oxford: Clarendon Press, 1993), 39.

9. See John J. Mearsheimer, "Back to the Future: Instability in Europe after the Cold War," in *The Cold War and After: Prospects for Peace*, ed. Sean M. Lynn-Jones and Steven E. Miller (Cambridge: MIT Press, 1993), 188.

10. Mearsheimer, "The False Promise," 340–341.

11. John J. Mearsheimer, "Why We Will Soon Miss the Cold War," *The Atlantic* 266, no. 2 (August 1990).

12. Kenneth N. Waltz, "The Emerging Structure of International Politics," in Brown, *The Perils of Anarchy*, 74.

13. Waltz, "The Emerging Structure," 73.

14. Richard K. Betts, "Systems of Peace as Causes of War? Collective Security, Arms Control, and the New Europe," in *Coping with Complexity in the International System*, ed. Jack Snyder and Robert Jervis (Boulder, CO: Westview Press, 1993), 272.

15. Stephen M. Walt, "Alliance Formation and the Balance of World Power," *International Security* 9, no. 4 (Spring 1985): 12.

16. Charles L. Glaser, "Realists as Optimists: Cooperation as Self-help," in Brown, *The Perils of Anarchy*, 400–405.

17. For further discussion see Michael Mastanduno, "Preserving the Unipolar Moment: Realist Theories and U.S. Grand Strategy after the Cold War," *International Security* 21, no. 4 (Spring 1997): 49–88.

18. Jack Snyder, "Averting Anarchy in the New Europe," in Lynn-Jones and Miller, *The Cold War and After*, 139.

19. Robert Axelrod and Robert O. Keohane, "Achieving Cooperation under Anarchy: Strategies and Institutions," in Baldwin, ed., *Neorealism and Neoliberalism*, 94.

20. Robert O. Keohane and Lisa L. Martin, "The Promise of Institutionalist Theory," *International Security* 20, no. 1 (Summer 1995): 42.

21. Robert O. Keohane, Joseph S. Nye, and Stanley Hoffmann, eds., *After the Cold War: International Institutions and State Strategies in Europe, 1989–1991* (Cambridge: Harvard University Press, 1994), 2–3.

22. Charles A. Kupchan, "The Case for Collective Security," in *Collective Security after the Cold War*, ed. George W. Downs (Ann Arbor: University of Michigan Press, 1994), 50–51.

23. Robert O. Keohane, "Institutional Theory and the Realist Challenge after the Cold War," in Baldwin, ed., *Neorealism and Neoliberalism*, 272.

24. John G. Ruggie, "The False Premise of Realism," *International Security* 20, no. 1 (Summer 1995): 65–66. These options included unilateral US security guarantees to one, several, or an organization of European states; one or more US bilateral alliances with European states; or a "dumbbell" model linking North American and European alliances. The US, Ruggie maintains, chose the model which most closely approximated collective security.

25. Stephen Weber, "Does NATO Have a Future?" in *The Future of European Security*, ed. Beverly Crawford (Berkeley: Center for German and European Studies, University of California, 1992), 369–370, 381.

26. John Duffield, "The North Atlantic Treaty Organization and Alliance Theory," in *Explaining International Relations since 1945*, ed. Ngaire Woods (Oxford: Oxford

University Press, 1996), 343–345. In a previous study, Duffield assessed NATO's role in helping to clarify boundaries for state behavior in Cold War Europe, reinforcing the US commitment to European security, and influencing military planning and capabilities: John S. Duffield, "Explaining the Long Peace in Europe: The Contributions of Regional Security Regimes," *Review of International Studies* 20, no. 4 (October 1994): 369–388. Duffield has also sought to demonstrate that NATO's Cold War conventional force posture was affected independently by the norms and rules of the institution, reinforced via rational incentives for compliance, which in turn reinforced a process within states affecting the views and calculations of decision-makers. See John Duffield, *Power Rules: The Evolution of NATO's Conventional Force Posture* (Stanford, CA: Stanford University Press, 1995), 251–257.

27. Robert McCalla, "NATO's Persistence after the Cold War," *International Organization* 50, no. 3 (Summer 1996).

28. See Ashton B. Carter, William J. Perry, and John D. Steinbruner, *A New Concept of Cooperative Security* (Washington, DC: The Brookings Institution, 1992); and Janne E. Nolan, ed., *Global Engagement: Cooperation and Security in the 21st Century* (Washington, DC: The Brookings Institution, 1994).

29. "US Wants to Expedite Entry of Eastern Nations into Alliance," *New York Times*, 27 October 1994, 5(A).

30. See Karl Deutsch, et al., *Political Community in the North Atlantic Area* (Princeton: Princeton University Press, 1957), 5–6.

31. Deutsch, *Political Community*, 203.

32. Weber, Does NATO Have a Future?" 369–372.

33. Secretary of State Madeleine K. Albright, *Statement before the Senate Foreign Relations Committee*, Washington, D.C. (7 October 1997).

34. See Emanuel Adler, *European Union: A Pluralistic Security Community* (Berkeley and Los Angeles: University of California Press, 1991).

Chapter 2

1. Richard Kugler, *Commitment to Purpose: How Alliance Partnership Won the Cold War* (Santa Monica, CA: RAND Corporation, 1993), 30–36.

2. Robert Osgood, *NATO: The Entangling Alliance* (Chicago: University of Chicago Press, 1962), 29–30.

3. Richard A. Best, Jr., *"Cooperation with Like-Minded Peoples": British Influences on American Security Policy, 1945–1949* (New York: Greenwood Press, 1986), 28.

4. See John Baylis, *Anglo-American Defence Relations, 1939–1980: The Special Relationship* (New York: St. Martin's Press, 1981); Joseph Smith, ed., *The Origins of NATO* (Exeter, UK: University of Exeter Press, 1990); and John Lewis Gaddis, *The Long Peace: Inquiries into the History of the Cold War* (New York: Oxford University Press, 1987).

5. "The Long Telegram (Kennan)" 22 February 1946. *Foreign Relations of the United States*, 1946, 4:706.

6. Don Cook, *Forging the Alliance: NATO, 1945–1950* (London: Secker and Warburg, 1989), 52–53.

7. Cook, *Forging*, 52–53.

8. See John Baylis, "Britain and the Dunkirk Treaty: The Origins of NATO," *Journal of Strategic Studies* 5 (June 1982): 236–247.

9. Message to a Joint Session of Congress, 12 March 1947, *Public Papers of the Presidents*, 1948 (Washington, DC: Government Printing Office, 1963), 178–179.

10. Marshall Plan aid was to be distributed to the recipient countries to promote self-help once they had first designed their own reconstruction programs.

11. Article 51 of the Charter of the United Nations states: "Nothing in the present Charter shall impair the inherent right of individual or collective self-defence if an armed attack occurs against a Member of the United Nations, until the Security Council has taken measures necessary to maintain international peace and security. Measures taken by Members in the exercise of this right of self-defense shall be immediately reported to the Security Council under the present Charter to take at any time such action as it deems necessary in order to maintain or restore international peace and security."

12. "Americas' Treaty Ratified, 72–1; Vandenberg Cites Bar to Veto," *New York Times*, 9 December 1947, 1, 4(A).

13. James Reston, "Need for Firm U.S. Stand in Support of Italy Is Seen," *New York Times*, 15 December 1947, 3(A). Also see Timothy Ireland, *Creating the Entangling Alliance: The Origins of the North Atlantic Treaty Organization* (Westport, CT: Greenwood Press, 1981), 37–41.

14 "The Chargé in London (Gallman) to the Secretary of State," London, 22 December 1947, *Foreign Relations of the United States*, 1948, 3:2.

15. Quoted by Theodore C. Achilles in "The Omaha Milkman: The Role of the United States in the Negotiations," in *NATO's Anxious Birth*, ed. Andre de Staercke (New York: St. Martin's Press, 1985), 30.

16. Charles E. Bohlen, *Transformation of American Foreign Policy* (New York: W. W. Norton & Co., 1969), 92–93.

17. "Summary of a Memorandum Representing Mr. Bevin's Views on the Formation of a Western Union," *Foreign Relations of the United States*, 1948, 3:5.

18. "Secretary of State to the British Ambassador," 20 January 1948, *Foreign Relations of the United States*, 1948, 3:8.

19. "Memorandum of Conversation, by Director of the Office of European Affairs (Hickerson)," *Foreign Relations of the United States*, 1948, 3:11. Hickerson had been advising Marshall that a regional security pact should be negotiated with Europe based on the Rio Treaty. In a memo to Marshall he wrote: "In my opinion a European Pact modelled on the treaty of Rio de Janeiro is the best answer to the security problem for Western Europe. For such a pact to be really effective, the United States would have to adhere." "Memorandum by the Director of the Office of European Affairs (Hickerson) to the Secretary of State," *Foreign Relations of the United States*, 1948, 3:7.

20. *Parliamentary Debates* (Commons), 1947–1948, 5th series, vol. 446 (1947–48), col. 383ff.

21. *Foreign Relations of the United States*, 1948, 3:76–78.

22. "Memorandum by the Director of the Policy Planning Staff (Kennan) to the Secretary of State," *Foreign Relations of the United States*, 1948, 3:7.

23. "The Secretary of State to the Embassy in the United Kingdom," 28 February 1948, *Foreign Relations of the United States*, 1948, 2:101.

24. Quoted in Alexander Rendel, "Secret Explorations: The Anglo-American Initiatives," in de Staercke, *NATO's Anxious Birth*, 12.

25. Lansing Warren, "De Gaulle, Asking for French Power, Seeks Our Arms Aid," *New York Times*, 8 March 1948, 1, 9(A).

26. See James Avery Joyce, *Broken Star: The Story of the League of Nations, 1919–1939* (Swansea: C. Davies, 1979), 45; and Byron Dexter, *The Years of Opportunity: The League of Nations, 1920–1926* (New York: Viking Press, 1967), 39.

27. Formally called "The Treaty of Economic, Social and Cultural Collaboration and Collective Self-Defense." *Department of State Bulletin* 18, no. 462 (9 May 1948): 600.

28. Address to a Joint Session of Congress, 17 March 1948, *Public Papers of the Presidents*, 184.

29. "Final Draft," undated, identified as "Pentagon Paper, 840.00/3–1748," *Foreign Relations of the United States*, 1948, 3:72–75.

30. Kennan summarized his and Bohlen's views in a note to Marshall and Lovett on 29 April 1948: "Memorandum by the Director of the Policy Planning Staff (Kennan) to the Secretary and Undersecretary of State (Robert Lovett), April 29, 1948," *Foreign Relations of the United States*, 1948, 3:108–109.

31. Robert H. Ferrell, "The Formation of the Alliance: 1948–1949," in *American Historians and the Atlantic Alliance*, ed. Lawrence S. Kaplan (Kent, OH: The Kent State University Press, 1991), 24.

32. Escott Reid, *Time of Fear and Hope* (Toronto: McClelland and Stewart, 1977), 135–136.

33. P. J. Philip, "Canada Endorses Free Nation Unity," *New York Times*, 30 April 1948, A(5).

34. "Attlee Ties Peace to Brussels Pact," *New York Times*, 28 May 1948, 10(A).

35. "Memorandum of Conversation, by the Acting Secretary of State," 11 April 1948, *Foreign Relations of the United States*, 1948, 3:82–83 and 93–94.

36. The Vandenberg Resolution was formally titled "Resolution of the Foreign Relations Committee Number 239." *Congressional Record*, 80th Cong., 2d sess., 11 June 1948, 4:7791.

37. The Dutch representative at the Washington talks suggested an alternative "peach" shape with the Brussels Pact serving as the "hard kernel in the center and a North Atlantic Pact the somewhat less hard mass around it." "Minutes of the Fifth Meeting of the Washington Exploratory Talks on Security," 9 July 1948, *Foreign Relations of the United States*, 1948, 3:171.

38. Cook, *Forging*, 173.

39. Clarence K. Streit, *Union Now: A Proposal for a Federal Union of the Free* (New York: Harper Brothers, 1949), 3–5. Later in his career Streit made a comparison of NATO and the Articles of Confederation in the US formative period. See Clarence K. Streit, *Freedom & Union* (February 1964): 4–5.

40. Theodore C. Achilles, "Fingerprints on History: The NATO Memoirs of Theodore C. Achilles," *Occasional Papers I* (Kent, OH: Lyman L. Lemnitzer Center for NATO and European Community Studies, 1992), 13. Achilles notes that after the US Senate approved the NATO treaty in August 1949, he said to Secretary of State Dean Acheson: "Dean, now that we've got this one wrapped up, let's go after a full Atlantic

federal union." Acheson responded that "I'd rather start with Britain, Canada, and ourselves." Achilles, "Fingerprints," 32–33.

41. Cook, *Forging*, 173.

42. "Minutes of the Second Meeting of the Washington Exploratory Talks on Security," 6 July 1948, *Foreign Relations of the United States*, 1948, 3:153. Escott Reid saw values that united the Western countries personally represented among the individual negotiators in Washington. Fourteen of the fifteen (St. Laurent was the exception) were "by origin, upbringing and careers members of the group of Protestant British and Protestant Irish origin which at that time dominated national political activities in the United States, Britain and Canada. It was thus natural for them to become advocates of a North Atlantic alliance of which these three countries would be the core." Reid, *Time of Fear and Hope*, 67.

43. "The Ambassador in France to the Secretary of State," *Foreign Relations of the United States*, 1948, 3:142.

44. Nicholas Henderson, *The Birth of NATO* (Boulder, CO: Westview Press, 1983), 38.

45. Cook, *Forging*, 185.

46. Cook, *Forging*, 185.

47. See Henderson, *Birth of NATO*, 52–54.

48. Achilles, "Fingerprints," 19.

49. On 18 March, Escott Reid had proposed in an internal Ministry of Foreign Affairs memo that a provision in the treaty include agreement by the Atlantic Nations to: organize their economic activities to produce the greatest possible returns by the elimination of conflict in their economic policies, the coordination of production, and the development of commercial exchanges; promote the attainment of a higher standard of living by their people and greater economic and social justice, and to develop on corresponding lines the social and other related services of their countries; work towards a better understanding of the principles which form the basis of their common civilization and to promote cultural exchanges between themselves; and use their best efforts to secure those amendments to the international instruments setting up the specialized agencies as are necessary to ensure that the agencies become the most effective possible instruments for the speedy attainment of the objectives set forth in the charter. Reid, *Time of Fear and Hope*, 168.

50. "Minutes of the Third Meeting of the Washington Exploratory Talks on Security, July 7, 1948," *Foreign Relations of the United States*, 1948, 3:159.

51. "Minutes of the Third Meeting," 159.

52. By fall 1948 the US supported inclusion of some nonmilitary issues in the treaty to make it more palatable to the Senate. However, in early 1949 the new US secretary of state, Dean Acheson, sought to dilute the Canadian initiative. Acheson felt that language stressing the "general welfare" would not be accepted in the Senate and he believed that such language was not practical without a mechanism for its implementation. The issue was settled permanently after a direct intervention by Canadian Prime Minister St. Laurent to President Truman, who subsequently endorsed the Canadian proposal. Lawrence S. Kaplan, *The United States and NATO: The Formative Years* (Lexington: The University Press of Kentucky, 1984), 117–118.

53. Henderson, *Birth of NATO*, 70.

54. "Memorandum by the Participants in the Washington Security Talks July 6 to September 9, Submitted to Their Respective Governments for Study and Comment," *Foreign Relations of the United States*, 1948, 3:237–245.

55. Achilles, "Fingerprints," 27.

56. Gaddis, *The Long Peace*, 63.

57. "Memorandum by the Director of the Policy Planning Staff, 29 November 1948," *Foreign Relations of the United States*, 1948, 3:283–289.

58. US Department of State, Policy Planning Staff (PPS), 43.

59. PPS, 43.

60. PPS, 43.

61. "Paraphrase of a Telegram from the British Secretary of State for Foreign Affairs (Bevin) of April 9th Regarding Recent Talks on North Atlantic Security Arrangements," *Foreign Relations of the United States*, 1948, 3:80.

62. Henderson, *Birth of NATO*, 37, 50.

63. "Minutes of the Fourth Meeting of the Washington Exploratory Talks on Security, July 7, 1948," *Foreign Relations of the United States*, 1948, 3:167.

64. See Henderson, *Birth of NATO*, 83–89.

65. Achilles, "Fingerprints," 28.

66. Albano Nogueira, "The Pull of the Containment: Portugal Opts for a European Role," in de Staercke, *NATO's Anxious Birth*, 70.

67. Reid, *Time of Fear and Hope*, 198.

68. Dean Acheson, *The Struggle for a Free Europe* (New York: W. W. Norton & Co., 1971), 61.

69. Kaplan, *The United States and NATO*, 110–112.

70. Western countries also tried to influence the election through overt and covert methods. The most important was a statement from Secretary of State George Marshall prior to the vote that Italy's application for Marshall Plan aid would be considered on the basis of whether or not the Communist party was defeated in the elections.

71. France opposed Italian participation. Paris felt that since Italy had been disarmed after World War II, it would not offer any tangible military contribution to Western defense plans. However, their position changed in relation to Algeria, which France wanted in the area covered by the treaty. Paris felt giving the institution a Mediterranean element via Italian membership might help its position vis-à-vis Algeria.

72. "Text of Acheson Remarks," *New York Times*, 27 January 1949, 4(A).

73. "Spaak Hails Publication of Treaty's Text as Victory for Diplomacy on Open Market," *New York Times*, 19 March 1949, 3(A).

74. Acheson, *Struggle*, 49.

75. "Text of Mr. Acheson's Broadcast on Atlantic Accord," *New York Times*, 19 March 1949, 4(A).

76. For formal interpretations of the treaty, see "Minutes of the Ambassadors' Committee," 15 March 1949, *Foreign Relations of the United States*, 1949, 4:222–223; The Department of State White Paper on the North Atlantic Treaty: "The North Atlantic Pact: Collective Defense and the Preservation of Peace, Security and Freedom in the North Atlantic Community," *Department of State Bulletin* 20, no. 507 (20 March 1949): 342–350; and "Signing Ceremony of the North Atlantic Treaty: Statements by

the Foreign Ministers and President Truman," *Department of State Bulletin* 20, no. 511 (17 April 1949): 471–482.

77. Text of the North Atlantic Treaty. Signed in Washington D.C., 4 April 1949.

78. Bohlen, *Transformation*, 114.

79. Dean Acheson, "Canada, 'Stern Daughter of the Voice of God,' " in *Neighbors Taken for Granted: Canada and the United States*, ed. Livingston Merchant (New York: Praeger, 1966), 141.

80. Henry Kissinger, *Diplomacy* (New York: Simon & Schuster, 1994), 460.

81. Hans J. Morgenthau, *Politics among Nations* (New York: McGraw-Hill, 1993), 530.

82. Dean Acheson, *Present at the Creation: My Years in the State Department* (New York: W. W. Norton & Co., 1969), 284.

Chapter 3

1. Each NATO ambassador would have a deputy chief of mission, or secondary representative, to do the primary senior-level preparatory work for the ambassadors. National delegations were given offices near the NAC and the Private Office of the Secretary General to facilitate communication between representatives. National delegations varied in size proportionate to the country and their relative influence within NATO.

2. Acheson, *Present at the Creation*, 329.

3. See Walter LaFeber, "NATO and the Korean War: A Context," in Kaplan, ed., *American Historians*, 33–51; and Walter LaFeber, *America, Russia, and the Cold War, 1945–1971* (New York: John Wiley and Sons, 1972), 95–145.

4. *Foreign Relations of the United States*, 1949, 4:353–356.

5. Gregory Pedlow, "The Politics of NATO Command," in *U.S. Military Forces in Europe: The Early Years, 1945–1970*, ed. Simon W. Duke and Wolfgang Krieger (Boulder, CO: Westview Press, 1993), 18.

6. For an overview of the development of NATO's bureaucracy and the role of the secretary general see Robert S. Jordan, *The NATO International Staff/Secretariat, 1952–1957* (London: Oxford University Press, 1967); and Robert S. Jordan, *Political Leadership in NATO: A Study in Multilateral Diplomacy* (Boulder, CO: Westview Press, 1979).

7. "Text of Letter from President Eisenhower to General de Gaulle," 20 October 1958, in *The Atlantic Alliance: Jackson Subcommittee Hearings and Findings*, ed. Sen. Henry M. Jackson (New York: Praeger, 1967), 285–286.

8. The foreign ministers were Gaetano Martino, Halvard Lange, and Lester Pearson, respectively.

9. "Report of the Committee of Three on Non-Military Cooperation in NATO," NATO Information Service, December 1956.

10. Harlan Cleveland, who was US Ambassador to NATO in the mid-1960s, notes that consultation in NATO included: imparting information unilaterally; exchanging information bilaterally or multilaterally; notifying others of national decisions already taken, but without expecting any reaction on their part; notifying others of decisions already taken, in such a way as to build consent for them; consulting in advance on national actions that affect the interests of others; consulting internationally to ascer-

tain in advance the possible reaction to a national decision not yet made (that is, as an input to the national decision itself); consulting in advance on a matter lending itself to separate parallel national actions by others; and consulting for the purpose of arriving at a decision which by its nature must be taken or carried into action collectively. Harlan Cleveland, *The Transatlantic Bargain* (New York: Harper & Row, 1970), 19.

As another former NATO official, Roger Hill, has shown, the institutional network gave rise to a heavy flow of information exchange, advice-giving, decision-making, communications to capitals, formal meetings, informal gatherings, distribution of documents, translations, visits back and forth, report writing, and collective drafting. The headquarters machine, bureaucracies in capitals, and other parts of the network continuously process the tide of inflowing requests, initiatives, draft documents, and memoranda. Roger Hill, *Political Consultation in NATO* (Toronto: Canadian Institute of International Affairs, 1978), 74.

11. This overview of NATO's political and military processes is based on information available from NATO, including *NATO: Facts about the North Atlantic Treaty Organization*; *North Atlantic Treaty Organization: Facts and Figures*; and the *NATO Handbook* published by the NATO Press Service in Brussels. That information is supplemented by interviews with former and current NATO officials.

12. As one study has shown, by the end of the Cold War, formal and ad hoc NATO structures totaled over four hundred. Dan Smith, *Pressure: How America Runs NATO* (London: Bloomsbury Publishing, 1989), 10.

13. Jordan, *Political Leadership*, 127, 184.

14. Initially SHAPE was based outside of Paris. Since 1966, it has been located outside of Mons, Belgium.

15. This cycle was initially conducted as an annual review begun in 1951. It evolved into a triennial review in the 1960s and a biennial review by the 1980s.

16. "Allied Interdependence: Trade and Cooperation in Military Equipment," *Transatlantic Policy Panel Report*, Center for Strategic and International Studies Special Report 16 (May 1977), 7.

17. Robert R. James, *Standardization and Common Production of Weapons in NATO* (London: International Institute for Strategic Studies, 1967), 1–11.

18. E. Vandervater, Jr., *Coordinated Weapons Production in NATO: A Study of Alliance Process* (Santa Monica, CA: The RAND Corporation, 1967).

19. James R. Carlton, "NATO Standardization: An Organizational Analysis," in *NATO after Thirty Years*, ed. Lawrence S. Kaplan and Robert W. Clawson (Wilmington, DE: Scholarly Resources, 1981), 211.

20. See James A. Huston, *One for All: NATO Strategy and Logistics through the Formative Period, 1949–1969* (Newark, DE: University of Delaware Press, 1984), 157–183.

21. See Francis A. Beer, *Integration and Disintegration in NATO: Processes of Alliance Cohesion and Prospects for Atlantic Community* (Columbus: The Ohio State University Press, 1969).

22. Roger Hilsman, "On NATO Strategy," in *Alliance Policy in the Cold War*, ed. Arnold Wolfers (Baltimore, MD: The Johns Hopkins University Press, 1959), 152.

23. De Gaulle's actions were not universally welcomed in France. For example, in the National Assembly, former Premier René Pleven launched a strong attack on the

unilateral nature of the decision and the fact that France appeared to be weakening NATO without any concessions from—or weakening of—the Warsaw Pact. L. Radoux, *France and NATO* (Paris: Western European Union, 1967), 65–78.

24. Named after Belgian Foreign Minister Pierre Harmel who led the study.

25. "The Future Tasks of the Alliance (Harmel Report)," December 1967, NATO Office of Information and Press, Brussels.

26. "Future Tasks." The proposal for mutual and balanced force reductions (MBFR) signaled acceptance of a Warsaw Pact offer for negotiations the year before. NATO's formal activities were expanded via the creation of a Committee on the Challenges of Modern Society (CCMS). The committee was chartered to improve "the exchange of views and experience among the allied countries with the deliberate objective of stimulating actions on problems of the human environment by member governments."

27. Robert Hunter, *Security in Europe* (London: Eleks Books, 1969), 54.

28. Simon Lunn, *Burdensharing in NATO* (London: Royal Institution of International Affairs, 1983), 49. American newspaper editorials were even more dramatic in their assessments of the European effort. For example, the *Chicago Tribune* opined: "The heirs of Talleyrand, Bismarck and Disraeli (and of Petain, Hitler and Chamberlain) tell us that we don't know how to deal intelligently with the Soviet colossus. We are hamhanded, they say, unsubtle, and simpleminded. But look at the record. These paragons of diplomacy managed twice in this century to get Europe in such an unholy mess that the U.S. was called upon to rescue it at a vast cost in wealth and blood." Quoted in Simon Serfaty, "Atlantic Fantasies," in *The Atlantic Alliance and Its Critics*, ed. Robert W. Tucker and Linda Wrigley (New York: Praeger, 1983), 122.

29. Free-riding is a public choice dilemma for collective action. During the Cold War, collective defense became a public good—a benefit which, once provided, is utilized by all recipients whether they contribute to the costs of service provision or not. If one nation has a greater demand for a public good than others, it will place a higher valuation on its provision. Ultimately, that state provides a disproportionate level of the collective good, as the smaller members of an alliance tend to supply only suboptimal amounts. Moreover, a small country that views defense costs as a burden could withdraw from (or not contribute to) the military obligations of an alliance, knowing that the larger power and its remaining allies would still come to its defense if attacked. See Mancur Olson and Richard Zeckhauser, "An Economic Theory of Alliances," *The Review of Economics and Statistics* 47:3 (August 1966): 266–279; and Mancur Olson, *The Logic of Collective Action: Public Goods and the Theory of Groups* (Cambridge, MA: Harvard University Press, 1965).

30. The figures on European and American defense expenditures as a percentage of GNP were compiled from the International Institute for Strategic Studies, *The Military Balance* (London: Brassey's, 1960–93). There were disputes over the best way to measure burdensharing in NATO, including: the military plans that are set out by NATO members; the ability of a country to contribute to those plans; and a variety of economic factors such as relative growth in defense spending over time. Nevertheless, the relevant figures prompting political disputes over NATO burdensharing were drawn from comparisons of the percentage of GNP allocated to national defense. See James R. Golden, *The Dynamics of Change in NATO: A Burden-Sharing Perspective*

(New York: Praeger, 1983), 24–54; and Simon Duke, *The Burdensharing Debate: A Reassessment* (New York: St. Martin's Press, 1993), 124–150.

31. Leonard Sullivan Jr. and Jack A. LeCuyer, *Comprehensive Security and Western Prosperity* (Washington, DC: The Atlantic Council of the United States, 1988), 48.

32. "Requests from the Brussels Treaty Powers to the U.S. Government for Military Assistance," 5 April 1949, *Foreign Relations of the United States*, 1949, 4:285–287.

33. See Lawrence S. Kaplan, *A Community of Interests: NATO and the Military Assistance Program, 1948–1951* (Washington: Office of the Secretary of Defense, Historical Office, 1980).

34. Harry S. Truman, *Memoirs, Volume II: Years of Trial and Hope* (Garden City, NY: Doubleday, 1956), 253.

35. Kaplan, *The United States and NATO*, 45.

36. See Edward Fursdon, *The European Defence Community: A History* (New York: St. Martin's Press, 1980).

37. The signators of the EDC were France, Belgium, the German Federal Republic, Italy, Luxembourg, and the Netherlands. The US and Britain provided support via protocols (signed the same day) on mutual security guarantees between EDC and NATO members. Britain did not sign the EDC as it did not accept the supranational element of the accord.

38. *Foreign Relations of the United States*, 1952–1954, 5:711–712.

39. *Protocol Modifying and Completing the Brussels Treaty*, Paris, 23 October 1954.

40. After its creation, the WEU could claim only one major achievement—aiding in the settlement of the Saar lands in 1955, which further eased the historical tensions between France and Germany. See Alfred Cahen, *The Western European Union and NATO: Building a European Defence Identity within the Context of Atlantic Solidarity* (London: Brassey's, 1989), 4–5.

The European members did apply some elements of economic integration to security, primarily through the creation of the EUROGROUP in 1968. This was an inner–NATO caucus of European ministers of defense. The EUROGROUP received a degree of institutionalization (though without French participation), with high-level staffing from European defense ministries responsible for coordinating European activity in communication (EUROCOM), logistics (EUROLOG), and defense procurement (EURONAD) designed to enhance Europe's commitment to NATO. In the European Community, France participated in the Independent European Programme Group (IEPG), which included all of the EC member states (except Ireland), Turkey, and Norway. The Single European Act of 1984 gave the IEPG a goal of creating a European defense industry. See Trevor Taylor, *European Defence Cooperation* (London: Routledge & Kegan Paul, 1984), 17–27; and Jeffrey Harrop, *The Political Economy of Integration in the European Community* (Brookfield, VT: Gower Publishing, 1989), 10.

41. See Gregory Treverton, *The Dollar Drain and American Forces in Germany: Managing the Political Economics of Alliance* (Athens, OH: Ohio University Press, 1978).

42. United States Senate, "United States Troops in Europe: Hearings Before the Combined Subcommittee of Foreign Relations and Arms Services Committees on the Subject of United States Troops in Europe," 90th Cong., 1st Sess., 26 April and 3 May 1967.

43. Joan Hoff-Wilson, " 'Nixingerism,' NATO, and Détente," in *American Historians and the Atlantic Alliance*, ed. Lawrence S. Kaplan (Kent, OH: Kent State University Press, 1991), 99.

44. Mansfield continued his efforts with an amendment to the Selective Service Act of 1971 requiring that US force levels in Europe be reduced by 50 percent—to about 150,000 troops by the end of the year. The White House enlisted former SACEURs, plus former secretaries of state George Ball and Dean Acheson, and former president Lyndon Johnson to lobby against the amendment, which was defeated by a vote of 61–36. In 1973, the Senate approved a similar Mansfield Amendment by a vote of 49–46. Caught by surprise, the Nixon administration campaigned successfully against a bill put forward by Sen. Alan Cranston (which contained virtually the same language as the Mansfield Amendment), thus assuring Mansfield's procedural defeat.

Senators Sam Nunn and Henry Jackson continued the Mansfield tradition through an amendment to the Defense Department Authorization Act of 1974. This amendment stated that a failure of the European members to offset fully the costs of troops in Europe would result in automatic reductions in troop levels. Had the amendment passed, it would have required the president to reduce US forces in Europe on a percentage equal to the amount of the balance-of-payments deficit the European members of NATO failed to offset.

45. Lawrence S. Kaplan, "NATO: The Second Generation," in Kaplan and Clawson, *NATO after Thirty Years*, 7.

46. Defence Planning Committee Communiqué, 18 May 1977, NATO Office of Information and Press. The DPC recommendations became formal NATO policy at a Washington, D.C., heads of state NATO summit in May 1978.

47. Quoted in Lunn, *Burdensharing*, 17–18. The official, Robert Komer (special assistant for NATO affairs to the secretary of defense) noted that in reality the US had already included increases into its own planning for the time period covered by the LTDP and that the only countries that would have to increase their percent of GNP toward defense would be European members of NATO.

48. Duke, *The Burdensharing Debate*, 73.

49. Foreign Policy Research Institute, *The Three Percent Solution and the Future of NATO* (Philadelphia: Foreign Policy Research Institute, 1981), 29–30.

50. North Atlantic Treaty, Washington, D.C., 4 April 1949.

51. North Atlantic Treaty, Preamble.

52. Ferenc A. Vali, *The Turkish Straits and NATO* (Stanford, CA: Hoover Institution Press, 1972), 83.

53. S. Victor Papacosma, "Greece and NATO," in *NATO and the Mediterranean*, ed. Lawrence S. Kaplan, Robert W. Clawson, and Raimondo Luraghi (Wilmington, DE: Scholarly Resources, 1985), 192.

54. Several of the coup leaders had served with the Greek Central Intelligence Agency (KYP), which had close ties to the American CIA. Coup leader Papadopoulos had served as liaison between the two services. Theodore Couloumbis, *The United States, Greece, and Turkey: The Troubled Triangle* (New York: Praeger, 1983), 51.

55. D. George Kousloulas, "The Origins of the Greek Military Coup, April 1967," *Orbis* 8, no. 1 (Spring 1969): 332.

56. Though the US embargoed heavy weapons sales to Greece, Washington contin-

ued to be the largest supplier of weapons to Greece. In fact, there were more US military supplies transferred to Greece in 1967–70 than there had been in the three years before the coup. In 1972 Washington negotiated an "open-ended" homeport agreement for the stationing of US Naval forces in Greece (rescinded in 1974 after the junta fell). Both France and Germany also traded with and sold military equipment to Greece. Benjamin Cameron Sharp, *NATO and the Mediterranean, 1949–1979: Deterioration on the Southern Flank* (Ann Arbor: UMI, 1981), 102–103.

57. Robert Jordan and Werner Feld, *Europe in the Balance: The Changing Context of European International Politics* (London: Faber and Faber, 1986), 216.

58. For example, in 1967 he withdrew a Greek brigade from Cyprus rather than allow tensions there to fester—much to Washington's and NATO's pleasure.

59. Couloumbis, *The United States, Greece, and Turkey*, 101–102.

60. See Laurence Stern, *The Wrong Horse: The Politics of Intervention and the Failure of American Diplomacy* (New York: Times Books, 1977). Stern notes similarities between Kissinger's willingness to overlook principles in Greece to the approach taken by Metternich during the Greek uprising against the Ottoman Empire in 1821.

61. See Thanos Veremis, "Greece and NATO: Continuity and Change," in *NATO's Southern Allies: Internal and External Challenges*, ed. John Chipman (New York: Routledge, 1988), 269–270.

62. Steven Erlanger, "Turkish Prime Minister's Islamic Tour Worries U.S.," *New York Times*, 10 August 1996, 2(A).

63. Jordan, *Political Leadership*, 136.

64. Sharp, *NATO and the Mediterranean*, 85–86. UN peacekeepers were eventually deployed to the region.

65. The Johnson letter was published in the *Middle East Journal* (Summer 1966): 386–389.

66. The Turkish response added: "If NATO members should start discussing the right and wrong of the situation of their fellow-member victim of a Soviet aggression, whether this aggression was provoked or not and if the decision on whether they have an obligation to assist this member should be made to depend on the issue of such a discussion, the very foundations of the Alliance would be shaken and it would lose its meaning." Published in the *Middle East Journal* (Summer 1966): 389–393.

67. Jordan, *Political Leadership*, 136.

68. James Brown, *Delicately Poised Allies: Greece and Turkey* (London: Brassey's, 1991), 9.

69. Interviews with US and NATO officials in Brussels and Washington, D.C., February 1996.

70. Sean Kay and Judith Yaphe, "Turkey's International Affairs: Shaping the U.S.–Turkey Strategic Partnership," *Strategic Forum* 122 (July 1997): 4.

71. Joint press conference by US President Bill Clinton and Italian Prime Minister Romano Prodi, *White House Information Service*, 12 June 1996.

72. Brown, *Delicately Poised Allies*, 5.

73. "The United States High Commissioner for Germany (McCloy) to the Secretary of State," 25 April 1950, *Foreign Relations of the United States*, 1950, 4:634.

74. John A. Reed, *Germany and NATO* (Washington: National Defense University Press, 1987): 37, 43.

75. Modified Brussels Treaty, Protocol Number III: Paris, 23 October 1954.

76. Declaration by the Government of the Federal Republic of Germany, Paris, 23 October 1954.

77. Declaration by the Governments of the United States of America, the United Kingdom, and France, Paris, 23 October 1954.

78. Richard Kugler, *Commitment to Purpose: How Alliance Partnership Won the Cold War* (Santa Monica, CA: RAND Corporation, 1993), 66.

79. Joseph Joffe, *The Limited Partnership: Europe, the United States, and the Burdens of Alliance* (Cambridge, MA: Ballinger Publishing Company, 1987), 184.

80. Quoted in Michael R. Beschloss and Strobe Talbott, *At the Highest Levels: The Inside Story of the End of the Cold War* (Boston, MA: Little, Brown & Co., 1993), 185–186.

81. See Esther Barbe, *España y la Otan: La problematica europea en materia de seguridad* (Barcelona: Editorial Laia, 1981), 51–90.

82. Antonio Sanchez-Gijon, "On Spain, NATO and Democracy," in *Politics and Security in the Southern Region of the Atlantic Alliance*, ed. Douglas Stuart (Baltimore, MD: The Johns Hopkins University Press), 99.

83. Angel Vinas, "Spain and NATO: Internal Debate and External Challenges," in Chipman, *NATO's Southern Allies*, 153–154.

84. See Javier Perez Royo, "Repercussions on the Democratic Process of Spain's Entry into NATO," in *Spain's Entry into NATO: Conflicting Political and Strategic Perspectives*, ed. Frederico G. Gil and Joseph S. Tulchin (Boulder, CO: Lynne Rienner Publishers, 1988), 20–28; and Javier Ruperez, *España en la Otan: Relato Parcial* (Barcelona: Plaza and Janes, 1986), 141–187.

85. Sanchez-Gijon, "On Spain," 112. Spain signed a Treaty of Accession to the Treaty of Rome admitting it to the EC in June 1985 and became a full member of the EC in January 1986.

86. Vinas, "Spain and NATO," 183.

87. Gregory F. Treverton, "Spain, the United States, and NATO: Strategic Facts and Political Realities," in Gil and Tulchin, eds., *Spain's Entry into NATO*, 129–132.

Chapter 4

1. Manfred Wörner, "European Security: Political Will Plus Military Might," in Manfred Wörner, et al., *What Is European Security after the Cold War?* (Brussels: The Philip Morris Institute for Public Policy Research, 1993), 12.

2. London Declaration on a Transformed North Atlantic Alliance, July 1990, NATO Office of Information and Press.

3. London Declaration.

4. "The Alliance's Strategic Concept," agreed by the heads of state and government participating in the meeting of the North Atlantic Council in Rome on 7–8 November 1991, NATO Office of Information and Press. The communiqué also specified potential challenges arising from the Mediterranean region and nuclear proliferation.

5. The Alliance's Strategic Concept.

6. Interview with a senior NATO military planner, January 1992.

7. See "Transatlantic Relations and the Management of Disorder," *Report to the*

Netherlands Atlantic Commission (The Hague: Netherlands Atlantic Commission, 1993), 27.

8. For further discussion, see Sean Kay, "NATO and the CSCE: A Partnership for the Future," in *Paradigms* 7, no. 2 (Winter 1993): 59–77; and Sean Kay, "NATO and the CSCE: A New Russian Challenge," in *NATO in the Post-Cold War Era: Does It Have a Future?*, ed. S. Victor Papacosma and Mary Ann Heiss (New York: St. Martin's Press, 1995): 113–133.

9. Off-the-record comments of a senior NATO planner, April 1992. At the London NATO meeting, the members proposed that the CSCE endorse, inter alia: CSCE commitments to respect and uphold the rule of law; CSCE guidelines for enhancing economic cooperation, based on the development of free and competitive market economies; and CSCE cooperation on environmental protection. NATO also encouraged the CSCE to adopt a structure for regular consultations among member governments, to meet at the heads of state or ministerial level at least once a year; a schedule of CSCE review conferences once every two years; a small CSCE secretariat to coordinate meetings and conferences and serve as a data and information center; a CSCE mechanism to monitor elections in all the CSCE countries; a CSCE Center for the Prevention of Conflict; and a CSCE Parliamentary Assembly.

10. CSCE Charter for a New Europe. Available from the CSCE (OSCE) Secretariat in Prague, the Czech Republic.

11. *North Atlantic Council Communiqué*, Copenhagen, 6–7 June 1991, NATO Office of Information and Press.

12. The ministers also agreed to strengthen the Conflict Prevention Center by reinforcing and increasing its role in fact-finding missions, the monitoring of disputes, and implementation and verification of arms control agreements. The CSCE thus sent an observer mission to Nagorno-Karabakh. Other such missions undertaken since 1992 included fact-finding, rapporteur, and monitoring in Albania, Chechnya, Estonia, Georgia, Kosovo, Moldova, Sandjak, and Vojvodina.

13. *Helsinki Document 1992: The Challenges of Change*. Available from the CSCE Secretariat in Prague.

14. *Rome Declaration on Peace and Cooperation*, November 1991. NATO Office of Information and Press.

15. North Atlantic Treaty Organization, *NATO Handbook* (Brussels: NATO Office of Information and Press, 1995), 44–45.

16. Off-the-record comments of a senior NATO planner, April 1992.

17. *Report of the NACC Ad Hoc Committee on Peacekeeping*, June 1993, NATO Office of Information and Press.

18. S. Nelson Drew, *NATO from Berlin to Bosnia: Trans-Atlantic Security in Transition* (Washington: National Defense University, 1995), 25–26.

19. Reuters. 10 June 1994.

20. Interview with a senior NATO official, Brussels, June 1994.

21. A formal version of the RAND paper appeared in Ronald D. Asmus, Richard L. Kugler, and F. Stephen Larrabee, "Building a New NATO," *Foreign Affairs* 4 (September/October 1993): 28–40.

22. US Department of Defense, Office of International Security Affairs, *United States Security Strategy for Europe and NATO* (Washington, DC: Government Printing Office, June 1995).

23. The name Partnership for Peace grew out of discussion in SHAPE about giving the NACC a "Partnership for Peacekeeping" function. While the PFP was the result of considerable interagency review in Washington, the primary impetus came from the Joint Chiefs of Staff and the Office of the Secretary of Defense.

24. William Drozdiak, "NATO Balks at Opening Pact to E. Europe," *Washington Post*, 1 September 1993, 25(A).

25. *Comments to the Press by NATO Secretary General Manfred Wörner*, 21 October 1993, NATO Office of Information and Press.

26. Les Aspin, "Partnership for Peace: Remarks as Prepared for Delivery by Secretary of Defense Les Aspin to the Atlantic Council of the United States," J. W. Marriott Hotel, Washington, D.C., 3 December 1993.

27. Aspin, "Partnership for Peace." For further discussion of the objectives behind the PFP, see Joseph Kruzel, "Partnership for Peace and the Transformation of North Atlantic Security," in Papacosma and Heiss, *NATO in the Post–Cold War*, 339–346.

28. Interviews, Washington, D.C., August 1997.

29. The decision-making process behind NATO enlargement was a complex one, involving a number of complicated international, bureaucratic, and personal dynamics among key individuals. While the full description of the process will have to await the memoirs of those involved in the process and eventual publication of records as in the early NATO negotiations of the late 1940s, an initial description can be found in James Goldgeier, "NATO Enlargement: Anatomy of a Decision," *The Washington Quarterly* 21, no. 1 (Winter 1998): 85–102.

30. Senator Richard G. Lugar, "NATO's 'Near Abroad': New Membership, New Missions." Speech to The Atlantic Council of the United States on 9 December 1993.

31. "Partnership for Peace Invitation," issued by the heads of state and government participating in the meeting of the North Atlantic Council held at NATO Headquarters, Brussels, on 10–11 January 1994, NATO Office of Information and Press.

32. Partnership for Peace Invitation.

33. The actual Planning Cell is located near the Allied Command Europe headquarters outside the SHAPE compound.

34. Partnership for Peace Invitation.

35. Partnership for Peace Invitation.

36. Partnership for Peace Framework Document. NATO Office of Information and Press, January 1994.

37. Partnership for Peace Framework Document.

38. United Press International, 12 January 1994.

39. White House Information Service, 27 May 1994.

40. Institute for National Strategic Studies, *Strategic Assessment 1995: U.S. Security Challenges in Transition* (Washington, DC: National Defense University Press, 1995), 44. To compensate, NATO created a Political Military Steering Committee (PMSC), which links civilian oversight of PFP programs and their military implementation. Under the PMSC (chaired by the deputy secretary general of NATO) countries can send representatives from whichever ministry is most relevant to the issue being raised in the 16-plus-1 format or among a number of partners coordinating activities.

41. Jeffrey Simon, "Partnership for Peace: Guaranteeing Success," *Strategic Forum* 44 (September 1995): 3.

42. *USNATO Wireless File: Security Issues Digest* 1088:5 (June 1992).

43. Michael Evans, "UK Reluctant to Use Troops in Bosnia," *The Times* (London), 3 June 1992, 11.

44. *Oslo Summit: Final Communiqué*, NATO Office of Information and Press, 10 June 1992.

45. Robert Mauthner, "NATO Agrees to Peacekeeping Role in Europe," *Financial Times*, 5 June 1992, 4.

46. Meeting on the sidelines of the summit, NATO and WEU members did agree to begin joint naval patrol exercises in the Adriatic Sea to enforce the UN arms embargo against the former Yugoslav republics. This was, however, a largely symbolic action, as the major violations of the embargo were occurring over land.

47. Drew, *NATO from Berlin*, 9–10.

48. *Communiqué Issued by the Ministerial Meeting of the North Atlantic Council*, 17 December 1992. NATO Office of Information and Press.

49. Drew, *NATO from Berlin*, 12.

50. John Kriendler, "NATO's Changing Role: Opportunities and Constraints for Peacekeeping," *NATO Review* 41, no. 3 (June 1993): 15–22.

51. Michael R. Gordon, "U.S. Is Urging NATO to Prepare Force for Duty in Bosnia," *New York Times*, 11 March 1993, 1, 16(A).

52. *Radio Free Europe/Radio Liberty (RFE/RL) Daily Reports*, 1 December 1993.

53. *RFE/RL Daily Reports*, 30 November 1993.

54. See Suzanne Crow, "Why Has Russian Foreign Policy Changed?" *RFE/RL Daily Report*, 6 May 1994; and Sean Kay, *The Political Victory of the Russian Armed Forces: Assessing the Impact in the New Military Doctrine* (Brussels: NATO Office of Information and Press, NATODATA, 1994).

55. "CSCE and the New Europe: Our Security Is Indivisible," CSCE Ministerial Final Communiqué, November 1993, CSCE Secretariat, Prague.

56. Reuters, 25 May 1994.

57. Reuters, 10 June 1994.

58. Reuters, 10 June 1994.

59. Joint NATO–Russia Declaration, 22 June 1994, NATO Office of Information and Press.

60. Associated Press, 2 May 1994.

61. Reuters, 30 June 1995.

62. Reuters, 20 November 1996.

63. These three were the brain trust of US action, not only in Bosnia, but toward NATO as a whole. This was particularly true regarding the PFP (Kruzel) and the Combined Joint Task Forces (Drew) proposals of the January 1994 NATO summit.

64. *IFOR Fact Sheet*, June 1996, NATO Office of Information and Press.

65. George Joulwan, "SHAPE and IFOR: Adapting to the Needs of Tomorrow," *NATO Review* 2 (March 1996): 6–9.

66. The thirteen were Austria, the Czech Republic, Estonia, Finland, Hungary, Latvia, Lithuania, Poland, Romania, Russia, Slovakia, Sweden, and Ukraine.

67. *Final Communiqué of the North Atlantic Council in Ministerial Session Meeting in Berlin, Germany*, 3 June 1996, NATO Office of Information and Press.

68. Jeffrey Simon, "The IFOR/SFOR Experience: Lessons Learned by PFP Partners," *Strategic Forum* 120 (July 1997).

69. See Carl Bildt, "Implementing the Civilian Tasks of the Bosnian Peace Agreement," *NATO Review* 5 (1996): 3–6.

70. Christine Wallich, "Policy Forum: Bosnia—After the Troops Leave," *Washington Quarterly* 19, no. 3 (Summer 1996): 82–83.

71. *IFOR Fact Sheet: Civil-Military Cooperation*, NATO Office of Information and Press, June 1996.

72. *IFOR Fact Sheet*, 20 August 1996.

73. *Joint Press Conference of Secretary General and Supreme Allied Commander Europe at NATO Headquarters*, 18 March 1996, NATO Office of Information and Press.

74. Reuters, 14 August 1996.

75. *President Bill Clinton, Address to the Nation*, 27 November 1995, The White House, Office of the Press Secretary.

Chapter 5

1. *Atlantic News*, no. 2711 (20 April 1995).

2. Interview with a senior US military planner, Washington, D.C., November 1994.

3. Reuters, 9 September 1994.

4. Walter Slocomb, *Presentation to the Defense and Security Committee of the North Atlantic Assembly*, North Atlantic Assembly Annual Session Meeting, in Washington, D.C., November 1994.

5. Interview, US Department of State, November 1994.

6. *White House Information Service*, 1 December 1994.

7. The US also suggested enhancing some OSCE capabilities to include dialogue on nonproliferation, peacekeeping within the CIS, preventive mechanisms for addressing ethnic conflict, and economic development, and proposed involving the institution more directly in the resolution of long-term problems in the Balkans. However, actual implementation of these goals was left for further discussion.

8. John Borawski, "Partnership for Peace and Beyond," *International Affairs* 71, no. 2 (1995): 245.

9. Associated Press, 1 December 1994.

10. NATO Office of Information and Press, 1 December 1995.

11. White House Information Service, 5 December 1994.

12. Reuters, 5 December 1994.

13. Reuters, 5 December 1994.

14. Reuters, 6 December 1994.

15. Richard Holbrooke, "America, A European Power," *Foreign Affairs* 74, no. 2 (March/April 1995): 45–46.

16. Holbrooke, "America," 46.

17. Zbigniew Brzezinski, "A Plan for Europe," *Foreign Affairs* 74, no. 1 (January/February 1995): 26–42.

18. Holbrooke, "America," 51. Holbrooke suggested that such an arrangement would require negotiation over a broad range of issues including the pace of NATO expansion, the state of other Russian–NATO ties such as the PFP, the degree to which

the OSCE has been turned into a more useful organization, and the implications of events such as Russia's policy towards Chechnya.

19. R. Jeffrey Smith and Daniel Williams, "Russia Intends to Pursue Guarantees from NATO," *Washington Post*, 11 March 1995, 21(A).

20. Reuters, 13 March 1995. Vice President Gore was invoking the language of Russian Foreign Minister Kozyrev from June 1994, when Kozyrev agreed to sign the PFP while insisting on first negotiating a detailed cooperation program that would formalize a relationship based on what he called "no mutual vetoes or no surprises."

21. Reuters, 18 and 19 March 1995.

22. Reuters, 20 March 1995.

23. Reuters, 20 March 1995.

24. Associated Press, 23 March 1995.

25. Reuters, 3 April 1995. The Russian military had been pushing for a renegotiation of the Conventional Forces in Europe Treaty since early summer 1993. The NATO linkage may have simply offered the Russian armed forces an excuse to push their case.

26. Interfax, 3 April 1995, in *Open Media Research Institute (OMRI) Daily Digest*, 4 April 1995.

27. Nezavismaya Gazeta, 4 April 1995, in *OMRI Daily Digest*, 5 April 1995.

28. Reuters, 3 April 1995.

29. Associated Press, 5 April 1995.

30. Associated Press, 14 April 1995.

31. Reuters, 24 April 1995.

32. Associated Press, 26 April 1995.

33. Izvestia, 27 April 1995, in *OMRI Daily Digest*, 28 April 1995.

34. Michael Dobbs and R. Jeffrey Smith, "US Offers Assurances on NATO," *Washington Post*, 7 May 1995, 1(A).

35. Associated Press, 8 May 1995.

36. Reuters, 11 May 1995.

37. Reuters, 11 May 1995.

38. NATO Office of Information and Press, 31 May 1995.

39. Associated Press, 30 May 1995.

40. Reuters, 31 May 1995.

41. Strobe Talbott, "Why NATO Should Grow," *New York Review of Books* XLII, no. 13 (10 August 1995): 27–30.

42. Talbott, "Why NATO Should Grow," 28.

43. *Study on NATO Enlargement*, NATO Office of Information and Press, September 1996, 2.

44. *Study on NATO Enlargement*, 2. New members would be expected to conform to basic principles embodied in the Washington Treaty: democracy, individual liberty and the rule of law; to accept NATO as a community of like-minded nations joined together for collective defense and the preservation of peace and security, with each nation contributing to the security and defense from which all member nations benefit; to be firmly committed to principles, objectives, and undertakings included in the Partnership for Peace framework document; to commit themselves to good faith efforts to build consensus within the alliance on all issues, since consensus is the basis of alli-

ance cohesion and decision-making; to undertake to participate fully in the alliance consultation and decision-making process on political and security issues of concern to the alliance; to establish a permanent representation at NATO Headquarters; to establish an appropriate national military representation at SHAPE/SACLANT; to be prepared to nominate qualified candidates to serve on the International Staff and in NATO agencies; to provide qualified personnel to serve on the International Military Staff and in the Integrated Military Structure if and as appropriate; to contribute to alliance budgets, based on budget shares to be agreed; to participate, as appropriate, in the exchange of allied intelligence, which would be based entirely on national contributions; to apply NATO security rules and procedures; and to accept the documents that provide the basis for the existing policies of the alliance, *Study on NATO Enlargement*, 24–25.

45. *Study on NATO Enlargement*, 9.

46. *Study on NATO Enlargement*, 9–10.

47. Reuters, 28 September 1995.

48. "NATO Seen Slowing Down Enlargement Process," *Der Spiegel*, 21 August 1995.

49. Interview with a senior European defense official, Washington, D.C., October 1995.

50. Interview with a senior US official, Washington, D.C., March 1996. According to NATO officials there was still some debate at this time as to whether or not Hungary should be invited to join.

51. Warren Christopher, *A Democratic and Undivided Europe in Our Time*, speech presented at Cernin Palace, Prague, 20 March 1996, US Department of State, Office of the Spokesman.

52. *Thesis of the Council for Foreign and Defense Policy*, May 1995.

53. Comments of Kohl and Perry at the annual *Wehrkünde* meeting of defense specialists, Munich, Germany, February 1996.

54. Michael Dobbs, "Enthusiasm for Wider Alliance Is Marked by Contradictions," *Washington Post*, 7 July 1995, 1, 6(A).

55. J. F. O. McAllister, "If you buy that, we know a bridge in Brooklyn," *Time* 150 (21 July 1997): 16.

56. Henry Kissinger, "The Dilution of NATO," *Washington Post*, June 8, 1997, 9(C).

57. The following overview of the analytical cases for and against NATO enlargement is not intended to be exhaustive. Many important figures have commented authoritatively on NATO enlargement and it would be impossible to address each one here. Instead, this section seeks to illustrate the main arguments with examples from the debates.

58. John Lewis Gaddis, "What History Teaches about Grand Strategy," speech delivered at the National Defense University, Washington, D.C., 7 October 1997.

59. Interview with a high level State Department official, April 1996.

60. Reuters, 28 June 1995.

61. Peter Rodman, "4 More for NATO," *Washington Post*, 31 December 1994. Rodman suggests that the question is "whether the West is prepared to consolidate the new status quo that emerged in Central Europe in 1989, the present reality that the

Central European and Baltic democracies are free and independent sovereign states that have opted to associate with the West." Peter Rodman, "Understanding with Moscow," *Washington Post*, 16 January 1996, 9(A).

62. Kissinger, *Diplomacy* (New York: Touchstone, 1993), 823–825.

63. Zbigniew Brzezinski, "A Plan for Europe."

64. William Safire, "Strategic Dilemma," *New York Times*, 1 December 1994, 32(A).

65. Jonathan Eyal, "Beware of Russians Bearing NATO Gifts," *Wall Street Journal Europe*, 19–20 April 1996, 6(A).

66. Conor Cruise O'Brien, "The Future of 'the West,' " *The National Interest* 30 (Winter 1992/1993): 9.

67. Henry Kissinger, "Expand NATO Now," *Washington Post*, 19 December 1994, 27(A).

68. Stephen Pelz, "The Case for Limiting NATO Enlargement," *National Security Studies Quarterly* 3, no. 3 (Summer 1997): 59–72.

69. Karsten Voigt, "NATO Enlargement: Sustaining the Momentum," *NATO Review* 2 (1996): 15–19.

70. Off-the-record comments by a senior German official, Washington, D.C., February 1996.

71. For discussion of why states might behave in this manner, see Randall L. Schweller, "Bandwagoning for Profit: Bringing the Revisionist State Back In," *International Security* 19 (Summer 1994): 79.

72. Joshua B. Spero and Frank Umbach, "NATO's Security Challenge to the East and the American–German Geo-Strategic Partnership in Europe," *Bericht des BIOst NR* 39 (1994): 16–17.

73. Michael Brown, "NATO Expansion: Wait and See," *Washington Post*, 26 December 1994, 29(A). Also see Michael E. Brown, "The Flawed Logic of NATO Expansion," *Survival* 37, no. 1 (Spring 1995): 34–48.

74. See Michael Mandelbaum, *The Dawn of Peace in Europe* (New York: The Twentieth Century Fund, 1996).

75. Michael Mandelbaum, "Preserving the Peace: The Case against NATO Expansion," *Foreign Affairs* 74, no. 3 (May 1995): 9–13.

76. Mandelbaum, "Preserving the Peace," 10. Actually, NATO is expanding to Russia's border in Kaliningrad. However, in this theoretical case, NATO would enlarge to up to the Russia-Ukrainian or Baltic-Russian borders.

77. Richard K. Betts, in *Coping with Complexity in the International System*, ed. Jack Snyder and Robert Jarvis (Boulder, CO: Lynne Rienner Publishers, 1995), 278.

78. George Kennan, *At Century's Ending: Reflections, 1982–1995* (New York: W. W. Norton & Co., 1996), 330.

79. Philip Zelikow, "The Masque of Institutions," *Survival* 38, no. 1 (Spring 1996): 14.

80. Zelikow, "The Masque," 15.

81. Owen Harries, "The Collapse of the West," *Foreign Affairs* 72, no. 4 (September/October 1993): 41–53.

82. Fred Iklé, "How to Ruin NATO," *New York Times*, 11 January 1995, 21(A).

83. Fred C. Iklé and Sergei A. Karagonov, *Harmonizing the Evolution of US and*

Russian Defense Policies (Washington, DC: Center for Strategic and International Studies, 1993). Members of the study group included Alexei Arbatov, Gen. John R. Galvin, Catherine Kelleher, Benjamin S. Lambeth, Gen. Edward Meyer, Nikolai V. Mikhailov, Serge Rogov, John D. Steinbruner, Dmitri Trenin, and Paul D. Wolfowitz.

84. See Charles L. Glaser, "Why NATO is Still Best: Future Security Arrangements for Europe," *International Security* 18, no. 1 (Summer 1993): 18.

85. Sam Nunn, *The Future of NATO in an Uncertain World*, speech to the SACLANT Seminar 95, 22 June 1995, Norfolk, VA.

86. Javier Solana, *Speech by the Secretary General at the North Atlantic Assembly Meeting*, Athens, 20 May 1996, NATO Office of Information and Press.

87. William E. Odom, "NATO's Expansion: Why the Critics Are Wrong," *National Interest* 39 (Spring 1995): 45.

88. Asmus, Kugler, and Larrabee, "Building a New NATO," 30.

89. Jamie P. Shea, "Enlarging NATO Eastward?" in *European Security and International Institutions after the Cold War*, ed. Marco Carnovale (New York: St. Martin's Press, 1995), 86.

90. Shea, "Enlarging," 87.

91. Shea, "Enlarging," 88.

92. Shea, "Enlarging," 94–95.

93. Ron Asmus, "NATO Enlargement: An Alliance Strategy for the Baltic States," January 1996.

94. Asmus, "NATO Enlargement," 13. Asmus maintained that of the three Baltic countries, Estonia is the most qualified for EU membership.

95. Jeffrey Simon, *Central European Civil-Military Relations and NATO Expansion* (Washington, DC: National Defense University Press, 1995); and Jeffrey Simon, *NATO Enlargement and Central Europe: A Study in Civil-Military Relations* (Washington, DC: National Defense University Press, 1996).

96. Adrian Karatnycky, "Open Up the Club," *Washington Post*, 7 July 1995, 21(A).

97. See Bruce Russett, *Grasping the Democratic Peace: Principles for a Post–Cold War World* (Princeton: Princeton University Press, 1993); Bruce Russett, "Can a Democratic Peace Be Built?" *International Interactions* 18, no. 3 (Spring 1993): 277–282; and Kim Edward Spiezio, *Beyond Containment: Reconstructing European Security* (Boulder, CO: Lynne Reinner Publishers, 1995).

98. Harlan Cleveland, *Birth of a New World: An Open Moment for International Leadership* (San Francisco: Jossey-Bass Publishers, 1993), 204–220.

99. Allen G. Sens, "Saying Yes to Expansion: The Future of NATO and Canadian Interests in a Changing Alliance," *International Journal* L (Autumn 1995): 684.

100. "Moving Forward from NATO's 'Study on NATO Enlargement,'" the Committee on Eastern Europe and Russia in NATO, November 1995.

101. Reuters, 28 August 1996.

102. See Hans Binnendijk and Sean Kay, "Measuring NATO's Outreach," *Washington Times*, 21 August 1997, 21(A).

103. See Lawrence S. Kaplan, "NATO Enlargement: Historical Aspects," in *NATO Enlargement: Opinions and Options*, ed. Jeffrey Simon (Washington: National Defense University, 1995), 21–42; and Condalezza Rice, "Now, NATO Should Grow," *New York Times*, 8 July 1996, 23(A).

104. Senate Foreign Relations Subcommittee on Europe, *Testimony of Former Deputy Undersecretary of State Arnold Horelick*, 25 April 1995.
105. Senate Foreign Relations Subcommittee on Europe, *Testimony of Horelick*, 25 April 1995.
106. Charles A. Kupchan, "Expand NATO—and Split Europe," *New York Times*, 27 November 1994, 11(E).
107. Charles A. Kupchan, "A More Perfect Atlantic Union," *Washington Post*, 18 April 1996, 25(A); and Charles A. Kupchan, "Reviving the West: For an Atlantic Union," *Foreign Affairs* 75, no. 3 (May/June 1996): 92–104.
108. Kupchan, "A More Perfect," 25(A).
109. Rick Atkinson and John Pomfret, "East Looks to NATO to Forge Links to West," *Washington Post*, 27 November 1994, 1, 16(A).
110. Jeff Gerth and Tim Weiner, "Arms Makers See a Bonanza in Selling NATO Expansion," *New York Times*, 29 June 1997, 1, 4(A).
111. See Jeffrey Simon and Hans Binnendijk, "Romania and NATO: Membership Reassessment at the July 1997 Summit," *Strategic Forum* 101 (February 1997).
112. Carla Anne Robbins, "Devil Is in Details of NATO Expansion: Cost Questions Cloud Plans to Add Three New Members," *Wall Street Journal*, 9 August, 1996.
113. See Sean Kay, "Budapest Needs to Get Serious about NATO," *Wall Street Journal Europe*, 6 October 1997, 11(A).
114. Brooks Tigner, "New NATO Cost Rift Threatens to Erode Support," *Defense News*, June 1997.
115. United Press International, 23 October 1997.
116. For a moderate example of Helms's views of international institutions, see Jesse Helms, "Saving the U.N.," *Foreign Affairs* 75, no. 5 (September/October 1996): 2–7.
117. John E. Reilly, "The Public Mood at Mid-Decade," *Foreign Policy* 98 (Spring 1995): 89.
118. "Americans Overwhelmingly Favor NATO Expansion, Poll Says." Associated Press, 7 October 1997.
119. United Press International, 30 March 1998.
120. "German Public Endorsement of NATO Enlargement Declines Sharply," *USIA Opinion Analysis*, April 1997, M-55–97.
121. A point made effectively by Michael Mandelbaum.
122. Reuters, 14 May 1996.
123. Nezavisimaya Gazeta, 11 April 1996, in *OMRI Daily Digest*, 12 April 1996.
124. For further discussion see Chris Layne, "Why Die for Gdansk? The Case Against NATO Enlargement." Paper Presented to a CATO Institute Conference, NATO Enlargement; Illusions and Reality, June 25, 1997.
125. Michael Dobbs, "Wider Alliance Would Increase U.S. Commitments," *Washington Post*, 8 July 1995, 1(A).
126. *OMRI Daily Digest*, 28 April 1995.

Chapter 6

1. See United Kingdom, Ministry of Defence, *Statement of the Defence Estimates 1994* (London: Ministry of Defence, 1994); French Ministry of Defence, *Livre Blanc sur la Défence* (Paris: France, Ministry of Defence, 1994); and Federal Ministry of Defence, *White Paper on the Security of the Federal Republic of Germany and the Situation and Future of the Bundeswehr* (Bonn: Federal Ministry of Defence, 1994).

2. Under President Bush, the US promised to retain some 150,000 US troops in Europe or available to the European theater. However, some proposals popular in the US Congress suggested 25,000 troops would suffice, while others counseled 50,000 to 70,000. For discussion of US force levels in Europe see Colin L. Powell, "The American Commitment to European Security," *Survival* 34:2 (Summer 1992): 1; and Don M. Snider, "US Military Forces in Europe: How Low Can We Go?" *Survival* 34, no. 4 (Winter 1992–1993): 24–39. Snider maintains that a militarily significant force would have to include 75,000 US ground forces. The Clinton Administration has settled on the figure of 95,000.

3. Based on interviews, Washington, D.C., March 1996.

4. Daniel Williams and John M. Goshko, "Reduced US World Role Outlined but Soon Altered," *Washington Post*, 26 May 1993, 1(A). The official was widely recognized to be Undersecretary of State for Political Affairs Peter Tarnoff.

5. Stanley R. Sloan, "Transatlantic Relations in the Wake of the Brussels Summit," *NATO Review* 42, no. 2 (April 1994): 27–31.

6. Les Aspin, Secretary of Defense, *Annual Report to the President and the Congress* (Washington: Department of Defense, 1994), 9.

7. William Drozdiak, "US and Europe in Serious Rift over Bosnia War," *Washington Post*, 27 November 1994, 1(A).

8. Quoted in Charles Krupnick, "Not What They Wanted: American Policy and the European Security and Defense Identity," in *Disconcerted Europe*, ed. Alexander Moens and Christoph Antsis (Boulder, CO: Westview Press, 1995), 130.

9. *Rome Declaration of Peace and Cooperation*, 7–8 November 1991, NATO Office of Information and Press.

10. Interviews with NATO political and military planners, March 1992.

11. The Gulf War borrowed heavily from NATO assets and command and control—including arrangements made for British and French forces under US command. Nonetheless, the European allies were reluctant to grant political credit to NATO for aiding the mobilization and operation of forces in the gulf while seeking to promote the WEU—even though the latter did very little.

12. *Agence Europe*, no. 5388 (10–11 December 1990): 3–4.

13. Catherine M. Kelleher, *The Future of European Security* (Washington: The Brookings Institution, 1995): 56–57.

14. *Maastricht Treaty on European Union*, J.4.1. The treaty entered into force in November 1993 after receiving approval from the twelve member state parliaments.

15. *Treaty on European Union*, Article J.4.2.

16. *Declaration on the Role of the Western European Union and Its Relations with the European Union and with the Atlantic Alliance*, Maastricht, the Netherlands, 10 December 1991.

17. The origins of Franco-German security cooperation lie in the Elysée Treaty of 1963, which outlined broad political and defense cooperation. In 1987 France and Germany created a joint brigade of 4,000 troops. In 1988 they established a joint Defense and Security Council to oversee the brigade and identify other areas for cooperation—including sharing information on nuclear issues.

18. William Drozdiak, "France, Germany Unveil Corps as Step toward European Defense," *Washington Post*, 23 May 1992, 15(A).

19. Robert J. Art, "Why Western Europe Needs the United States and NATO," *Political Science Quarterly* 111, no. 1 (Spring 1996): 29.

20. Peter Schmidt, "ESDI: A German Analysis," in *Reforging the Trans-Atlantic Relationship*, ed. Charles Barry (Washington: National Defense University Press, 1996), 42. Shortly after activation, the Eurocorps began limited exercises, including training maneuvers in the French and Belgian Ardennes. Additionally, the Eurocorps and WEU conducted a joint exercise called Crisex, dealing with decision-making procedures, command and control, and eventual deployment of forces. Crisex took place in Brussels, in Metz, and on the Canary Islands for the three respective elements of the exercise. European Information Service, European Report, "Defense/Security: From Bit Player to Major Actor for WEU," 11 November 1995.

To complement the Eurocorps, France, Italy, Spain, and Portugal have organized a land force (EUROFOR) and a maritime force (EUROMARFOR).

21. Beyond the corps, France and Germany were pursuing further military cooperation including: regular meetings of ministerial working and expert groups, the purpose of which is to further develop common projects; an exchange of officers, including between staffs; intensification of leadership and language training by means of officer and officer candidate exchanges; cooperation in training and exercising, for instance by temporarily establishing Franco-German exercise naval forces; use and development of training facilities, for instance, the combined Army Aviation training center in Rennes, France; conduct of analyses and studies, for instance, in the field of air defense; promotion of friendly ties by way of over sixty affiliations; and furnishing of mutual support in humanitarian operations, for instance, in the operations in Cambodia and Somalia, doing so at the conceptual level by elaborating common airlift plans for providing humanitarian aid and by devising a common medical training concept for humanitarian operations. Federal Ministry of Defence, *White Paper*, 60.

22. Western European Union Council of Ministers, *Petersberg Declaration*, Bonn, 19 June 1992. In accordance with these objectives, the WEU created a planning cell in Brussels as part of its WEU international secretariat (which was moved from London to Brussels). The cell was activated in October 1992, consisting of a forty-member coordinating group of military officials tasked to prepare contingency plans for the employment of forces under WEU auspices; prepare recommendations for the necessary command, control, and communication arrangements, including standing operating procedures for headquarters that might be selected; and keep an updated list of units and combinations of units which might be allocated to the WEU for specific operations.

23. Address by Andrei Kozyrev, minister of foreign affairs of Russia, to the WEU Parliamentary Assembly, Paris, 1 December 1994.

24. WEU Press Release, 11 November 1994. To compensate for this technological weakness, a WEU Satellite Center was inaugurated at Torrejon, Spain on 28 April 1993. The center receives its instructions from the WEU permanent council and is responsible for intelligence gathering, the verification of arms control agreements, monitoring crises affecting European security, and monitoring environmental hazards. The Torrejon project became a priority for France, which hoped to give the WEU advance-warning supervision of disarmament treaties, collection of strategic and wartime intelligence data, navigational assistance, electronic warfare capabilities, and so

forth. France and Germany have also begun a joint project to develop a new line of military spy satellites; in July 1996 Italy joined the project. The program was well funded at $2.1 billion and is thus a priority for the EU.

25. On the record interview with Sir Hugh Dudley Smith, President of the WEU Assembly, Washington, DC, 18 November 1994.

26. Claude Carlier, "NATO and the European Union," in Papacosma and Heiss, *NATO in the Post–Cold War*, 145.

27. Morton B. Berman, et al., *The Independent European Force: Costs of Independence* (Santa Monica, CA: The RAND Corporation, 1993).

28. A major initiative under this framework has been a feasibility study for a Future Large Aircraft, begun in 1993. Additionally, an industrial consortium (EUROFLAG) has been established within the EU to conduct other feasibility studies for joint projects.

29. NATO Office of Information and Press, *NATO Handbook* (Brussels: North Atlantic Treaty Organization, 1995), 358.

30. Willy Claes, *Address to the Fortieth Annual Session of the North Atlantic Assembly*, Washington, DC, 18 November 1994.

31. Lecture by Volker Rühe at the Johns Hopkins School for Advanced International Studies, "The New NATO," *German Information Center: Statements and Speeches* XIX, no. 7 (30 April 1996): 3.

32. Charles Barry, "NATO's Combined Joint Task Forces in Theory and Practice," *Survival* 38, no. 1 (Spring 1996): 84.

33. *Press Briefing by Secretary of the Treasury Lloyd Bentsen, Secretary of State Warren Christopher, and Secretary of Defense Les Aspin*, The White House, Office of the Press Secretary, 7 January 1994.

34. *Remarks by the President to the North Atlantic Council Summit*, The White House, Office of the Press Secretary, 10 January 1994.

35. *Declaration of the Heads of State and Government Participating in the Meeting of the North Atlantic Council Held at NATO Headquarters*, 10–11 January 1994, NATO Office of Information and Press.

36. Charles Barry, "ESDI: Toward a Bi-Polar Alliance?" in Barry, *Reforging the Trans-Atlantic*, 77.

37. Stanley R. Sloan, "Combined Joint Task Forces (CJTF) and New Missions for NATO," *CRS Report for Congress* 94–249 S (17 March 1994): 2–3.

38. See Sean Kay, "Common Defence, Common Burden," *European Brief* 2, no. 3 (December 1994): 13–15.

39. On the record interview with Simon Lunn, deputy secretary general of the North Atlantic Assembly, Washington, DC, 18 November 1994.

40. Barry, "ESDI," 77.

41. Interview, Washington, DC, November 1994.

42. This internal NATO military adaptation would have included regional coordination of NATO commands with specific tasks including transportation; command, control, communications and intelligence; and logistics. Additionally, SACLANT proposed development of a common simulation and training system to help NATO militaries coordinate high technology warfare.

43. Theresa Hitchens and Robert Holzer, "Commanders: Reform NATO to Address New Missions," *Defense News* (26 June): 4, 50.

44. Raphael Estrella, "The Reformation of NATO," *Draft General Report of the North Atlantic Assembly Defence and Security Committee*, DSC (96) 2 (May 1996).

45. Daniel W. Christman, "NATO's Military Future," *Joint Forces Quarterly* (Spring 1996): 79.

46. Reuters, 29 February 1996.

47. Reuters, 29 February 1996.

48. Reuters, 7 May 1996.

49. Reuters, 12 March 1996.

50. Paris also dropped a request for a form of CJTF to be organized around NATO headquarters, where France had assigned officers, and another based on national commands. See "Way Is Cleared for Joint European Forces," *Jane's Defence Weekly*, 27 March 1996.

51. Craig R. Whitney, "NATO Looks to Peacekeeping by Europeans on Their Own," *New York Times*, 3 March 1996, 6(A).

52. Within the International Military Staff, a "Capabilities Coordination Cell" would be established to aid the Military Committee in providing planning guidance to the Major NATO Commander and aid the Military Committee providing advice to the NAC.

53. Barry, "NATO's Combined," 86.

54. *Ministerial Meeting of the North Atlantic Council*, Berlin, 3 June 1996, NATO Office of Information and Press.

55. According to the final communiqué this would be based on: identification, within the alliance, of the types of separable but not separate capabilities, assets, and support assets, as well as, in order to prepare for WEU-led operations, separable but not separate, headquarters, separate joint quarters elements, and command positions that would be required to command and conduct WEU-led operations and which could be made available, subject to decision by the NAC; and elaboration of appropriate multinational European command arrangements within NATO, consistent with and taking full advantage of the CJTF concept, able to prepare, support, command, and conduct the WEU-led operations. This implies double-hatting appropriate personnel within the NATO command structure to perform these functions. Such European command arrangements should be identifiable and the arrangements should be sufficiently well articulated to permit the rapid constitution of a militarily coherent and effective operational force.

56. *Ministerial Meeting of the North Atlantic Council*, Berlin. Such planning would, at a minimum: prepare relevant information on objectives, scope, and participation for illustrative WEU missions; identify requirements for planning and exercising of command elements and forces for illustrative WEU-led operations; and develop appropriate plans for submission through the Military Committee and NAC to the WEU for review and approval.

57. The Berlin communiqué also expressed satisfaction with the growing ties between NATO and the WEU. The ministers endorsed the completion of a new agreement between NATO and the WEU on security measures for the protection of shared classified information and expressed a desire to build on consultative mechanisms based on joint NATO–WEU Council meetings and those between the WEU Permanent Council and SACEUR.

58. Anthony Cragg, NATO assistant secretary general for defense planning, "The Combined Joint Task Force Concept: A Key Component of the Alliance's Adaptation," *NATO Review* 44, no. 4 (July 1996): 7–10.

59. Barry, "NATO's Combined," 82–83.

60. See "Allocution de Monsieur Charles Millon, ministre de la défence, le 19 decembre 1995, lors du colloque organisé par la fondation pour les études de défence," *Défense Nationale* (April 1996): 12–13; and Charles Millon, "Vers une défense nouvelle," *Défense Nationale* (14 July 1996): 13–19.

61. Robert P. Grant, "France's New Relationship with NATO," *Survival* 38, no. 1 (Spring 1996): 65.

62. Charles Miller, "France, U.K. Strike Defense Pact," *Defense News* 15 (6–12 November 1995): 4.

63. *News From France* (8 December 1995): 3.

64. See *News From France* (3 May 1996): 4; and Mariano Aguirre, "L'OTAN au service de quelle sécurité," *Le Monde Diplomatique*, April 1996.

65. Roger Cohen, "France to Rejoin Military Command of NATO Alliance," *New York Times*, 6 December 1995, 1(A).

66. Address to a Joint Session of Congress by French President Jacques Chirac, 1 February 1996.

67. Estrella, "The Reformation of NATO," 10.

68. *OECD Economic Outlook*, June 1996.

69. See Arthur Paecht, "La défense: Le temps des choix," *Défense Nationale* (February 1996): 7–16.

70. *The Economist*, 2 March 1996, 45.

71. See Craig R. Whitney, "Cold War Over, France Plans a Slim, Volunteer Military," *New York Times*, 23 February 1996, 3(A); and *The Economist*, 2 March 1996, 45–46. Restructuring the armed forces also stemmed from the difficulty Paris had in putting together a rapid deployment force during the Persian Gulf conflict. As the conservative parliamentarian and defense expert Pierre La Lellouche told the *New York Times*, 23 February, "We had to beg, borrow and steal from 47 separate regiments to put together a 15,000-man intervention force during the war in the Persian Gulf. At the same time, the British army, which is less than half the size of the French Army now, managed to deploy more than 30,000 soldiers to the same theater of operations."

Movement toward such national rapidly deployable forces has become common practice in national military planning with Germany, developing a crisis reaction force of 55,000 deployable in 1999. On 1 August 1996, Britain announced the formation of a new Joint Rapid Deployment Force (JRDF), to be drawn from the army, navy, marines, and air force. The British force will have some units on twenty-four-hour standby and quickly deployable at a reinforced brigade strength of 6,000 to 8,000 troops.

72. Interviews, April 1998.

73. Off-the-record comments of a high level European official addressing the Annual Meeting of the Society of Civil Defense Courses, Helsinki, Finland, 6 May 1996.

74. Drew, *NATO from Berlin*, 11.

75. For example see Charles Barry, *Reforging the Trans-Atlantic Relationship*; Stanley Sloan, "Negotiating a new Transatlantic Bargain," *NATO Review* 2 (March 1996): 19–23; and Simon Serfarty, *Stay the Course: European Unity and Atlantic Solidarity* (Washington: Center for Strategic and International Studies, 1997).

Chapter 7

1. William Drozdiak, "Ex-Antagonist Leading Alliance to New Century," *Washington Post*, 6 July 1997.

2. Reuters, 17 December 1997.

3. This data is from the Institute for National Strategic Studies, *Strategic Assessment 1995: U.S. Security Challenges in Transition* (Washington, DC: National Defense University Press, 1995), 42; and Norbert Wieczorek (Federal Republic of Germany), "Europe and North America: Partners and Competitors," *Draft General Report, The North Atlantic Assembly Economic Committee* EC (96) 7 (May 1996).

4. Remarks by the President to the Nixon Center for Peace and Freedom Policy Conference, The Mayflower Hotel, Washington, DC, 1 March 1995.

5. Reuters, 18 June 1996.

6. William Drozdiak, "NATO Finds an Expansive Sense of Purpose," *Washington Post*, 6 July 1997, 1, 19(A).

7. William Drozdiak, "European Allies Balk at Expanded Role for NATO, *Washington Post*, 22 February 1998, 27(A).

Selected Bibliography

Acheson, Dean. *Present at the Creation: My Years in the State Department*. New York: W. W. Norton & Co., 1969.

Baldwin, David, ed. *Neorealism and Neoliberalism: The Contemporary Debate*. New York: Columbia University Press, 1993.

Barry, Charles, ed. *Reforging the Trans-Atlantic Relationship*. Washington, DC: National Defense University Press, 1996.

Beer, Francis. *Integration and Disintegration in NATO: Processes of Alliance Cohesion and Prospects for Atlantic Community*. Columbus: The Ohio State University Press, 1969.

Beschloss, Michael R., and Strobe Talbott. *At the Highest Levels: The Inside Story of the End of the Cold War*. Boston: Little, Brown and Company, 1993.

Bohlen, Charles E. *Transformation of American Foreign Policy*. New York: W. W. Norton & Co., 1969.

Brown, Michael, Sean Lynn-Jones, and Steven Miller, eds. *The Perils of Anarchy: Contemporary Realism and International Security*. Cambridge: MIT Press, 1995.

Buchan, Alistair. *NATO in the 1960's: The Implications of Interdependence*. New York: Praeger, 1963.

Calleo, David. *The Imperious Economy*. Cambridge: Harvard University Press, 1982.

Carr, E.H. *The Twenty Years Crisis, 1919–1939*. London: Macmillan Press, 1940.

Carter, Ashton B., William J. Perry, and John D. Steinbruner. *A New Concept of Cooperative Security in the 21st Century*. Washington, DC: The Brookings Institution, 1994.

Chernoff, Fred. *After Bipolarity: The Vanishing Threat, Theories of Cooperation, and the Future of the Atlantic Alliance*. Ann Arbor: The University of Michigan Press, 1995.

Claude, Inis L. *Swords into Plowshares: The Problems and Progress of International Organization*, 4th ed. New York: Random House, 1984.

Cook, Don. *Forging the Alliance: NATO, 1945–1950*. London: Secher and Warburg, 1989.

Couloumbis, Theodore. *The United States, Greece, and Turkey: The Troubled Triangle*. New York: Praeger, 1983.

Crawford, Beverly, ed. *The Future of European Security*. Berkeley: University of California, 1992.

Deutsch, Karl, et al. *Political Community in the North Atlantic Area.* Princeton, NJ: Princeton University Press, 1957.

Downs, George, ed. *Collective Security after the Cold War.* Ann Arbor: University of Michigan Press, 1994.

Drew, S. Nelson. *NATO from Berlin to Bosnia: Trans-Atlantic Security in Transition.* Washington: National Defense University Press, 1995.

Duffield, John. *Power Rules: The Evolution of NATO's Conventional Force Posture.* Stanford: Stanford University Press, 1995.

Duke, Simon. *The Burdensharing Debate: A Reassessment.* New York: St. Martin's Press, 1994.

Fursdon, Edward. *The European Defence Community: A History.* New York: St. Martin's Press, 1980.

Gaddis, John Lewis. *The Long Peace: Inquiries into the History of the Cold War.* New York: Oxford University Press, 1987.

Gilpin, Robert. *War & Change in World Politics.* New York: Cambridge University Press, 1981.

Goldstein, Judith, and Robert O. Keohane, eds. *Ideas & Foreign Policy: Beliefs, Institutions, and Political Change.* Ithaca: Cornell University Press, 1993.

Goodman, Elliot R. *The Fate of the Atlantic Community.* New York: Praeger Publishers, 1975.

Hill, Roger. *Political Consultation in NATO.* Toronto: Canadian Institute of International Affairs.

Hunter, Robert. *Security in Europe.* London: Eleks Books, 1969.

Ireland, Timothy. *Creating the Entangling Alliance: The Origins of the North Atlantic Treaty Organization.* Westport, CT: Greenwood Press, 1981.

Jervis, Robert. *Perception and Misperception in International Politics.* Princeton, NJ: Princeton University Press.

Joffe, Joseph. *The Limited Partnership: Europe, the United States, and the Burdens of Alliance.* Cambridge: Ballinger Publishing Company, 1987.

Jordan, Robert S. *The NATO International Staff/Secretariate, 1952–1957.* London: Oxford University Press, 1967.

Jordan, Robert S. *Political Leadership in NATO: A Study In Multilateral Diplomacy.* Boulder, CO: Westview Press, 1979.

Kaplan, Lawrence S. *A Community of Interests: NATO and the Military Assistance Program, 1948–1951.* Washington, DC: Office of the Secretary of Defense, Historical Office, 1980.

Kaplan, Lawrence S. *The United States and NATO: The Formative Years.* Lexington: University of Kentucky Press, 1984.

Kaplan, Lawrence S. *NATO and the United States: The Enduring Alliance.* New York: Twayne's Publishers, 1994.

Kaplan, Lawrence S., and Robert W. Clawson, eds. *NATO after Thirty Years.* Wilmington, DE: Scholarly Resources, 1981.

Kaplan, Lawrence S., Robert W. Clawson, and Raimondo Luraghi, eds. *NATO and the Mediterranean.* Wilmington, DE: Scholarly Resources, 1985.

Kelleher, Catherine. *The Future of European Security.* Washington, DC: The Brookings Institution, 1995.

Kennan, George F. *At Century's Ending: Reflections, 1982–1995.* New York: W. W. Norton & Company, 1996.

Keohane, Robert O. *Neorealism and Its Critics.* New York: Columbia University Press, 1986.

Keohane, Robert O. *International Institutions and State Power.* Boulder, CO: Westview Press, 1989.

Keohane, Robert O., Joseph S. Nye, and Stanley Hoffmann, eds. *After the Cold War: International Institutions and State Strategies in Europe, 1989–1991.* Cambridge: Harvard University Press, 1993.

Kissinger, Henry. *Diplomacy.* New York: Simon & Schuster, 1994.

Krasner, Stephen D. *International Regimes.* Ithaca, NY: Cornell University Press, 1981.

Krauss, Melvin, ed. *How NATO Weakens the West.* New York: Simon & Schuster, 1986.

Kugler, Richard. *Commitment to Purpose: How Alliance Partnership Won the Cold War.* Santa Monica, CA: RAND Corporation, 1993.

LaFeber, Walter. *America, Russia, and the Cold War, 1946–1971.* New York: John Wiley and Sons, Inc., 1972.

Lunn, Simon. *Burdensharing in NATO.* London: Royal Institute of International Affairs, 1983.

Lynn-Jones, Sean, and Steven Miller, ed. *The Cold War and After: Prospects for Peace.* Cambridge: MIT Press, 1993.

Mandelbaum, Michael. *The Dawn of Peace in Europe.* New York: The Twentieth Century Fund, 1996.

Morgenthau, Hans J. *Politics among Nations*, 3d ed. New York: Knopf, 1978.

Nolan, Janne E., ed. *Global Engagement: Cooperation and Security in the 21st Century.* Washington, DC: The Brookings Institution, 1994.

North Atlantic Treaty Organization. *NATO Handbook.* Brussels: NATO Office of Information and Press, 1995.

Nye, Joseph S. *Bound to Lead: The Changing Nature of American Power.* New York: Basic Books, 1990.

Olson, Mancur. *The Logic of Collective Action: Public Goods and the Theory of Groups.* Cambridge, MA: Harvard University Press, 1965.

Osgood, Robert. *NATO: The Entangling Alliance.* Chicago: University of Chicago Press, 1962.

Papacosma, S. Victor, and Mary Ann Heiss, eds. *NATO in the Post–Cold War Era: Does it have a Future?* New York: St. Martin's Press, 1995.

Reid, Escott. *Time of Fear and Hope.* Toronto: McClelland and Steward, 1977.

Rittberger, Volker. *Regime Theory and International Relations.* Oxford: Clarendon Press, 1993.

Ruggie, John G. *America and the New World Order: Multilateralism after the Cold War.* New York: Columbia University Press, 1996.

Ruggie, John G., ed. *Multilateralism Matters: The Theory and Praxis of an Institutional Form.* New York: Columbia University Press, 1993.

Russett, Bruce. *Grasping the Democratic Peace: Principles for a Post–Cold War World.* Princeton: Princeton University Press, 1993.

Serfaty, Simon. *Stay the Course: European Unity and Atlantic Solidarity* (Washington, DC: Center for Strategic and International Studies, 1997).

Simon, Jeffrey. *Central European Civil–Military Relations and NATO Expansion.* Washington, DC: National Defense University Press, 1996.

Simon, Jeffrey, ed. *NATO Enlargement: Opinions and Options.* Washington, DC: National Defense University Press, 1995.

Sloan, Stanley R. *NATO's Future: Beyond Collective Defense.* Washington, DC: National Defense University Press, 1995.

Sloan, Stanley R., ed. *NATO in the 1990s.* Washington, DC: Pergamon-Brassey's, 1989.

Snyder, Jack, and Robert Jervis, eds. *Coping with Complexity in the International System.* Boulder, CO: Lynne Rienner Publishers, 1995.

de Staercke, Andre, ed. *NATO's Anxious Birth.* New York: St. Martin's Press, 1985.

Stuart, Douglas, and William Tow, *The Limits of Alliance: NATO Out-of-Area Problems since 1949.* Baltimore: The Johns Hopkins University Press, 1990.

Treverton, Gregory R., ed. *The Shape of the New Europe.* New York: Council on Foreign Relations, 1992.

Truman, Harry S. *Memoirs Volume II: Years of Trial and Hope.* Garden City, NY: Doubleday, 1956.

Ullman, Richard. *Securing Europe.* Princeton: Princeton University Press, 1991.

Walt, Stephen M. *The Origins of Alliances.* Ithaca: Cornell University Press, 1987.

Waltz, Kenneth N. *Theory of International Politics.* Reading, MA: Addison-Wesley Publishing Company, 1978.

Weiner, Jarrod, ed. *The Transatlantic Relationship.* London: Macmillan Press, 1996.

Williams, Phil. *The Senate and US Troops in Europe.* New York: St. Martin's Press, 1985.

Wolfers, Arnold, ed. *Alliance Policy in the Cold War.* Baltimore: The Johns Hopkins University Press, 1959.

Zelikow, Philip, and Condoleeza Rice. *Germany Unified and Europe Transformed: A Study in Statecraft.* Cambridge: Harvard University Press, 1995.

Index

About the Author

Dr. Sean Kay is an assistant professor in the Department of International Studies at Rhodes College in Memphis, Tennessee, specializing in US foreign and security policy, international security, and international organization. Previously he was a visiting assistant professor of government at Dartmouth College. Dr. Kay has worked as a specialist on US foreign policy and international relations at the Institute for National Strategic Studies in the US Department of Defense in Washington, been a co-recipient of a NATO research fellowship, and worked on the international staff of the North Atlantic Assembly in Brussels. Dr. Kay is the author of numerous book chapters, journal articles, and editorials in major national newspapers dealing with NATO and European security. Sean Kay received his Ph.D. in international relations from the University of Massachusetts at Amherst.